Ireland Abroad: Politics and Professions in the Nineteenth Century

Ireland Abroad

Politics and Professions in the Nineteenth Century

EDITED BY

Oonagh Walsh

FOUR COURTS PRESS

Set in 10 on 12.5 point Bembo for
FOUR COURTS PRESS LTD
Fumbally Lane, Dublin 8, Ireland
e-mail: info@four-courts-press.ie
and in North America
FOUR COURTS PRESS
c/o ISBS, 5824 N.E. Hassalo Street, Portland, OR 97213.

A catalogue record for this title
is available from the British Library.

ISBN 1–85182–606–8

Printed in Great Britain
by MPG Books, Bodmin, Cornwall

Contents

Preface

The essays in this volume represent a selection of the papers delivered at the 'Ireland Abroad' conference held at the University of Aberdeen in April 2000, under the auspices of the Society for the Study of Nineteenth Century Ireland. The editor would like to thank the Officers of the Society, in particular Margaret Kelleher and James Murphy, for their encouragement throughout.

I would like to gratefully acknowledge the financial assistance given by the British Academy, and the Faculty of Arts and Divinity of the University of Aberdeen. Thanks are also due to the Research Institute of Irish and Scottish Studies, for hosting the conference, and to Aberdeen City Council for their hospitality. Permission to reproduce J. Hodgson's painting for the jacket cover was granted by Aberdeen City Council.

I am also grateful to Michael Adams, Martin Fanning and Anthony Tierney of Four Courts Press for their support and assistance in the course of editing this volume.

In memory of
Dickon Walsh (1932–2002)

Introduction

OONAGH WALSH

Interest in migration and diaspora studies shows little sign of abating. In recent years, indeed, the field has not merely grown, but expanded beyond its principal original focus on immigrant studies, to embrace a broader and more complex appreciation of the topic.[1] The increasing use of the term 'diaspora' to suggest a wide-ranging examination of parent as well as host countries and cultures indicates that the field will continue to expand, allowing for an interdisciplinary and multicultural world view. Diaspora furthermore suggests a more complex perspective on the process of migration, with its implication of classification by racial or religious, as well as national, allegiance.[2]

As far as Ireland is concerned, this shift in emphasis is evident in a number of ways. From a position where much of the focus was upon the Irish experience in the United States, and to a lesser extent, the Antipodes, work is now being undertaken on South America, South Africa, India, and Asia, as well as what was actually the principal destination for the Irish, Britain.[3] What this new work has revealed is the manner in which Irish migrants responded to the opportunities as well as pressures offered by host countries, and how ethnicity and religion were frequently utilised to advantage. The loosening of theoretical frameworks with regard to migration has allowed for the imaginative reading of groups such as missionaries,[4] soldiers,[5] or civil servants, many of whom would not have considered themselves

---

1 Migrants from Europe who settled in the New World in the nineteenth century have long been a topic of interest, and the experiences of the Jewish and African diasporas explored in various ways, but the nineteenth and twentieth century movements of Asians, for example, are only now beginning to be undertaken. See for example C. Bates (ed.), *Community, Empire and Migration: South Asians in Diaspora* (Basingstoke, 2001); D. Dabydeen & B. Samaroo (eds), *India in the Caribbean* (London, 1987); C. Clarke, C. Peach, & S. Vertovec (eds), *South Asians Overseas: Migration and Ethnicity* (Cambridge, 1990), M.S. Wokeck, *Trade in Strangers: the Beginnings of Mass migration to North America* (Pennsylvania, 1999). 2 For an Irish combination of both of these elements, see for example D. Keogh, *Jews in 20th Century Ireland* (Cork, 1998). 3 For an indication of the sheer scale of Irish migration, see P. O'Sullivan's six-volume work on *The Irish World Wide* (Leicester, 1992). See also P. McKenna, 'Irish Emigration to Argentina: a different model' in A. Bielenberg (ed.), *The Irish Diaspora* (Harlow, 2000), pp. 195–212; D.H. Akenson, *Occasional Papers on the Irish in South Africa* (Grahamstown, 1991); D.M. MacRaild, *Irish Migrants in Modern Britain* (Basingstoke, 1999). 4 E.M. Hogan, *The Irish Missionary Movement: A Historical Survey, 1830–1980* (Dublin, 1990); M. Holmes & D. Holmes (eds), *Ireland and India: Connections, Comparisons, Contrasts* (Dublin, 1997). 5 K. Jeffery (ed.), *'An Irish Empire?': Aspects of Ireland and the British Empire* (Manchester, 1996); T. Bartlett & K. Jeffery (eds), *A Military History of Ireland* (Cambridge, 1996).

to be 'immigrants', but who certainly fit comfortably within the Irish diaspora. Moreover, with the reconfiguration of the image of the migrant has also come a wider appreciation of Irish roles in social, political, and military movements throughout the globe. Active as pro- and anti-slavers, as radical and conservative politicians, as governmental administrators and anti-government agitators, and fighting on both sides of campaigns from the American Revolution through to the Boer War, Irish influence in all these fields proves wide-ranging and contradictory. As essays within this volume also show, the concept of 'diaspora' as a 'de-centred approach in which migration, migrants and their multi-generational societies and cultures are seen as phenomena in themselves'[6] allows for the examination of migrant representation and construction through literature and memoir, as well as more traditional forms of migrant record. As scholars continue to explore the diversity of Irish influences abroad, another dimension is emerging closer to home: the impact on Ireland itself of returning migrants. And the recent media preoccupation with the issue of refugees and asylum seekers throughout Europe suggests that there are yet more chapters to be added to the history of migration.

This is a collection of essays that reflect on the state of being 'abroad', rather than engage with the minutiae of cohort depletion, passenger lists, or patterns of settlement. That is not to say that the essays fail to wrestle with the fundamental issues associated with migration, such as displacement, opportunity, and disappointment. These inescapable elements of the migrant experience are reflected in the careers of individuals and groups under study, and in the literature that survived them. Some contributions emphasise the role of the individual as participant in the migratory process, or as an agent in cultural and political transmission. Others look at groups or organisations who whole-heartedly embrace the host culture, seeking to re-make themselves through a process of assimilation. Still more focus on the liberation to be found through imagining an Ireland that is projected 'abroad'.

A striking thread through the essays is the sense of opportunity associated with 'abroad'. The majority of the subjects, either as individuals, or groups of professionals, were relatively privileged; they were for the most part literate, several were very well educated, and some were wealthy, and do not for the most part conform to the stereotypical image of the impoverished Irish migrant. Thus arguably many left Ireland in an attempt to improve their professional or political prospects, rather than as a last desperate act of survival. This appears to have had a considerable impact upon their perceptions of the host country. With the exception of those whose residency abroad was by nature of their occupation temporary, many sought to assimilate with the new society, while still retaining a distinct sense of ethnicity. They were, however, traditional migrants in the sense that most did not return to Ireland once they had established themselves elsewhere.

The volume is divided into three sections: 'Imaginings', 'Professions', and 'Transmissions'. The first includes those essays that engage with the means through

6 P. MacÉinrí, 'Introduction' in A. Bielenberg (ed.), *The Irish Diaspora*, p. 1.

which Ireland has been both represented, and self-created, by individuals who left it to travel abroad, or, in one case, never visited the country at all. This section, and the book, begins with Declan Kiberd's reading of Wolfe Tone's journal, kept when Tone cut a youthful swathe through Irish, American and French society. Tone begins the long nineteenth century, his actions signalling a world of political and philosophical possibility for Ireland. Although it is he who travels abroad, it is his journal that brings abroad to Ireland, placing Belfast and Irishtown at the heart of European thought, and drawing comparisons between the French Revolution, and what he hoped might be achieved in Ireland. As the originary moment for this volume, Tone's memoir is, as Kiberd remarks, remarkable for its poignancy. The reader carries the uncomfortable burden of knowledge that Tone lacked: that his optimistic journeys will end in military failure and suicide. Clíona Ó Gallchoir's essay on Madame de Genlis' responses to a country she had never visited, continues this theme of an imagined Ireland. Freed from the burden of personal experience, Ireland becomes for Genlis 'an idealised eighteenth-century state of mind', a tabula rasa on which her characters progress may be charted, without the inconvenience of historical or political realities. Ireland is an Eden, an uncorrupted backdrop against which heroic figures fulfilled their romantic destinies, and in which religious, economic, and political differences could be elided for the sake of a good story. Genlis' stories constructed a version of Ireland that drew upon, but did not accurately reflect, historical reality, while insisting upon their validity as 'national tales'. The issue of literary constructions of Ireland is also charted by Liam Harte, although from the perspective of Irish immigrants to Britain. Ostensibly accounts of individual successes and failures, these autobiographies actually constitute national as well as personal acts of 'self-fashioning'. The memoirs under discussion assume several guises – moral tales, testimonials, political biographies, and narratives of self-improvement – yet all share an implicit concern to 'challeng[e] negative stereotypes of the immigrant Irish'. Immigrant success was an automatic rebuttal to those who viewed the Irish as inherently shiftless and untrustworthy, and the biographers recount with pride the occasions on which their achievements were recognised by the British establishment. The narratives reveal a basic tension with regard to self-construction, however; British acceptance of the Irish immigrant was predicated on assimilation. For some, this was an unproblematic position; for others, it provoked a sense of personal and cultural anxiety, quieted only through emphatic declarations of allegiance with Ireland.

Peter Denman further explores the ambiguities at the heart of the creative immigrant experience, but raises the liberating potential to be found through the location of Irish narratives abroad. Being abroad is an 'enabling resource', freeing writers from the necessity of engaging with domestic politics, yet drawing upon (as Ó Gallchoir also suggests), an established conception of Ireland as a site of drama and romance. The novel *Vandeleur* draws upon these presumptions, but reflects the potentially liberating effect of migration: Irish characters did not simply change location, they could also reinvent themselves culturally. However, it is

Charles Wolfe's poem, 'The Burial of Sir John Moore', that indicates the extent to which 'abroad' was a crucial element in Irish historical literature. An 'Irish poem of expatriation which is universalist and inclusive, if not unionist, in effect', the work emphasised the potential for integration represented by military service, but steered away from any emphatic statement of political or national assimilation. The final essay in this section also examines themes of ethnic 'disguise'. While other authors in this volume have raised the potentially liberating elements in residence 'abroad', Kate Costello-Sullivan engages with the awkward position of the Irish in the Empire. Kim, the titular hero of Rudyard Kipling's tale, occupies an ambiguous middle ground between 'English' and 'Indian'. In this case, 'abroad' becomes the place in which anxieties regarding Ireland's own position in the Empire are played out. Kim is variously described as 'Indian', 'Asiatic', 'Oriental', 'British', 'English' and 'Irish' by critics and by Kipling alike, reflecting not merely the character's indeterminate status, but the broader position of Irish immigrants throughout the British empire. The question asked repeatedly by Kim – 'Who is Kim?' – finds echoes in the experiences of several of the groups and individuals presented in this volume: the state of being 'abroad' bringing the troubled issues of ethnicity, race, and culture very much to the fore.

The second section of this volume focuses upon some of the professions followed by Irish immigrants, and the reasons for the congregation of individuals in certain fields. Louise Miskell opens with an examination of an immigrant group doubly neglected by diaspora scholars: medical practitioners. As she points out, little work has been done on the Irish professional experience abroad, and even less on the experiences of Irish medical practitioners, a considerable body of men by the 1880s. In an interesting reversal of the traditional image of the disadvantaged unskilled migrant, Miskell traces the careers of several newly qualified Irishmen in Wales, finding that increasing industrialisation offered opportunities to ambitious individuals who faced unemployment at home. Opportunity is also a central theme in the succeeding essay, on the Irish presence in police forces abroad. Elizabeth Malcolm points to the enormous numbers of Irishmen serving in police forces in Britain, and especially Australia, where in the 1860s almost 70 per cent of recruits were Irish born, and 45 per cent had previously served in a police force, in the majority of cases the Royal Irish Constabulary. It is a striking instance of how the Irish transmitted not merely culture, but professional organisation and expertise abroad, and shaped fundamental societal structures. Ironically, political developments at home, in the shape of land agitation and boycott, significantly influenced the movement of Irish policemen overseas, as large numbers resigned from the RIC. As with Miskell's examination of Irish doctors, the importance of informal networks of communication is clear in the testimony of Irish police, as information regarding territories with the best opportunities was rapidly transmitted to the discontented forces at home.

Diane M. Hotten-Somers moves the focus back to somewhat more familiar territory with her examination of the relationship between Irish domestic servants and their middle-class employers in the United States. Like their male counterparts in the Australian police force, Irishwomen dominated domestic service, forming over 50 per cent of the service in cities such as Massachusetts in the late nineteenth century. The domestic servant, argues Hotten-Somers, was increasingly viewed as a commodity, purchasable (and expendable) in a manner similar to the mass-produced consumer goods that flooded the American market in this period. Indeed, the 'commodification' of the domestic servant encouraged greater regulation of the public and private lives of domestic servants, as employers sought to standardise the profession. The ideal end-product was an identically trained servant, endlessly replicated in training institutes across the country, and instantly replaceable. The next essay in this section, by Nini Rodgers, follows the career of an individual who saw 'abroad' as a place of varied opportunity. Richard Robert Madden travelled extensively, adapting his talents to the opportunities that presented themselves wherever he landed. Madden was no mere adventurer, though. He is best remembered for his courageous role in combating slavery in the Americas, and as an historian of the United Irishmen. In this sense, Madden was a man who literally saw Ireland abroad – his anti-slavery work informed his writing of Irish history, and his natural sense of justice. Oonagh Walsh ends this section with an examination of aspects of the life of Robert Alexander Crawford, a Presbyterian missionary to Manchuria in the late nineteenth century. Crawford was a multi-faceted individual, revelling not merely in his role of Christian missionary, but in the opportunities that missionary work gave him to travel extensively in remote regions. A skilled cartographer, he was elected a Fellow of the Royal Geographical Society for his detailed and accurate maps of Manchuria. His papers reveal a depth of insight into the complexities of Chinese life, but also the struggle he had in accommodating the European impact on Chinese life, and his own role in that process.

The third segment of this volume is entitled 'transmissions', a term designed to suggest the manner through which cultures are constructed as a result of migrant contact. It also refers to the construction of an Irish migrant identity, one in which certain kinds of migrants, such as the elite, may have been simply elided. Irish emigration demonstrates both elements of this process in an obvious manner. The essays in this section demonstrate how British domestic politics, the Roman Catholic church in Scotland, and the development of an alternative Irish ethnicity in Australia, all reflect the manner in which Irish emigration helped to re-construct host cultures. The authors engage with the literal transmission of culture by immigrants to their hosts, and the absorption of alien cultures at home.

The first essay in this unit, by Martin J. Mitchell, raises the issue of politically contaminating visitors, in its concentration upon the Catholic church in Scotland's anxieties regarding the suitability of Irish born and trained priests. Despite a huge increase in the numbers of Roman Catholics in the western lowlands of Scotland, boosted for the most part by Irish migrants between 1790 and 1830, and a chronic lack of priests to minister to them, the Scottish Catholic hierarchy were loath to recruit Irish priests. Driven at times by desperation to employ such men in their dioceses, the hierarchy frequently found that ethnic and national tensions made the situation impossible. The Irish claimed bitterly that they were passed over for senior posts because of their nationality, while the hierarchy feared the control they exercised over their congregations, especially the Irish-born. As the century advanced, tensions also increased over the politically inflammatory role Irish priests were seen to play in Scotland, encouraging the spread of organisations such as the Repeal Association. National identity took precedence over religious obligation, as the priests continued to actively participate in politics, in the face of opposition from their superiors.

Máirtín Ó'Catháin's essay on the activities of republican activists in Scotland continues this theme of a host society desperately seeking to contain its dissenting Irish elements. Unlike the Irish-born priests of Mitchell's study, many of these activists were Scottish born, but their political allegiance was to Irish militantism. They represented therefore not merely non-assimilated migrants, but a group who sought the literal destruction of the Union. Ó'Catháin examines two phases of the 'dynamite war' in Scotland in the 1880s and 1890s, and demonstrates the importance of cross-national political links. The dominant influence as far as Scottish activism was concerned was Irish-America, not necessarily Ireland, a fact that may have influenced the Scottish trend towards the dynamiting campaign. But the consequences of emigration go beyond this factor. The author argues that the dynamiters and their supporters were doubly alienated from influences that might have moderated their activities. They had rejected what they regarded as the cautious approach of the Irish Republican Brotherhood, and their 'heightened sense of exile', exacerbated by the appalling conditions under which they laboured in Glasgow, encouraged a hopeless faith in violent action as a means of political, and presumably economic, advance.

Irish migration has had a world-wide impact, with certain destinations such as the United States and Australia receiving large numbers of Irish settlers, and consequently a good deal of scholarly attention. Given the numbers involved, a surprising element has been the presumption that all Irish migrants shared a common religious and cultural heritage. Lindsay Proudfoot's contribution to this volume proposes a revision to the predominant image of Irish migrants as Catholic and Gaelic, examining instead the Anglo-Irish and Scots-Irish migrants who also travelled to Australia. Drawing attention to the large numbers of both – Protestants accounted for almost 45 per cent of Irish-born migrants in New South Wales in 1844–5 – Proudfoot draws attention to the means through which alternative Irish identities were constructed in Australia, and how these were expressed geographically. The disruption of a homogenous Australian-Irish culture allows for a more sophisticated appreciation of colonial Australia's relationship with Britain.

Ian McClelland further develops this theme of alternative identities in Australia, through his examination of Anglo-Irish gentry migrants to that country. He argues that this particular group exerted an influence on Australian society out of all proportion to their numbers. Ironically, these particular migrants have been ignored by historians, principally because of their relative wealth. While impoverished migrants travelled in large numbers on assisted passages, and so are recorded in governmental and other records, the gentry are noted by name only at points of departure and arrival. They have therefore been less examined than other migrant groups, yet assumed the same influential positions in Australia – landowners, clerics, doctors, bureaucrats, and pillars of society – as they had enjoyed in Ireland. Their position of relative privilege, McClelland argues, caused gentry migrants to view the Australian landscape in a significantly different manner from many of their fellow-Irish, and caused the landscape to be differently, and demonstrably, inscribed by their preoccupations and interests. In this, their shaping of new settlements 'reflected similar activities undertaken by other Anglo-Irish gentry members back in Ireland', suggesting that for this class at least, 'Ireland Abroad' was a literal fact, a theme that links many of the pieces in this collection. The final essay in this section, and in the book, raises some far-reaching questions regarding the associations between Irish Famine migrants of the nineteenth century, and those refugees, economic and political, currently seeking asylum in Ireland. Individuals seeking residence in Ireland today, argues Jason King, are interpreted both as the modern equivalent of the Irish displaced in mid-century, and as 'bogus' refugees, unworthy of humanitarian consideration. King examines the contradictory attitudes towards migrants, when a sense of guilty obligation towards new migrants – because of the Irish historical experience – clashes with anxieties regarding the protection of contemporary prosperity. What emerges from the rhetorical thicket of 'obligation' and 'continuity' is a shared desire on the part of Victorian authorities, and European Union legislators, to ensure that migrants remain in perpetual motion, moving constantly towards an imaginary refuge in another country.

For many Irish, 'abroad' is in fact 'home'. Long association with migration, and the creation of hyphenated communities in the United States, Britain and mainland Europe, means that a sense of membership in other countries exists for a considerable proportion of the population. Yet, as the essays in this collection indicate, migrant response is enormously varied. 'Abroad' may be imagined, constructed, a place of new beginnings or a shadow of 'home', and yet still trigger an emotional, uneasy response. It is to this interface between one place and another, but also between our myriad and evolving sense of 'self', that these essays are directed.

Republican self-fashioning:
the journal of Wolfe Tone*

DECLAN KIBERD

If Theobald Wolfe Tone had never kept a journal, and if his wife Matilda hadn't gathered his texts together it is probable that his life and death would not have the significance which now attaches to them. He died, like hundreds of others in 1798, fighting to create a republic, but it is because he left a moving and witty chronicle of his struggle that he is celebrated as the prophet of Irish independence.

Because that record is fragmentary, and because parts of it were lost by other people, it has the radiant quality of a romantic artwork. In it a man who has no sure sense of how events will turn out writes at the mercy of each passing moment, revealing a soul in all the vulnerability of its self-making. Tone's journal is the Irish *Prelude*, an account of the growth of its author's mind which by its very nature must remain unfinished, being a mere overture to something more interesting which will follow, the identity of a free citizen. The reader who knows how the tale ended must feel the poignant vulnerability of the writer in every line. The identity towards which Tone moves so gracefully is not the 'I' with which he began. It cannot, as it turns out, be written by Tone himself: and it is left to be inferred by his son William. He, one of the earliest intended readers, must write the introduction and fill the gaps in the broken narrative.

The extraordinary sense of involvement of all subsequent readers of the journal is due in great part to the space which it leaves for a readerly role. The identity of Tone which emerges at the end is shaped as much by the attentive reader as the patriot writer, defined from day to day amidst the fluctuations of the 1790s world in Ireland, the United States and France. Tone begins the memoir with some feeling of positional superiority over the more naïve, youthful fellow whom he was in the 1780s, and the chronicle begins with a sense of perfectly understandable self-division. Tone has not gone far before he is assigning pseudonyms to himself and his circle of friends, for whom everything, even revolution, takes on the quality of a great game. But this is a merely adolescent trying-on of various possible roles. What really captures the reader's imagination is a promise of an identity which will emerge in Tone from the very act of writing his life down. If his style represents a version of his current self, it contains the possibility of a richer personality yet to emerge out of the diarist's own self-division (for now Tone is 'Hutton' in the journal, 'James Smith' to the wider world).

At the start Tone is so superior about his youthful self that he seems quite invulnerable in the present: but as the present moment approaches in his narrative and yields to daily journalising, he loses that control. The text is turned over to the reader, who at once feels ashamed of knowing something that its author could never have known: that the adventure of bringing the French to Ireland ended in his death. Yet somehow, Tone seems to have suspected that this was how it might all turn out, for his entries are written in the hope that some structure of future meaning will be discernible in the fragments of a chaotic life, a structure which is less imposed by the writer than discovered by the reader. In this, of course, he anticipates the gapped autobiographies and confessional narratives of W.B. Yeats and Samuel Beckett.

Edmund Burke emerges soon enough as the major antagonist of Tone in the journal, but had he known of its existence, he would probably have endorsed its method. He believed that the attempt to overcome modern fragmentation was *morbid*, leading only to a life-denying abstraction. Tone's refusal to reduce the journal to 'system', to a premature coherence, would have been applauded by him. W.B. Yeats also endorsed such an approach, for in his own *Autobiographies* (the plural title was deliberate), he observed their forward thrust: 'it is so many years before one can believe enough in what one feels to know what the feeling is'.[1] His description of Salvini, a great actor stuck with the bad part of the gravedigger in *Hamlet*, might well have been applied to Tone: 'when the world fails his ideal, as it must, and as he knows instinctively it must, he catches a glimpse of his true self before uttering his swansong'.[2] Tone's text too is offered as a promissory note to the future in compensation for a botched life. Every autobiography is in some sense a confession of guilt. Ostensibly, Tone was expelled from his native Ireland in 1795 for writing a seditious letter to a French revolutionary agent; that was, in the eyes of some, his fitting punishment. He found the United States disagreeable enough: the life of a Princeton farmer humiliated his sense of merit, as did the prospect of seeing his children marry among boorish peasants. But his self-accusation is rather different: it is of abandoning his beloved family in the United States for a private mission as a secret emissary of the United Irishmen in Paris. If there is some residue of a Protestant 'search for evidences' in Tone's nakedness before the moment, it may be found in his condition as a romantic solitary or wanderer, cast out from life's feast, a restless consciousness, travelling vast distances often incognito, unable to make normal social contacts with other people's families.

To experience Tone must now daily add the consciousness of it, as he submits to the humiliations of self-analysis. Like all romantic artists, 'he pleads to be forgiven, condoned, even condemned, so long as he is brought back into the wholeness of people and things'.[3] His attempt to describe seemingly indescribable experiences

---

1 W.B. Yeats, *Autobiographies* (London, 1955), p. 69. 2 Ibid., p. 84. 3 S. Spender, 'Confessions and Autobiography', in J. Olney (ed.), *Autobiography: Essays Theoretical and Critical* (Princeton, 1980), p. 120.

is the start of this re-entry process, for what Tone writes is a quest-romance. At the end should be the establishment of an Irish republic and the heaping of honours and comforts on his family as its first and foremost citizens, now rewarded for all their sufferings. All of Tone's pleasures are in that sense forepleasures, anticipations of a greater joy to come. Whether he is recalling the popularity of his young family on a ship to America, as they shared wine and food with other grateful emigrants, or an earlier moment when they climbed McArt's fort on a lovely day with a community of like-minded Belfast republicans, Tone finds in such past experiences of solidarity a microcosm of the republic of the future.

The quest has, therefore, strong roots in past epiphanies, the memory of which is so potent that it triggers a wish for renewed fulfilment. The voyage to America is dangerous, but sweetened by the wine and cakes donated by the friends in Belfast and the gratitude of fellow passengers. The only discordant note is struck when the ship is boarded by callous captains of British frigates, who press some sailors and abuse the passengers. But the moments of solidarity seem all the more worthy of repetition, especially after such attack. The search of the romantic quester is for a society that will deliver him from the anxieties of reality, yet somehow contain that reality. His fear is self-absorption: hence the need for some grand ideal to serve. The danger is vanity, best avoided by strong doses of self-mockery and of real devotion to others. The search for enlightenment which was once the sole preserve of religion must now be conducted in a secular narrative because, for a modern republican, the only legitimate myth is art.

Tone wants a republic, but fears increasingly that he may have to find it first of all in himself. His journal becomes a virtual society, in which he trades quips and quotations with his wife, children, friends. It, at least, will fill the gap that is a result of his solitary mission to distant places. All this is one romantic author's attempt to come to terms with his own isolation: the almost unbearable poignancy is the knowledge that Tone, unlike the Ancient Mariner or the Leech-Gatherer, never did fully re-enter the human community. It is we eavesdroppers on his private conversation who must restore him, by a tender reading of his work.

Although a man of the Enlightenment, Tone was born late enough in the eighteenth century to be an early romantic. His memoir glosses quickly over his childhood in a distinctly Augustan fashion, which would have appalled Rousseau or Wordsworth. After that, however, he appears as a determined romantic, viewing his life as an experiment in living, worthy of analysis for the sake of those who come after. His emphasis is as often on the private as on the public world, for it is his own state of mind that provides the linking material between these disparate zones. Because the forms of autobiography are unique in each specific case, there can be no rigid rules. Everything is notionally admissable, for even acts of literary criticism or accounts of military manoeuvres may allow the writer to divulge some aspect of himself. The self and world, though apparently opposed, are fused in the consciousness by the very act of writing.

In that sense all writing, including his political pamphlets or memorials to the

French government, becomes for Tone a version of autobiography. At the same time, he comes to recognise that any unmediated autobiography is impossible, though always desirable, for the *I* becomes a *me*, the subject an object in the gesture of reportage, even as T. W. Tone becomes John Hutton or James Smith. The self isn't directly knowable in the conditions of modernity, nor should it necessarily seek to make itself available to outside decoders. It is known, rather, through its effects, from which its unknown qualities may be inferred. Like the poet John Keats, Tone knows that he can grasp only a part of the truth at a time: he too is the artist of half-knowledge, capable of living in doubts and uncertainties with no irritable reaching after fact and reason.[4] And, like Keats also in this, he leaves his texts as if they were traces which will not only survive his own death but be seen as a rehearsal for it. Compared with other rebels, Tone did very little, apart from fight gallantly when the *Hoche* was about to be overpowered: we know him less through military action than through the consciousness revealed in the journal

Living on the cusp between eighteenth and nineteenth centuries, Tone understood that one really was an extension of the other rather than an alternative to it. For him the Imagination was not opposed to Reason so much as a heightened version of it. Imagination was the capacity to see things as they were; fantasy the resort of those who wished to see them as they were not. Repeatedly in the journal he uses humour as a defensive wit, forestalling mockery of romantic idealism by another person. The perils of sincerity are never perils for Tone, because he is too continuously aware of his own multiplicity to make the mistake of stabilising one identity over others. His choice of James Smith as a code-name seems almost a joke, for this most common name of Englishmen cries out to be seen through. Likewise, his playing at different roles – that of Irish roisterer, French lover, or American farmer – is done with an excess that borders on disavowal. Tone knows the dangers of singularity, for he has seen the word 'honest' become a term of abuse in the plays of Sheridan. The new Enlightenment protagonist was Diderot's Rameau, the man who knew that any one person has half a dozen selves to be true to. This was the spirit as praised by Hegel: 'to be conscious of its own distraught and torn existence, and to express itself accordingly – this is to pour scornful laughter on existence, on the confusion pervading the whole and on itself as well'.[5] There is a lot of that laughter in the journal, which never invests any entry with more emotion than it deserves from the reader.

The refusal of romantic artists to work in tired, old forms was based on a shrewd judgement of just how necessary it was for form to follow function. The object was to abolish the notion of art as a separate activity of a specialist caste, by substituting for it the example of autobiography as a complete expressiveness to which any citizen might aspire. Tone's journal is that of a dreamer, but one who is seeking to engage with real things; hence the fact that, like the notebooks kept by

---

4 *Letters of John Keats,* ed. F. Page (London, 1968), p. 53.   5 Quoted by L. Trilling, *Sincerity and Authenticity* (Oxford, 1972), p. 25.

romantic poets and painters, it often takes the form of quasi-scientific note-taking, as if strange new ideas were being sketched or new forms essayed. 'The subjective emphasis is not egotistical', says Jacques Barzun in *Classic, Romantic and Modern*: 'rather is it a condition of the search and the modesty of the searcher'.[6] Tone was imbued with the scientific spirit of experiment: but also with the idea that the role of language was to inform and to raise feeling. Insofar as he contained within himself certain contradictions, he found in the nation a concept to reconcile individual energy and transcendent tasks, a notion vast enough to hold contrasting elements. He could conceive of Ireland as a nation uniting Catholic, Protestant and Dissenter because he himself had in a few years traversed the society: a coachmaker's son turned gentleman-scholar of Trinity College Dublin, a Protestant lawyer turned Catholic propagandist, a former empire man become a republican militant. Because he passed through so many levels of his society, he achieved an anthropologist's view of its codes; his diaries are proof that he could see it from an outside vantage-point, even as he continued to care passionately about what was happening within.

Tone had no compunction about applying the word 'romantic' repeatedly to himself and his siblings (most of whom travelled to the ends of the earth while young). Theatre posed for him in a particularly direct way the related problems of sincerity and authenticity. As a young tutor of twenty, he found himself like Rousseau in the home of an aristocratic couple and promptly fell in love with the lady, Eliza Martin of Galway. She teased him mercilessly, when they were male and female leads in a play called *Douglas*, during which he had to utter the lines

> Her manifest affection for the youth
> Might breed suspicion in a husband's brain . . .[7]

She was beautiful, influential and bored with her husband: and Tone knew it. 'Being myself somewhat of an actor', he recalled a decade later, 'I was daily thrown into particular situations with her, both in rehearsals and on the stage'. His suffering was inconceivable, 'without, however, in a single instance overstepping the bounds of virtue, such was the purity of the extravagant affection I bore her'.[8] Some years later, Eliza Martin absconded with another man after a notorious affair: Tone came to feel that she had been simulating onstage an emotion which in his case was all too real ('an experiment no woman ought to make').[9] He was challenged by her acting abilities as well as her beauty, but he was a conflicted lover: 'Had my passion been less pure, it might have been not less agreeable'[10] – but not more either, for Tone had 'a puritanical attitude towards female virtue'[11] and would

6 J. Barzun, *Classic, Romantic and Modern* (London, 1962), p. 63.   7 M. Elliott, *Wolfe Tone: Prophet of Irish Independence* (London, 1989), p. 27.   8 T. Bartlett (ed.), *Life of Wolfe Tone* (Dublin, 1998), p. 19. This volume contains both the autobiographical memoirs and the journals which are the main subject of this essay.   9 Ibid., p. 19.   10 Ibid., p. 20.   11 Elliott,

soon elope with the teenaged Martha (Matilda)Worthington on the rebound from Eliza.

Ever afterwards theatre haunted him, the cavalier in him delighting in its display even as the puritan worried about its insincerity. Despite these scruples, he could never abstain for long. Country house theatricals often posed such challenges. In Jane Austen's *Mansfield Park* Sir Thomas Bertram bans them lest his daughter be enabled to express in her part onstage words of tenderness for the man she truly loves rather than for the one to whom she is engaged. All through the ensuing century men and women who acted in such theatricals were pronounced morally suspect by writers as different as Disraeli and Thackeray.[12]

Tone was histrionic and also something of a gallant. No sooner had he married Matilda and fathered children than he left them for a legal training in London. There he enjoyed dalliances because 'the Englishmen neglect their wives exceedingly' and the wives were not cruel to willing substitutes.[13] The thought that he might be similarly neglecting a loyal wife never seems to have entered Tone's head. On the other hand, the question of *trust* haunts him in early pages of the journal. The optimism of the Enlightenment tells him to trust appearances, yet all around is evidence of man's fallen nature. His own family are tied up by robbers in Kildare and he spends a terrible night bound and gagged, wondering whether his pregnant wife and his parents are dead. Yet with the intrepidity of a man, Matilda breaks free and bravely re-enters the house, freeing her husband. Later, when Tone agrees to work as secretary to the Catholic Committee (even though he has never met most of the Catholics before), he is a victim of two attempted robberies as he goes about its work by stagecoach. The more you trust, it seems, the more you are betrayed: and the more likely you are to betray those who trust you. All these scenes are, of course, screen-versions of the anxiety that now assails the writer – the man who has no idea how much longer he'll live or of what the future holds for Matilda and the children. Yet as always he resolves to trust the future, even as he abandons his family to the mercy of time's arrow.

Like Wordsworth in *The Prelude*, Tone recollects past emotion in present tranquillity, and he also is moved more by past or future moments than by present ones. So an early moment of revolutionary solidarity is to be found in the memory of happy days spent by his young family with Tom Russell of the United Irishmen in and around their small house at Irishtown. Tone recollects 'the delicious dinners, in the preparation of which my wife, Russell and myself were all engaged; the afternoon walks, the discussions as we lay stretched on the grass . . .'[14] This is an image of perfected community, whose men gladly assume domestic work and whose women partake fully in political debate. Neither Tone's wife nor his sister left the table, but were often joined for poetry-making and political repartee by Russell's

Wolfe Tone, p. 30. Martha Worthington was either fifteen or sixteen when they eloped. Tone preferred to call her Matilda. **12** On this see Trilling, p. 75ff. **13** Bartlett, *Life*, p. 26. **14** Ibid., p. 33.

old father. Such experiments offered the sort of plain living and high thinking that
was sought by Wordsworth and Coleridge, a sort of Grasmere Cottage with sex:
'She loved Russell as well as I did. In short, a more interesting society of individuals, connected by purer motives and animated by a more ardent attachment and
friendship for each other, cannot be imagined'. For Tone the personal is at least as
important as the political, which is little more than an organised extension of the
proper relations between individuals.

Tone had the eighteenth-century gregariousness made possible by an increase
in leisure, as more people lived in towns. It is significant that his Irishtown
epiphany should have been social in nature, whereas that experienced at the end
of the nineteenth century by James Joyce across Dublin Bay on Dollymount Strand
would be utterly solitary. As a moment, Tone's epiphany would repeat itself wherever United Irishmen gathered in a romantic setting – on Rams Island in Lough
Neagh or at the summit of McArt's Fort, from which they looked down at the radical city of Belfast and vowed to subvert the authority of England in their country. It would be hard to overstate the importance of that recollected moment as
Tone lay in the grass alongside his wife and best friend in Irishtown (the poor people's city parish by the sea). What is achieved in the recollection is an electric link
between location and patriotic sentiment. The poignancy involves the possibility
that such a golden moment may be recaptured and shared with the whole community. In this way Tone looks at once back and forward with something like the
emotion which would be felt by soldiers dying for their land in foreign wars.

The linkage between *locale* and *self* also heightened an awareness of the significance of *time* in the construction of an identity. The Memoir was interpellated by
Tone in the journal kept in France in September 1796, as if to emphasise the point.
But the Memoir of his earlier life yields to the journal, kept intermittently from
1789 onwards. If the Memoir accepts the pastness of the past, the journal challenges
it with the immediacy of each moment. Until the age of Rousseau and Tone, a life
was assumed to be an accumulation of facts: the self of a writer and the self
reported were assumed to be one and the same. Thereafter, an awareness grew of
the effects of time as a form of experience on the making of an identity. People
recognised that there was a personal past as well as a public past, even as they
remained somewhat naïve in their confidence that they could recover past emotion. They soon discovered, like Wordsworth, that memory played many a trick and
that the experience recollected was often usurped by the act of recollection, which
itself became a more pressing alternative emotion. The real relationship was less
between rememberer and remembered than between the subject and time. Tone
was sophisticated in recognising time as an opportunity as well as an enemy: perhaps the fact that he was writing at the end of a momentous century helped him
to theorise time in this self-aware way.

It is his sharp awareness of tradition as an invention of the present that informs
Tone's running commentary on the previous century of Irish writing in English,
from Swift through Goldsmith and Sheridan, down to Burke. They (along with

Shakespeare and Henry Fielding) are the authors most often quoted and they were not conjoined in this fashion by any text earlier than Tone's. He becomes in a sense the first professor of Anglo-Irish Literature and Drama, a defender of that tradition, yet at the same time a fomentor of revolution. There is no necessary contradiction between these roles, for a similar ambivalence existed in Swift. Tone had no doubt of the moral of Swift's writing, 'that the influence of England was the radical vice of our government'.[15]

Tone's use of quotation is far more subtle than that of a clubman capping famous lines with a comrade over a frothy beer, for he often unfreezes the seemingly familiar aphorism, inflecting it with unexpected meanings in its new context. The entire journal might in fact be read as a parody of Swift's *Journal to Stella*, its coded names being a version of the 'little language' between the Dean and his friend. Early on, Tone jokes that his is 'a thousand times wittier than Swift's . . . for it is written for one a thousand times more amiable than Stella'.[16] As a parody, it is also an act of homage, but in neither role is it limited by its target. Tone is conscious of doing more fully what Swift *should* have done. In an essay of 1790 Tone had praised Swift for using *The Drapier's Letters* to question 'the imaginary dependence of Ireland on England. The bare mention of the subject had an instantaneous effect on the nerves of the English government.'[17] Yet even Swift, 'with all his intrepidity, does not more than hint at a crying testimony to the miserable depression of spirits in this country'.[18] The value of living after Swift is the chance to take up work that he left incomplete.

The code used in the journal is easy to crack: Tone is Mr John Hutton; Russell (a noted anticlerical) is the P.P. (parish priest); William Sinclair is the Draper; and Sinclair's native city of Belfast Blefescu (sic). Relieved of their everyday identities and using this special code, the friends could by absolutely frank with one another in a mode of playful delight. Their masks were slippery and kept falling off or being confused with the face beneath, as happens so often with the devices used by Swift: but they allowed the comrades to play certain roles before themselves as a prelude to their attempt to strike the popular imagination. The theory of it all was based on yet another disavowal of sincerity: wearing his own face a man speaks with caution, but from the confines of a mask, he may blurt out the truth, especially when tongues are loosened by drink. A recurrent theme is captured in Tone's entry from his early weeks in Belfast in 1790: 'Huzza. Generally drunk – Broke my glass thumping the table. Home, God knows how or when . . .'[19] Since the heyday of Sheridan, heavy drinking had been seen as a sign of sociability and libertinism – so much so that when a spy sent from London tried to keep up with Tone's progress through the hostelries of Dublin, he was soon paralysed with an excess of claret. The shared assumption of the members of his club is that revolution is nothing if it is not great fun:

15 Ibid., p. 30. **16** Ibid., p. 125. **17** Cited in ibid., p. 438. **18** Ibid., p. 439. **19** Ibid., p. 135.

> The Tanner (Mr Robert Simms) looks extremely wise and significant. Gog (Mr Keogh), Mr Hutton and he worship each other and *sign an article with their blood: flourish their hands three times in a most graceful manner (see Goldsmith's Citizen of the World)*, and march off into town. *Ho, but they are indeed most agreeable creatures* (do.)[20]

Belfast in those years was a centre of radical activity, especially among its Presbyterian merchant class, who had little respect for inherited privilege. Tone loved the free-thinking ethos and reported it in his diary. One hairdresser, though a Presbyterian himself, had two children christened by a Catholic priest 'with a wish to blend the sects'.[21] Tone's own comments on the Catholic majority are filled with less warmth than Swift's. The ignorance of Catholics is 'a benefit just now as the leaders being few will be easily managed and the rabble are by nature and custom prone to follow them'. There is no affection in the reference, merely a clinical appraisal of the sheer force of Catholic numbers against the British.

What attracted Tone most of all to Belfast was its modernity, which allowed him to study the interactions between street and stage:

> Oct 17 1791: Came into town early, went to the theatre; saw a man in a white sheet on the stage, who called himself a Carmelite . . . NB A gentleman, indeed a nobleman, on the street in a white wig, vastly like a gentleman whom I had seen in the morning, walking the streets in a brown wig; one Mr Atkins, a player. QUARE Was he a lord or not? PP incapable of resolving my doubts; but one pretty woman in the house. Came home before the play was half over; the parties appearing all so miserable that I could foresee no end to their woes. Saw a fine waistcoat on the man who said he was a Carmelite, through a tear in the sheet which he had wrapped about him; afraid after all that he was no Carmelite, and that PP was right in his caution.[22]

Five days later comes a cryptic *sequitur*:

> Oct 22 Mem: Met the man who said on stage he was a Carmelite, walking the streets with a woman holding him by the arm; the woman painted up to the eyes; convinced, at last, that he was no Carmelite.[23]

The bad play *The Carmelite* allows Tone to make some points at a time when boundaries between street and stage have blurred and men behave like actors in

---

20 Ibid., p. 136.   **21** Ibid., p. 120. Tone's youthful support for empire was not inconsistent with his anti-Englishness: he simply wanted an independent Ireland to be in a position to found an empire of its own. He voiced (at various times) sympathy for Louis XVI and George III. As a republican, he did not *have* to be anti-monarchical, at least until the 1790s, when republicanism became strongly separatist.   **22** Ibid., p. 122.   **23** Ibid., p. 124.

order to be sociable.[24] Tone exploits that ambiguity in order to expose the aristocracy as no more than an unconvincing impersonation of 'gentlemen'. The other suggestion is linked: that Catholic priestcraft is also based on magical nonsense and on a similarly deceptive assumption of a falsely authoritative identity.

There is a lot of joking about Catholic ideas in the journal, and humour at the expense of their critics: 'See an apparition of Jordan, who is in London; find on speaking Latin to the said apparition that it is Jordan himself . . .'[25] On 5 November Tone pretends to see a vision of Guy Fawkes who, on being questioned in Latin, turns out to be a policeman: nonetheless, with tongue firmly in cheek, Tone says that he sent for fire-engines in his hotel bedroom. Like other United Irishmen, Tone believed in civil rights for all Catholics and that the arming of the citizenry would curtail clerical influence, 'so fatal to superstition and priestcraft is even the smallest degree of liberty.'[26] He questioned the widespread Protestant prejudice that Catholics were incapable of liberty: 'We plunge them by law, and continue them by statute, in gross ignorance, and then we make the incapacity we have created an argument for their exclusion from the common rights of man'.[27] Compared with the 'rights of man' argument, the limited freedoms and franchise of Grattan's Parliament (1782) were so much sham: an edifice of freedom built on a foundation of monopoly. 'Be mine the unpleasing task to strip it of its plumage and its tinsel, and show the naked figure.'[28] Again, his obsession with the difference between latent and manifest content, between appearance and underlying reality, emerges in these strictures. The common Protestant complaint against Catholics – that they judge only by surface imagery and neglect substantive content – is here deftly flung back in the face of a patriotic Protestant like Grattan by a thoroughgoing radical.

Tone believed that Catholics must be freed from their sense of dependence on the British government, and Presbyterians from their fears of enfranchising Catholics. The Catholic Relief Bill of 1793 was a minor relief, he admitted, but it was accompanied by a gunpowder act. Edmund Burke had been advising the British government on the need to ameliorate Catholic grievances and to drive a wedge between the emerging Catholic and Presbyterian radicals. The setting up of a national seminary for Catholic priests at Maynooth in 1795 did not impress Tone one jot: he foresaw that the clergy rather than laity would gain control of the educational institutions thus allowed. Towards Burke himself, Tone was ambivalent. He was fascinated by his aesthetic theories and recognised the greatness of his writing. Although Burke affected to be a great defender of traditional privilege, Tone was aware that he was in fact a *parvenu* in England, who had used his immense abilities to win the favour of the mighty and powerful. His career, though glittering,

---

24 R. Sennett, *The Fall of Public Man* (New York, 1978), pp. 64–6.   **25** Bartlett, *Life,* p. 131. **26** Ibid., p. 138.   **27** Ibid., p. 288.   **28** Ibid., p. 281. This may be a boost for Paine at the expense of Burke, who was accused by Paine of noticing only the plumage of society and missing the dead bird underneath.

constituted an act of national betrayal. Yet the sense of engagement with Burke in the journal goes well beyond the political into the personal, as if he is the real antagonist, the man to beat. Burke had been a precursor of Tone at Trinity College Dublin, also an auditor of its debating society and a man of burning ambition like himself. His *Reflections on the Revolution in France* (1790) had turned British people against the Jacobins, as Tone bitterly observed, by playing upon their competitive feelings towards French power and commerce. Ireland, however, was a different case (in Tone's view 'an oppressed, insulted and plundered nation'),[29] but this didn't deter Burke from fearing rather than encouraging a revolution in that country.

Burke had launched his beloved son Richard on a political career in the lucrative post of secretary to the Catholic Committee in Ireland: but he proved incompetent. By 1792 they were paying him off to make way for Tone: but the father continued to woo members of the committee on behalf of his son. Tone's diary for 5 September is written with cryptic eloquence in the sort of interior monologue later made famous through Joyce's Leopold Bloom:

> Sad. Sad. Edmund wants to get another 2000 guineas for his son, if he can: dirty work. Edmund no fool in money matters. Flattering Gog (Keogh) to carry his point. Is that *sublime* or beautiful?[30]

In contrast to the self-seeking of the Burkes, Tone believed that his own actions were purged of all self-interest and solely for the welfare of the Catholics. He believed that Burke was in the pay of the British government, and the award of a Civil List pension in 1794 only confirmed this suspicion.

In Tone's mental landscape, Edmund Burke occupies a position as polar opposite to Tom Paine: the one a reactionary, the other a radical. While Burke is smooth, emulsive and eloquent, Paine is jagged, challenging and awkward. After reading Paine, Tone can only marvel: 'His wit is, without exception, the very worst I ever saw. He is discontented with the human figure, which he seems to think is not well constructed for enjoyment. He lies like a dog . . . He has discovered that a spider can hang from the ceiling by her web, and that a man cannot, and this is *philosophy*'[31] By his own admission not the handsomest of men, Tone nonetheless took delight in all bodily pleasures. After his arrival in Paris in 1796, he noted how drapes were removed from windows, even as women adopted a *negligée* appearance in the streets, which were to be places without masks. Tone's own diary worked to a similar aesthetic of casual undress: its body also was revealed in its basic lineaments. The Augustans had sought to distort and conceal the body's natural shape, but now the French were willing to expose it in all its vulnerability. Of the French soldiers Tone observed: 'every one wears what he pleases; it is enough if his coat be blue and his hat cocked.'[32] In the Conseils des 500, he noted the refusal of parliamentarians to dress up. As so often before, he felt conflicting thoughts about this. The puritan in

29 Ibid., p. 39.   **30** Ibid., p. 151.   **31** Ibid., p. 475.   **32** Ibid., p. 562.

him endorsed those French lawyers who foreswore wigs and gowns, but the dandy missed them.

The mockery of Paine's distrust of the body has, then, strong roots in Tone's experience of the streets of post-Thermidorian Paris. He met Paine in Paris in 1797 and they fell to talking of Burke. As so often when caught between the claims of two charismatic men, Tone couldn't help voicing some fellow-feeling with Burke, even as he repudiated his politics, Once again, the defender of feeling against intellect could strike Tone where he was most vulnerable – on the subject of family feeling. Paine attributed Burke's depression to the success of his own *Rights of Man*, but Tone knew that it had more domestic roots:

> I am sure *The Rights of Man* have tormented Burke exceedingly, but I have seen myself the workings of a father's grief on his spirit, and I could not be deceived. Paine has no children?
>
> – Oh. my little babes, if I was to lose my Will, or my little Fantom![33]

Tone was amused by Paine's vanity, and certain that Burke's mind had been shattered by the sudden death of his son.

Even in the 1790s, the passage in Burke's *Reflections on the Revolution in France* about the flight of Marie Antoinette was famous. A band of 'ruffians', Burke wrote, had invaded the bedroom from which she fled 'almost naked', the very image of the newly freed bodies in Parisian streets; but for Burke this was not liberation but disenchantment: 'All the decent drapery of life is to be rudely torn off.[34] He might have expected ten thousand swords to leap from their scabbards in vengeance but no, the age of chivalry was dead, making way for an age of sophisters and calculators. The Tone of the journal is as haunted by that passage as anyone. Visiting Versailles, he is struck less by its majesty than by the *ennui* of a confined life in its *Château*.

The central issue raised by Burke's passage is an ideal of womanhood. Tone admired women possessed of 'manly' spirit and men capable of 'womanly' virtues, in keeping with the androgynous styles promoted by the French revolution. Yet Paris proved to him that truly democratic women were few and far between: most were secret royalists. Nor was he fully sure that he admired the new freedoms. He had failed to respond to the promptings of Eliza Martin in Galway: now in his lodgings in Paris he rejected the advances of a pushy landlady who wanted to take him to bed: 'I have no great merit in my resistance, for she is as crooked as a ram's horn (which is a famous illustration) and as ugly as sin besides; rot her, the dirty little faggot, she torments me.'[35] On such a subject, he was more ambivalent than

33 Ibid., p. 734.   **34** E. Burke, *Reflections on the Revolution in France* (London, 1969), pp. 85–6, 92.   **35** Bartlett, *Life,* p. 573. Matilda Tone was very tolerant in including this passage in the first edition of 1826.

ever, the puritan and cavalier cancelling one another out. Tone's landlady is a further image of the revolution, a sort of comic alternative to the tragic Burkean narrative of Marie Antoinette, for she invites invasion of the bed-chamber, being at
once ugly and aggressive. The treatment of the image suggests that Tone had more
in common with Burke than he cared to admit.

Burke had seen France of the revolutionary terror as sublime and peacetime
England as beautiful. Though haunted by the immensity of the former, he settled
gladly for the latter, but not without struggle, for as an *arriviste* himself he would
always harbour some smouldering resentments towards those who inherited rather
than earned their privileges. Burke was shrewd enough to recognise that, as an outraged Irishman, he might easily have identified with the rebels, as Tone did. Tone
in the journal repeatedly compares the Parisian Terror with the current British policy of suppression in mid-1790s Ireland: and so the possible equation is clear. What
Ronald Paulson has written of Burke – 'the ambivalence of the rebel towards the
act of revolt is both because it is an aggressive act and because the object remains
beyond comprehension'[36] – might apply also to Tone's feelings about his French
landlady.

For Burke the women in the mob which dragged Marie Antoinette from her
bed were monstrous: an example of the 'false sublime' in their awful energy even
as the outraged queen was beautiful. Mary Wollstonecraft argued against Burke that
such turbulent women were badly needed, to tear away the *in*decent draperies and
reveal to men the true nature of the world – an image of stripping already used by
Tone of Grattan's Parliament. In *A Vindication of the Rights of Women* (1792) she
argued that women should not seek power over men but over themselves: and the
state of widowhood was an ideal model, she suggested, allowing women to double
as father and mother in one.[37] This was exactly the situation of Matilda Tone in all
but name, and after 1798 she would be a famous revolutionary widow for many
years. Her husband may have shrunk from the advance of one unaccompanied
woman in fear that the one he had abandoned for the sake of the revolution might
feel her own situation to be no different from that of the landlady.

It could be said of Tone that he makes a clean breast of his flaws, while being
careful to admit only likeable ones. There are moments when he seems anxious to
present himself as a man attractive to women but one who never falls, and yet he
was frank enough in confessing the London amours of his student years. The over-
riding impression conveyed, as in Rousseau's *Confessions*, is of a search for absolute
transparency, 'a true republican frankness'.[38] Tone was an *honnête homme* but one
who realised just how disintegrated a modern consciousness could be. He was
capable of playing the rake, chatting up a Dutch beauty in a carriage, but he was
also a child of the age of sensibility, and so rebuked Lord Chesterfield for encouraging his son to sleep with happily married women (including his best friend's

---

36 R. Paulson, *Representations of Revolution 1789–1820* (New Haven, 1983), p. 70.   **37** M.
Wollstonecraft, quoted in ibid., p. 71.   **38** Bartlett, *Life*, p. 477.

wife). In such passages of the journal, the revolt of the laughing as opposed to the satiric comedy is re-enacted. Tone was fond of the sentimental comedies of Sheridan: a great grievance in Paris is that he may never see *The School for Scandal* in an English theatre again. The French production irritates him because the soliloquies are not uttered to the self, as in romantic rumination, but to the gallery. Worse still, the singing of civic airs at plays seems often done without real sincerity: after a few short years of revolution, the new rituals have already grown perfunctory. Yet the French retain the power to intrigue, removing the bloody conclusion of Shakespeare's *Othello* for a more uplifting closure: 'I admire a nation that will guillotine sixty people a day for months, men and women and children, and cannot bear the catastrophe of a dramatic exhibition.'[39]

'The catastrophe of a dramatic exhibition': the phrase is telling. Though Tone frequented the playhouses as a cure for his loneliness in Paris, he could not help feeling the theatre 'trivial', almost unworthy as a subject: 'but I must write something to amuse me'.[40] His reservations are puritanical in basis – acting encourages people to assume personalities not their own and to usurp those of others. Many passages of the journal are devoted to detecting and exposing imposters: swindlers in hotels, mountebanks in carriages, and so on. When, finally, Tone meets the ambitious French naval leader Lazare Hoche, the seaman says that 'he got me by heart' and Tone wonders what he means: if he has mastered the detail of his Memorials (political analysis of Ireland prepared for the French government), fine, but if he is pretending to have plumbed Tone's character to the depths, that is not so flattering and probably untrue. The French revolution, even as it sought transparency in human exchanges, nevertheless insisted that no citizen was obliged to possess a personality that was 'believable' in traditional terms. The new simplicity of dress added to the 'mystery within'. Tone, already possessed of one name and two pseudonyms, has no desire to be too easily read or decoded.

For him, the theatre was at once an immoral institution, which encouraged persons to simulate emotions they did not feel, and a glorious utopian zone in which a person might throw off the constraints of a jaded role and assume a new, altogether unprecedented character. By the time he reaches Paris, Tone can hardly conceal his excitement at being able to attend Racine's *Iphigénie* at the Grand Opera. The period costumes are utterly accurate and the muslin *negligée* dresses of the heroine beyond praise, 'entirely in white, without the least ornament'.[41] The ballet *L'Offrande à la liberté* was even more striking: and Tone deliberately uses a Burke-word to describe it: 'All this was at once pathetic and sublime, beyond what I had ever seen, or could almost imagine.'[42] This is the only moment in the journal when Tone feels that words cannot fully render what he has seen. For one majestic instant onstage, the gap between a reality and a representation of it has been closed, as the symbolic and real meanings coincide. In a stroke, those moral scruples touched off in him by theatrical performances have been resolved and the

39 Ibid., pp. 504–5.　**40** Ibid., pp. 567, 576.　**41** Ibid., p. 404.　**42** Ibid., p. 464.

degradation of all actors – from the Carmelite in Belfast to the ham-soliloquists in Sheridan – has been removed. 'What heightened it beyond all conception was that the men I saw before me were not hirelings acting a part; they were what they seemed, French citizens flying to arms to rescue their country from slavery.'[43]

What Tone felt in those moments was something rather like what Jean-Jacques Rousseau had recommended years earlier in his *Lettre à M. d'Alembert sur les Spectacles*. He also felt his self to be multiple and was aware of the problems this posed for the potentially sincere man: he had concluded that hope lay in the dedication of the honest soul to a transcendent task outside the self. Such a task was the creation of republican virtue: and the only entertainments worthy of a republic would be those in which the citizen was no longer just a spectator but also a participant:

> People think that they come together in the theatre and it is there that they are isolated. It is there that they go to forget their friends, neighbours and relations in order to concern themselves with fables . . .[44]

Rousseau's ideal spectacle was a memory of an impromptu communal festival during his childhood, a memory not unlike that of Tone of the Irish Volunteers linking hands in the Phoenix Park. Rousseau recalled 'the unity of five or six hundred men in Uniform, holding one another by the hand and forming a long band that snaked about in rhythm and without confusion'.[45] While the original moment witnessed by Rousseau had a beautiful spontaneity, the attempt to describe it thereafter in programmatic fashion for others might seem forced, even insincere. Tone himself was quite scathing about the unconvinced rendition of civic airs at the Opera, as has been seen.

At another military spectacle, *Serment de la Liberté,* at the Opera on 13 March 1796, Tone watched as a procession of beautiful women presented a line of youths with their sabres, each man saluting his mistress and kissing the sabre on receipt:

> I do not know what Mr Burke may think, but I humbly conceive from the effect all this had on the audience that the age of chivalry is not gone in France. I can imagine nothing more suited to strike the imagination of a young Frenchman than such a spectacle as this . . .[46]

The context of the diary animates this analysis: for the journal is written by a man who seeks only the good opinion of his wife, referring all his thoughts, hopes and judgements back to her. If Hector's bravery against Achilles owed much to his desire for approval from the Trojan women, human nature hasn't changed over

---

43 Ibid., p. 465. **44** Rousseau, quoted in Trilling, *Sincerity*, p. 65. **45** Rousseau, quoted in J. Starobinski, *Jean-Jacques Rousseau: Transparency and Obstruction*, trans. By A. Goldhammer (Chicago, 1988), p. 93. **46** Bartlett, *Life*, p. 495.

three millennia: Tone sees himself as gripped by the same emotion, such as was appealed to by Fielding's Lady Bellaston in working upon Lord Fellamar. The journal is, in fact, daily testimony that chivalry has never been stronger than in the new revolutionary world, though Tone is honest enough to include within its range the comically reduced anti-heroes of Fielding as well as the more austere heroes of Homer. There is, he sees, a demonstrable link anyway between the comic and heroic. The idea that a man may be laughed to scorn can only have meaning in the wider context of his dignity as a viable possibility.

The sheer pace of change in the 1790s amazes even Tone. Rereading entries from the previous winter he is 'very curious to see what pains I took to prove fifty things which are now regarded as axioms'.[47] That sense of movement makes him all the more aware of how much he lives from moment to moment: the significance of events is often lost at the time of their happening. In the absence of any wider sense of significance into which things might be cast, it seems wiser not to impose even the beginnings of a pattern on entries: 'but as that would be something approaching to system, I despair of ever reaching it'.[48] The work of piecing together the shreds of an integral personality can safely be left to others: his task is simply to show how he came to be the man he now is.

Although Tone never accuses himself of deserting his family, and therefore never seeks formal forgiveness, the whole journal is composed with that implicit object. Proceeding more by implication than statement, he trusts that the narrative of his exile will suggest a truth he is too modest to assert. His absence is, in fact, but a sign of his deep love. He removes himself from his family for a great task, but is forever present to them through his written words. They are all exiled from Ireland (the others in America, he in France), but then so is the truth that his country needs but cannot yet see. In this his dilemma is identical to that of Rousseau in the *Confessions*: 'To hide without writing would be to disappear. To write without hiding would be to give up the idea that he is different from other people ... The goal is to be recognised as a "noble soul". He breaks with society only in hopes of making a triumphal return.'[49] The willingness to undress the soul before the world's tribunal is tantamount to an assertion of republican virtue, for a person so free of dissimulation, a character so *unrehearsed*, cannot have any sin to repent of. On the contrary, he will expect to be given credit by every single reader.

The mesmeric power of Tone's candour to later generations is straightforward enough in its origins: readers give credence to an image of Tone that they have largely constructed for themselves. His truth seems to come without mediation, unobstructed, even as his language hardly draws attention to itself. The self is so engrossed in itself that it gives little thought to the medium or to the techniques of sincerity. The prose, though beautiful, is deliberately styleless, suggesting a self not exceptional, just one man speaking to others in a search for the conditions in which that self might further grow. The reader has to help in the release of that

---

47 Ibid., p. 154.   **48** Ibid., p. 198.   **49** Starobinski, *Jean-Jacques Rousseau*, pp. 125–6.

future self and bring the story to its completion of that unfinished business. One consequence is that for almost two centuries Tone's journal has not even been treated as a work of literature. Like the Bible in the days before the higher criticism, it was a point of origin, the word unmediated, holy writ. Its theme was grand: being itself. And the challenge posed was not to be like Tone but to awaken every reader to the artist-hero who lies within himself or herself.

So far is Tone from notions of warrior-heroism that he repeatedly quotes Fielding's Parson Adams ('I do not desire to have the blood even of the wicked upon me'), and Sheridan's Bob Acres ('that I could be shot before I was aware').[50] Much of his time in France is spent – like that of his illustrious successor Beckett – pondering the meaning of waiting for something that may never happen: in this case a naval expedition. The arrest of Russell in October 1796 is traumatic news, leading to the collapse of the code: suddenly, revolution is no longer a game. As one expedition is cancelled and another aborted, Tone lives on an emotional roller coaster, unsure whether he will live as an Irish citizen or French officer. Although he never discusses the medium of language as such, he often ruminates upon the processes of his own mind. A journal is a daily process, whereas a book would be only a finished object: Tone is less interested by the object than by the ways in which an imagination can reach out to an object. For him, meaning isn't preformed: rather it emerges in the process of the search, the mind being attracted and excited by the pleasures of that search itself. In the virtual society of the journal, he regrets that so many good ideas are lost for want of an interlocutor to make them seem real. As the day of departure for Ireland draws near, the *anomie* brought on by prolonged isolation astonishes him. The expedition may 'change the destiny of Europe', emancipating three nations and opening the seas. Before either Karl Marx or James Connolly, Tone could see that Ireland might be the Achilles heel of the British empire, but somehow he is under-whelmed:

> The human mind, or at least my mind, is a singular machine. I am here in a situation extremely interesting and, on the result of which, every thing most dear to me as a citizen and as a man depends, and yet I find myself in a state of indifference . . .[51]

Tone monitored his responses with the precision of a brain-surgeon, and was astounded by what he found. On his first expedition to Bantry Bay in December 1796, he was on the ship that stood becalmed within a few yards of Ireland, utterly unable to land. It was a moment like that, months earlier, in which he had looked down with his friends from McArt's Fort on the townscape of Belfast. In Tone's writings, distance is always the necessary condition of love. Only those who can stand back from a city, a family or a nation, and conceive of it, can know precisely what it can be made to mean. Yet estrangement is also a condition of that inten-

50 Bartlett, *Life*, pp. 591, 853.   51 Ibid., p. 791.

sity. A few years later a solitary romantic soul would define itself against the void on a mountain peak or at the lonely prow of a ship facing into storm, but for Tone such moments are ultimately *social*. His hope was always to make the inhabitants of Ireland share in that developed consciousness: 'Poor Pat . . . who knows what we may make of him yet?'[52] Nevertheless, when he finally reaches the desired moment on the Irish coastline, all he feels is an unexpected estrangement:

> I am now so near the shore that I can in a manner touch the sides of Bantry Bay, with my right and left hand, yet God knows whether I shall ever tread again on Irish ground. There is one thing which I am surprised at, which is the extreme *sang froid* with which I view the coast. I expected I should have been violently affected, yet I look at it as if it were the coast of Japan; I do not however, love my country the less, for not having romantic feelings with regard to her.[53]

Nothing, in fact, could have been more romantic than such an attitude. The landscape is no longer seen here as a mere backdrop to the human drama, but as a wholly unknown world with a mysterious life of its own, full of redemptive possibilities, but essentially inscrutable. In that respect it is akin to the Catholic masses, defined and defended but never really animated in Tone's writing. What Rainer Maria Rilke wrote of the strange disconnection of landscape from human figure in the Mona Lisa might be invoked in this scene:

> It had been necessary to see the landscape in this way, far and strange, remote and without love, as something living a life within itself, if it ever had to be the means and notion of an independent art; for it had to be far and completely unlike us – to be a redeeming likeness of our fate. It had to be almost hostile in its exalted indifference, if, with its objects, it was to give a new meaning to our existence.[54]

Because Tone had been so intently monitoring the workings of his inner self, the landscape had become estranged. This would be a characteristic experience of four generations of romantic and republican militants afterwards in Ireland: the same sense of tragic separation from the very people in whose name they risked their lives, and the same sense of the remote, ungraspable beauty of the landscapes through which they moved on their dangerous errands. *On Another Man's Wound*, Ernie O'Malley's account of the War of Independence, may be the consummation of a tradition that had its source in that paragraph of Tone. What was thought to be the discovery of a new intensity of feeling in the face of a natural setting was

52 Ibid., p. 628. **53** Ibid., p. 465. **54** R.M. Rilke, *Von der Landschaft, Ausgewählte Werke*, 1938, II, p. 218: cited by J.H. Van den Berg, 'The Subjsect and his Landscape', in H. Bloom (ed.), *Romanticism and Consciousness: Essays in Criticism* (New York, 1970), p. 61.

revealed in the entry to be really the revelation of a loss: the sense that nature, far from being in harmony with the human mood, was unspeakably other, indescribable, unavailable to ready meaning. The Tone who, when he became secretary to the Catholic Committee, could admit to never having known a single one of its Catholics, was in the same predicament as the romantic protagonist who finds himself standing *before* a landscape rather than *in* it.

Tone was born to be estranged, for he was a play-actor: even the revolution for which he gave his life was but another role. However, he was estranged for a very good reason from the world as he found it: his 'true' self, the one that would signal an end to all the acting, lay up ahead. His autobiography, like Rousseau's, confronted taboo subjects in seeking to make that better self. Written like many subsequent diaries of Irish republicans in conditions of quarantine – one thinks of John Mitchel's *Jail Journal*, Máirtín Ó Cadhain's *As an nGéibheann* or Brendan Behan's *Borstal Boy* – his journal was a plea for understanding and forgiveness. Of another Irish autobiographer, James Clarence Mangan, it would be said that he had two personalities, one well known to the Muses and the other to the police.[55] The greatness of Tone's journal is that it renders the life of both, of Theobald Wolfe Tone and of Citizen James Smith. It gives the *auto*, the life of the mind, even as it chronicles the *bios*, the experience of the body.

Yet, precisely because he could divulge such a range of public and private sentiment, and at the same time control that sentiment, Tone remained to his readers as mysterious as the shores of Bantry Bay were to him. His readers, like his biographers, help to construct him, but soon realise that they are simply indulging a fantasy of the romantic performer and of what he might really be like.[56] To some he is a rationalist patriot; to others a colonial outsider; to others again a conflicted romantic whose ideas were less original than he took them to be. There is nothing especially false about any of these partial interpretations, but they all ignore one salient fact: Tone was an artist. He was so good an artist, so adept at using art to conceal art, that for all but two centuries he convinced his readers that he was no more than an interesting diarist. 'As to literary fame', he recalls of his London days in the Memoir of 1796, 'I had *then* no great ambition to attain it.'[57] That sentence is as near as he comes to admitting that the autobiography will constitute his present attempt.

Tone finally landed on the shores of Lough Swilly (from which the Gaelic earls had fled in 1607) in 1798. He was captured, identified by a Trinity College classmate, and arrested to be tried for his life. He wounded himself in the throat and died after some days of terrible pain. Whether he was attempting suicide or seeking to delay the hangman remains uncertain. He wanted to be shot like a soldier,

55 J. Mitchel (ed.), *James Clarence Mangan: Poems* (New York, 1859), introduction, p. 32. **56** Authoritative examples are Elliott's ground-breaking biography; T. Dunne's *Theobald Wolfe Tone: Colonial Outsider* (Cork, 1982); and F. MacDermott, *Theobald Wolfe Tone* (Dublin, 1926). **57** Bartlett, *Life*, p. 23.

not hanged like a dog. 'I am sorry that I have been so bad an anatomist', he said.[58] He was only thirty-five. His enemy and likeness, Edmund Burke, had died of old age just the previous year, still desolate after the death of his son. Burke was so terrified that Jacobins would dig up his remains and vandalise them that he carefully choreographed a secret burial. Tone was buried at the family home in Bodenstown. So defeated were republicans that his grave was not properly marked for half a century, until Thomas Davis helped his widow to raise a black slab.

It was unveiled at a private ceremony, in order to prevent embarrassment to Daniel O'Connell, the Catholic emancipist.[59] Since those days, however, it has become a place of annual pilgrimage for political parties and revolutionary cadres of modern Ireland. Tone refused to recognise the received identities of Catholic, Protestant and Dissenter, challenging their supporters to reimagine themselves under the 'common name of Irishmen'.[60] But he did more than that. In his journal, he left a model of how such a freed consciousness might move through the modern world.

58 Ibid., xxxviii.   59 Kevin Whelan, *The Tree of Liberty* (Cork, 1996), p. 168.   60 Bartlett, *Life*, p. 40.

Orphans, upstarts and aristocrats: Ireland and the idyll of adoption in the work of Madame de Genlis

CLÍONA Ó GALLCHOIR

Madame de Genlis' name appears in Irish history due to the fact that it was widely assumed that Pamela FitzGerald, wife of the United Irish leader Lord Edward FitzGerald, was her natural daughter. The significance of Pamela's parentage is more often considered in relation to her supposed father, the duke of Orleans, who was both Mme de Genlis' employer and the cousin of Louis XVI. The duke later became known as 'Philippe Egalité' when he embraced the principles of the revolution. The potent mix of royal blood, radical politics and sexual scandal that surrounded Pamela's birth and upbringing ensured that, even as a child, she possessed a degree of celebrity, or notoriety. Her marriage to Edward FitzGerald added to her iconic status, and also added to the glamour surrounding FitzGerald himself. As his aunt, Sarah Napier, remarked: 'Edward FitzGerald has acted a romance throughout all his life, and it is finished by his marriage to Pamela Seymour'.[1] Katherine Tynan's edited collection of Edward FitzGerald's letters, published in 1916, is subtitled 'A Study in Romance'.[2] Everyone, it seems, agrees that Edward and Pamela FitzGerald existed on the plane of romance, rather than reality. In the case of both, image and representation are as important as fact. As the historian Marianne Elliot comments, for instance, Pamela's assumed parentage contributed significantly towards establishing the image of Edward FitzGerald as a key figure in the United Irishmen:

> the myth [of Pamela's birth] played such a part in creating the reputation of Lord Edward as an advanced democrat that it has survived two centuries of scholarly research, and with Edward's style of dressing and of cropping his hair in the French republican style, long before it became common United Irish practice, [William] Drennan was correct in thinking that 'he and his elegant wife will lead the fashion of politics in a short time.'[3]

One response to this intoxicating mix of romance and politics has been ignored, and that is the response of Mme de Genlis herself. This is surprising, given

---

1 S. Tillyard, *Citizen Lord: Edward FitzGerald, 1763–1798* (London, 1998), p. 152.   2 K. Tynan, *Lord Edward: A Study in Romance* (London, 1916).   3 M. Elliott, *Partners in Revolution: The United Irishmen and France* (London, 1982) pp. 25–6.

that she was an accomplished author of novels, tales and educational works, and published her memoirs in eight volumes. Genlis lived in interesting times, and she appears to have materially contributed to their interest. Born in 1746, she married the Comte de Genlis, who later became the Marquis de Sillery. She was an extremely prolific, successful, and highly regarded writer, many of whose works were translated into English. In 1785 she was awarded an honorary doctorate by Oxford University, and it was also proposed that she should be made the first ever woman member of the Académie Française. She was also a controversialist, a public figure, reputed to be a political intriguer, in the best tradition of French 'boudoir politics'.[4]

Genlis was thus a talented, ambitious and intellectually gifted woman whose life and work have attracted scholarly and critical attention. Few of these commentaries, however, make any extended reference to her attitude either to Edward FitzGerald or to Ireland's history or political situation. One of the few such comments is provided by Patrick Byrne, in his 1955 study of Edward FitzGerald. It is perhaps significant that in describing Genlis' attitude towards Pamela's marriage Byrne adopts her perspective, thus creating an implied sense of her attitudes and motivations, without providing any support for these claims:

> [FitzGerald] shared an admiration for Rousseau with Pamela herself, this was no defect; perhaps it was merely the enthusiasm of youth. His political views, if not very clearly defined, were what we should now call definitely left-wing, but he was not committed to any dangerous association, and Madame reflected that in England it was always difficult for a man to make trouble for himself by being involved with the left; Tom Paine's case was merely an exception. As for Ireland, Madame never thought of that country at all. She had heard little about Ireland and she seldom thought of Lord Edward in connection with it.[5]

Byrne's speculations, however, do not bear scrutiny. It is certainly true that Genlis' political views are notoriously difficult to define, given her associations with both Jacobinism and Royalism. She was credited, for instance, with converting her employer, the duke of Orleans, to the principles of the Revolution and was supposed to have introduced her pupils as members of the Jacobin Club. Genlis herself, however, disputed these claims in a number of autobiographical texts, and was moreover associated with the Royalist faction in the years after the Revolution. In the 1820s she carried on a brief correspondence with the British Tory journalist John Wilson Croker, who was planning to write a history of the French Revolution; in her letters Genlis declares herself a friend of the church and

4 See J. Harmand, *The Keeper of Royal Secrets: Being the Private and Political Life of Madame de Genlis* (London, 1913) and G. de Broglie, *Madame de Genlis* (Paris, 1985). **5** P. Byrne, *Lord Edward FitzGerald* (Dublin, 1955), pp. 119–20.

conveys an image of herself as a conservative along the lines of Croker himself.[6] The evidence of Genlis' own writing is that her attitude towards the marriage underwent change as the political climate changed, and public events overtook private lives. The alteration is evident in two different accounts that Genlis gives of the marriage, one in *A Short Account of the Conduct of Mme de Genlis since the Revolution*, published in 1796, and another much later account given in her *Memoirs* of 1825. Although her account of FitzGerald in 1796 is glowing, and she describes the marriage as the culmination of all her efforts in educating and rearing Pamela, in her *Memoirs* she suggests that FitzGerald's 'exaggerated political opinions' had become apparent to her and caused her disquiet as early as 1796![7] Byrne's other assumptions about Genlis, that she regarded Rousseau with suspicion, knew nothing about Ireland, and did not in any case associate FitzGerald with the country, are equally unreliable. In fact, Genlis was heavily influenced by Rousseau, and the evidence of her 'Irish tale', 'The Great Earl of Cork', first published in France in 1805, is that not only did she associate Ireland quite explicitly with Edward FitzGerald, but that she chose Ireland as the location for a distinctly Rousseauvian narrative of independence and self-reliance.

There is evidence that Genlis had heard something about Ireland, even before she met Lord Edward. In her *Tales of the Castle* (1784), one of the stories concerns an Irish émigré or refugee, a Madame de Varonne, 'descended from one of the best families in Ireland', who was a loyal subject of James II and followed him into exile in France.[8] What is certain is that after Pamela's marriage to FitzGerald, Genlis became more interested in Ireland, to the extent that in 'The Great Earl of Cork; or the Artless Seduction', she based her story on the biography of Richard Boyle, the first earl of Cork, who was born in 1566. Given the great number of her writings, it is perhaps less than surprising that Genlis quite often drew on historical and biographical sources as material for her fiction, though it was unusual for her to depart from French sources. 'The Great Earl of Cork' is the title story in a collection of six tales, and in a prefatory 'Historical Notice' Genlis assures the French reading public that although the characters in the story may not be widely known in France, the extraordinary nature of their lives and achievements makes them figures of justifiable interest. In fact, Genlis self-deprecatingly dismisses her attempts to incorporate Boyle's biography into her fiction:

> Not being able to offer anything more to the public than this rather mediocre tale, I wanted at least to add to it some historical anecdotes, and to use the interest of truth to compensate for the meagre charm of fiction.[9]

6 J. Bertaud, 'Mme de Genlis, John Wilson Croker et la révolution française', *Revue de la littérature comparée* 51 (1977), pp. 356–65.   7 Genlis, *Memoirs*, 8 vols (London, 1825), iv, 290. 8 Genlis, 'The Brazier; or, Reciprocal Gratitude', in *Tales of the Castle; or, Stories of Instruction and Delight*, trans. T. Holcroft (Dublin, 1785), i, 63. Aside from this reference, however, the tale does not have other references to Ireland.   9 Genlis, *Le Comte de Corke, surnommé le Grand;*

Her acknowledged source is an unspecified British biographical dictionary, but this is liberally embellished with fictional episodes and characters, and is full of inaccuracies and anachronisms. These errors are, I suggest, partly purposeful, or at the very least significant, since they provide an insight into how Ireland was viewed from Genlis' complex and politicised perspective.

Genlis describes Richard Boyle as having been born in Ireland, in Blackrock Co. Dublin, the only surviving child of a young and beautiful widow who lived in a cottage near to a venerable and virtuous man named Mulcroon. Boyle was, however, born in England, in Kent, was not an orphan, and did not set foot in Ireland until 1588, after he had completed his education. In Genlis' tale, Mulcroon adopts the orphan boy and educates him, treating him as his own child. However, he is prevented from ensuring Richard's financial future because his estate is entailed. The main action of the tale concerns Richard's efforts to achieve renown, in spite of his humble origins, and lack of wealth and of family connections. In this he is ultimately motivated by his love for a Lady Ranelagh. Bizarrely, Genlis here chooses to give this fictional beloved the name of Boyle's daughter, Catherine, who on marriage became Lady Ranelagh; in reality, Boyle was married first to Joan Ansely, who died in 1599, and subsequently to Catherine Fenton. Boyle's association with the earl of Essex is represented here as the dramatic crux of the tale; he is thrown into prison on suspicion of involvement in Essex's rebellion, but pleads his case before the queen so effectively that he is cleared and provided with lucrative career opportunities.

It is very easy to find Genlis' departures from historical fact or even historical probability hilarious. It is evident that, for the most part, she is untroubled by the need to establish an 'authentic' sixteenth-century background. The description of the cottage in which Richard was born is just one example. Unable to give his ward any kind of inheritance, it is claimed that Mulcroon contented himself with making improvements to the cottage in which he was born, extending it and decorating it with 'elegant simplicity'. When Richard invites some visitors into his simple but elegant parlour, we are told that it features a large white marble table, and mahogany bookcases decorated with antique busts and alabaster vases. This conjures up a very neo-classical scene, and, in fact, mahogany, which is not native to western Europe, was not used in furnishings in Britain or Ireland until much later. Although Genlis appends a footnote to her description of Blackrock, claiming that it is absolutely authentic, it is clearly an eighteenth- rather than a sixteenth-century location. Blackrock as described by Genlis is a popular and fashionable seaside resort: she breezily informs us that the mineral waters in the area ensure that during the summer time it boasts a glittering society. In Genlis' version of the tale, the earl of Essex is among these notable summertime visitors, which is used to explain Boyle's acquaintance with him. Constantia Maxwell confirms that

ou, la séduction sans artifice. Suivi de cinq nouvelles 2 vols (London, 1808), i, v. Quotations given are my own translation.

Blackrock was an extremely popular spot in the eighteenth century, and that parties did indeed travel out from Dublin to take the waters there, but needless to say this practice was not established in the late sixteenth century.[10]

Genlis also appears to have little sense of the social, religious and political tensions of the time. Above all else, Richard Boyle was a representative of the New English, an 'adventurer'. Nicholas Canny has described him as 'a typical member of the New English elite in Ireland'; his career to an extent exemplifies the clashes between Old and New English, and between the New English and the government administration.[11] As Canny has shown, the mistrust and suspicion with which the New English were regarded played a highly significant part in shaping perceptions of Boyle's character, and in his own defensive response to attacks on his conduct and character. Genlis' ignorance of, or possibly lack of interest in, the detail of Irish history and culture is also evident in her description of a visit to Wicklow, undertaken by her hero. Boyle visits Lover's Leap near Dargle, and hears the tale associated with the rock. Again, Genlis observes in a footnote that the description of the rock and the account given of the tale are authentic. Boyle hears a voice singing a song relating to this same tale; later he is told that it is a traditional song, well known by the inhabitants of the area. Genlis clearly does not recognise or acknowledge the gap which would have separated a man of Boyle's background, class, religion and language from the popular culture of the rural Irish. Genlis' failure to register crucial aspects of Boyle's biography might cast doubt on the idea that this tale is anything other than a conventional romance with a nominally Irish setting. The comment of Patrick Byrne, quoted above, which suggested that Genlis made no distinction between Ireland and England might thus seem justified. But Genlis' rewriting of Richard Boyle's life suggests that Ireland represented for her a distinct range of imaginative possibilities.

As remarked above, Genlis is keen to point out to her readers that the scenery and the topographical detail in her tale are 'factual and perfectly exact'.[12] All the Irish scenes take place either in Blackrock or in Wicklow. Given that Genlis never visited Ireland, we can only assume that her knowledge of these places derived either from Pamela or from Edward FitzGerald himself, who of course spent his early childhood in Frescati House in Blackrock. He and Pamela lived at Frescati for a period after they returned to Dublin as a married couple; letters written by him to his mother from Frescati are filled with details of gardening and emphasise the happiness of the young family. FitzGerald was in fact reluctant to leave Blackrock, although he needed to decide on a more permanent home. Before settling in Kildare, he considered the possibility of living in Wicklow, and it seems reasonable to assume that he and Pamela made visits to the county.

Genlis' use of two locations associated with FitzGerald indicate that her version

---

10 C. Maxwell, *Dublin under the Georges, 1714–1830* (Dublin, 1979), p. 98. 11 N. Canny, *The Upstart Earl: A Study of the Social and Mental World of Richard Boyle, first Earl of Cork, 1566–1643* (Cambridge, 1982), p. 40. 12 Genlis, *Le Comte de Corke*, i, 1.

of the earl of Cork's life is more than simply factually inaccurate. Like all historical recreations, Genlis' tale is, ultimately, a more informative source on its own
period. Genlis extracted from the life of Richard Boyle a tale of the triumph of
natural merit, unaided by birth. This is in itself not a complete distortion of Boyle's
career: one of the reasons why Boyle was a figure of fascination both in his own
lifetime and later was precisely because of his phenomenal rise from obscurity to
power and wealth. Canny has described his career as 'truly exceptional' and as
'remarkable by the standards of any generation'.[13] Genlis' version of this fable is,
however, heavily influenced by eighteenth-century philosophies, and is characterised by both suspicion of excessive worldliness and faith in the power of a well-
directed education to shape human personality and character. Both principles are,
famously, elaborated in the most influential educational work of the eighteenth
century, Rousseau's *Emile* (1762).

As a successful educationalist, Genlis was thoroughly familiar with the works of
Rousseau. Her *Adelaide and Theodore* (1782) was a particularly highly-regarded
work on education, in an era in which such works proliferated. Genlis' response to
Rousseau is far from being uniformly negative; as Jean Bloch has pointed out, it
has much in common with that of her female contemporaries in Britain and
Ireland, such as Mary Wollstonecraft and Maria Edgeworth.[14] Although her educational programme has much in common with Rousseau's, she expresses a great deal
of resistance to his insistence that the education of girls should be tailored to their
dependent and subordinate role, encouraging their supposedly 'natural' traits of
manipulation and deception. Genlis' quarrel with Rousseau is thus focused on his
views on gender, rather than on the core principles which underpin *Emile*. The
eighteenth-century preoccupation with education was predicated on a general
acceptance that character formation had less to do with birth than with early influences, and in both *Adelaide and Theodore* and 'The Great Earl of Cork' Genlis
endorses this view. Genlis tell us for instance that the young Richard Boyle was
educated by Mulcroon, and that, although his education contained conventional
subjects such as mathematics and Latin, Mulcroon focused on efforts to inculcate
him with correct and just ideas, and to establish moral principles, thus indicating
the primary role of environmental influences in the formation of character. The
young Richard's orphan status and lack of money further emphasise his reliance on
character and cultivated talents alone, as well as representing a potentially radical
critique of systems of wealth and privilege.

This is reflected in the description of Blackrock as a retreat from worldly concerns. Blackrock is, in other words, an idealised eighteenth-century state of mind.
Mulcroon, we are told, has experienced unhappiness, and has been the victim of
ingratitude and injustice. However, his disillusionment is not accompanied by

---

13 Canny, *The Upstart Earl*, p. 8.   **14** J.H. Bloch, 'Women and the Reform of the Nation',
in *Women and Society in Eighteenth-Century France*, ed. E. Jacobs et al. (London, 1979), pp.
3–18, p. 17.

bitterness; thus his experiences have made him wise and have confirmed him in his decision to live an independent life. The environment into which Richard is born, therefore, represents the elusive eighteenth-century ideal of intellectual refinement and moral purity, in which all the advantages of cultivation can be achieved, without falling prey to the corrupting vices of over-refinement and excessive sophistication. At fifteen Richard is described as follows:

> The young Richard, born with a noble and sensitive soul, a good memory and superior intelligence, responded excellently to the pains taken by his generous benefactor. As modest and as simple as he was amiable, at 15 he was as handsome as an angel, though he never thought of his appearance; and, full of spirit and imagination, he believed that he simply possessed common sense.[15]

Richard's combination of well-cultivated talents and lack of worldly power are set against a character whom Genlis calls Sir Charles Manwood (in reality, Boyle had been briefly employed by a Sir Richard Manwood immediately before he arrived in Ireland). They are rivals for the hand of Lady Ranelagh. Boyle (naturally) triumphs, in a manner which Genlis describes as an 'artless seduction', once again suggesting Richard's position as a version of a child of nature.

The phenomenally successful sixteenth-century adventurer has, therefore, been transformed into an embodiment of eighteenth-century ideas about the primary importance of character as formed in an idealised educative process. In so far as this conviction is opposed to the belief in inherent or essential qualities, it is inevitably at odds with support for the aristocratic system. The location of Genlis' tale in areas associated with Edward FitzGerald suggests, furthermore, that the changes to Richard's character and background were inspired partly by Genlis' personal acquaintance with FitzGerald. As such, they are not randomly anachronistic, but indicative of Genlis' ideas about nobility and suggest that her use of an Irish setting is congruent with the ideas she sought to express in her tale.

Although one can imagine the ire of the FitzGerald family (by far the most respected of the Anglo-Norman or Old English elite) at the idea that they could be confounded with a New English 'upstart', the Boyle of Genlis' tale has a great deal in common with Lord Edward FitzGerald. The education of the large Leinster family in Blackrock was inspired by Rousseau's writings, which were greatly admired by the duchess of Leinster. The location was chosen because it favoured an informal lifestyle; the duchess wanted her children to develop qualities of independence, and to learn to value natural abilities more highly than birth. She wanted to employ Rousseau himself as a tutor for her children; failing that she employed a Scot named Ogilvie. After her husband's death she demonstrated her egalitarian principles and scandalised polite society by marrying Ogilvie and moving the fam-

---

15 Genlis, *Le Comte de Corke*, i, 3–4.

ily to the French countryside. Edward's education certainly seemed to 'take'. When serving with the army in Canada he revelled in the primitive lifestyle; later, when he was bitterly disappointed by being turned down as a suitor for Georgiana Lennox, he reflected that the values which separated him from his beloved were absent from more primitive, less artificial societies. Furthermore, by the time he met Genlis and Pamela he had renounced his title, committed himself to democratic principles and been ejected from the Army. In spirit, if not in fact, Edward presented himself as one who no longer relied on birth and position to smooth his way in the world.

Both Edward and Pamela occupied paradoxical positions in the debates around aristocracy and democracy. Edward's case is relatively straightforward: an aristocrat who embraced democracy. However, this is further complicated by his marriage to Pamela. One version of Pamela's birth makes her an (illegitimate) member of a royal house; the other depicts her as an obscure orphan, possessed of a rare 'natural' beauty. The whole is further complicated by the duke of Orleans' conversion to republicanism. According to Stella Tillyard, Pamela's marriage chances were blighted because she was 'damned as an aristocrat by many republicans, and as a republican by many aristocrats'.[16] The 'orphan' Richard Boyle, as represented by Genlis, thus is partly indebted to Edward FitzGerald for his fictional background, but Genlis' character combines aspects of the myths surrounding *both* Edward and Pamela FitzGerald.

At a more general level than individual biography, 'The Great Earl of Cork' contains some features which suggest that even in the minds of relatively poorly-informed foreigners such as Genlis, Irish scenes, characters and events prompted some very persistent associations. As we have seen, in the finest tradition of those who treat of Ireland, Genlis prefaces her tale with an apology for her fiction, remarking that the facts are much more interesting and strange than anything she could invent. It is also significant that Genlis accounts for Richard Boyle's appearance before the Star Chamber by claiming that he was accused of involvement in the rebellion of the earl of Essex. It seems that rebellion and revolution are for Genlis necessary elements of any 'Irish Tale'. Even independently of specific incidents of violence, Genlis' references to two apparently vastly different times and characters are linked by one coherent idea: the association of Ireland with an instability in social status and with disruption in the social order. As an 'adventurer' taking advantage of the opportunities offered by the colonial regime in Ireland, Richard Boyle was able to far exceed the social rank into which he was born. Edward FitzGerald, by contrast, voluntarily relinquished the privileges which had been his by birth. But whilst it is commonplace to observe that commentary on Ireland is informed by the vocabulary of disruption and strangeness, it is interesting to note that Genlis' tale, and in particular its conflation of a number of biographical narratives, suggests the persistence of another metaphor, that of adoption.

16 Tillyard, *Citizen Lord*, p. 150.

Given the eighteenth-century preoccupation with the influence of environment and education on the formation of character, adoption in this period
acquired renewed interest as a form of scientific or sociological experiment, in
addition to the inevitable romance surrounding obscured or mysterious origins.
Clarissa Campbell Orr affirms Genlis' belief 'in the power of the human will to
make and remake human personality and social practices', a belief that she explored
in her educational systems and in her decision to adopt Pamela and a younger girl,
Hermione, and to bring them up effectively as part of the Orleans household.[17]
The Edgeworth circle, who were admirers of Genlis' work, explored the meanings
of adoption in a number of ways. The English radical Thomas Day, a close friend
of Richard Lovell Edgeworth's, famously adopted two young girls in order to create, through a process of education, an ideal wife along the lines of Rousseau's
Sophie.[18] Richard Lovell Edgeworth himself expressed an interest in adopting an
infant or young child from a lower class and educating him in the manner of a gentleman, largely in the interests of scientific experimentation.[19] In the work of
Maria Edgeworth, adoption and guardianship of children are the norm, featuring
in *Belinda* (1801), *The Absentee* (1812), *Ormond* (1817), and, most prominently, in
Ennui (1809); reflecting both Edgeworth's interest in education and her response to
the complexities of personal and national identity. Although Edgeworth's contemporary and fellow-novelist, Sydney Owenson, is usually associated with the alle-
gory of the 'national marriage', adoption is at least as important a metaphor in *The
Wild Irish Girl* (1806). The marriage of the Anglo-Irishman Henry Mortimer and
the 'Princess of Innismore', Glorvina, is preceded by the metaphorical 'adoption'
of each by the other's father. The earl of M— claims that his plan to marry
Glorvina was actuated entirely by charitable and benevolent, rather than sexual
motives; when he learns of his son's passion for her he abandons the planned marriage, and announces that 'henceforth I shall consider her as the child of my adoption'.[20] Mortimer addresses the prince of Innismore in a letter, telling him that so
profound was the effect of meeting him that 'the first tye of nature was dissolved;
and from your hands I seemed to have received a new existence'.[21]

In the specific context of Ireland immediately after the rebellion of 1798 and
the Union of 1800, exploring the malleability of biological ties and the extent of
human adaptability was clearly linked to anxiety over the persistence of historical
enmity and the instability of the newly-inaugurated political order. The use of the
adoption metaphor, however, was a local application of a symbol that was characteristic of progressive and Enlightened thought across Europe. For committed pro-
gressives, the phenomenon of adoption was an irrefutable proof that human nature

17 I am very grateful to Clarissa Campbell Orr for permission to read and cite from her
unpublished essay, 'Mme de Genlis, Emigrée, the Republic of Letters and the Politics of
Adoption', given originally at 'French Emigrés' Conference II, London, 2 July 1999 (p. 1).
18 R.L. Edgeworth and M. Edgeworth, *Memoirs of Richard Lovell Edgeworth*, 2 vols (London,
1817), i, 214–15. 19 *Memoirs of Richard Lovell Edgeworth*, ii, 95–7. 20 S. Owenson, Lady
Morgan, *The Wild Irish Girl*, ed. K. Kirkpatrick (Oxford, 1999), p. 243. 21 Ibid., p. 221.

was characterised by potential rather than fixed identity; it was a living demonstration of the power of education and seemed to promise that radical and beneficial change was guaranteed.

By marrying Edward FitzGerald, Pamela might be seen to have exemplified the way in which humble birth could be nullified by education and environment. In the revolutionary climate of the day, the marriage carried an even more radical message, that of the imminent overthrow of the hierarchical social order. Ultimately these promises were not realised. Pamela FitzGerald was one of the casualties of the rebellion of 1798. After her husband's death she was ordered to leave Ireland and lived for a time in the émigré community in Hamburg. Her later life was one of misery and was marred by alcoholism and unsuccessful relationships. The disillusionment and disappointment that Genlis felt can be detected in the changes to her account of Pamela's character from the *Short Account* of 1796 to the *Memoirs* of 1825. In 1796 Genlis describes her adoption of Pamela as 'the best action of my life', and claims that her adopted daughter is 'a model for the wives and the mothers of the age'.[22] In her memoirs, however, Genlis provides a different account of Pamela, one which is clearly motivated by the events of the intervening years:

> Pamela had a beautiful face; candour and sensibility were the basis of her character; she never told a single falsehood, nor employed the slightest deception in the whole course of her education [. . .] I was deeply attached to her, but my attachment was an unfortunate one. This child, who was so charming, had the least application I ever saw in anyone; she had no memory, and was very volatile [. . .] Her mind was lazy to the last degree, and she turned out the least fit person possible for reflecting. Her fate threw her into extraordinary situations; she found herself without an adviser or a guide in a thousand dangerous circumstances; yet she always conducted herself admirably, as long as her husband lived, and, in some cases, in a manner that was truly heroic.[23]

Whilst maintaining a sympathetic view of Pamela, Genlis indicates here that she possessed faults of character which could not be remedied by education – or, at least, not remedied by a guardian as fond and attached as Genlis represents herself to be.

In 'The Great Earl of Cork', by contrast, Richard Boyle more than rewards the care of his guardian and educator, Mulcroon. His character and talent are recognised in spite of his low birth and lack of wealth, and by marrying Lady Ranelagh he acquires membership of the nobility. In effect, Genlis here provides an idealised account of the process of adoption and education, which, in her own experience,

---

22 Genlis, *A Short Account of the Conduct of Mme de Genlis since the Revolution* (Perth, 1796), p. 41. **23** Genlis, *Memoirs*, iii, 137–8.

was more complex and tragic. It is undoubtedly significant that Genlis' fictional-ized hero is male rather than female, and thus culturally permitted to 'make a name' for himself based on his talents and achievements. In the complex interactions between gender and social structure, women's 'names', identities and reputations were in effect determined by family affiliation and association. Thus, the utopian notion of self-determination which some versions of adoption imply is not, it seems, gender-neutral.

In this tale, I would argue, Genlis approaches Irish history as a vehicle for the representation of events which combine historical causality with lived human experience. The use of fictional narratives which insistently allegorize political and historical events is a marked feature of Irish culture in the early nineteenth cen-tury. Genlis' version of the 'national tale' indicates firstly that the allegorical poten-tial of Irish culture was acknowledged even by those with no direct experience of it. But Genlis' 'mistakes' and anachronisms suggest, more significantly, that Irish his-torical examples provided her with a way to explore and recreate the consequences of social and political upheaval for herself and those close to her. 'Irish Tales' of the early nineteenth-century involve, therefore, more than the introduction of 'local colour' and glamorized marginality: Genlis' use of the genre demonstrates its potential to express the aspirations and disillusionments of the post-Revolutionary condition.

Immigrant self-fashioning: the autobiographies of the Irish in Britain, 1856–1934

LIAM HARTE

It has been recognised for some time now that historians of the Irish in nine-teenth- and twentieth-century Britain have a sizeable body of autobiographical lit-erature to draw upon. For the most part, however, scholars have tended to use autobiographical testimony as a documentary supplement to empirical analysis, with very little attention being paid to it as a literary discourse. There are few crit-ical works that serve as navigational charts to Irish autobiography in general, let alone Irish immigrant self-writing, and those that do exist tend to concentrate on literary as opposed to plebeian self-writing.[1] Why this should be so is an open question. It may have something to do with the seemingly self-evident, artless nature of the genre, or the fact that autobiography is, in the words of John Sturrock, 'a kind of writing that, more than any other, is intended to work on our sympathies', and as such deters or even resists theorisation.[2] But whatever the rea-sons, it is perhaps time that we began to subject the autobiographical narratives of the Irish in Britain to more sustained literary analysis by inquiring into their tex-tual and contextual workings. Such an inquiry brings forth several complex ques-tions. Is there a discernable typology of Irish immigrant autobiography? What functions did self-writing serve for the immigrant subject? What were the motive forces behind this literature? How did immigrant subjects imagine and represent themselves? How did they construct and negotiate their identity both as individ-uals and as members of a particular cultural group?

In this essay I want to suggest answers to some of these questions based on my reading and research for a critical anthology of autobiographical writings by Irish immigrants in nineteenth- and twentieth-century Britain.[3] I will confine myself to

---

1 See T. Brown, 'Literary Autobiography in Twentieth-Century Ireland' in A. Martin (ed.), *The Genius of Irish Prose* (Dublin, 1984), S. Deane, 'Autobiography and Memoirs, 1890–1988' in *The Field Day Anthology of Irish Writing* (Derry, 1991), iii, pp. 380–3 and G. O'Brien's entry on autobiography in W.J. McCormack (ed.), *The Blackwell Companion to Modern Irish Culture* (Oxford, 1999), pp. 45–7. For Irish immigrant autobiography, see B. Canavan, 'Story-tellers and writers: Irish identity in emigrant labourers' autobiographies, 1870–1970' in P. O'Sullivan (ed.), *The Irish World Wide: The Creative Migrant* (Leicester, 1994), pp. 154–69. 2 J. Sturrock, 'Theory Versus Autobiography' in R. Folkenflik (ed.), *The Culture of Autobiography: Constructions of Self-Representation* (Stanford, 1993), p. 21. 3 Liam Harte, *Writing Home: An Anthology of Autobiography by the Irish in Britain* (Dublin, forthcoming).

self-narratives produced by first and second-generation nineteenth-century immigrants which appeared in print between the 1850s and the 1930s. Most of the texts
to which I will refer belong to the category of plebeian rather than literary autobiography, and many were the authors' only published work. I want to state at the
outset that I offer here no comprehensive, overarching theory of autobiography in
general or of Irish self-writing in particular. Indeed I am both wary and sceptical
about the possibility of arriving at any such grand theory, given the intensity of
theoretical debate about the nature of autobiographical discourse. My own
approach is based on a view of autobiography as a cultural practice and a narrative
artifice as much as a form of personal expression. Rather than seeing a self-narrative
as a more or less straightforward reflection of an autonomous pre-existing self, I
concur with those critics who conceptualise autobiography as a constitutive act,
whereby the subject's identity is configured by the act of autobiographical narration.[4] In this perspective, identity is seen as dynamic and evolutionary, 'a "production" which is never complete, always in process, and always constituted within, not
outside, representation'.[5] This leads to a narrative concept of the self as a rhetorical, fictive construct which is historically and culturally contingent. As Keya
Ganguly argues: 'It is important to underscore the ways in which identities are fab-
rications – that is, both invented and constructed – because doing so is a necessary
step in accounting for the centrality of representation in the constitution of the
real'.[6] Moreover, Michael Mascuch's formulation of autobiography as 'a perform-
ance, a public display of identity, even when composed secretly for an audience of
one'[7] usefully alerts us to the performative dimension of self-writing. Such insights
seem to me to have much validity, and can be of qualified use to us in our analysis of
the narrative self-representations of Irish immigrant autobiographers in nineteenth-
century Britain. Let us begin, however, with the question of typology.

It is possible to divide immigrant autobiographies of the period under review
into four broad narrative categories: moral, testimonial, political and self-improving. Caveats gather quickly around this statement. Not only are the borders
between these categories fluid rather than fixed, they also cut across two other
important classificatory modes, namely, gender and generation. Furthermore, not
all autobiographies fall neatly into a single category; some, indeed, such as Patrick
MacGill's *Children of the Dead End* (1914), contain elements of all four narrative
types. That said, such a typology provides us with a serviceable if rudimentary map
to what is largely uncharted literary territory, and affords us a discursive entry point
to the subject. Thus, we can assign to the first category autobiographies by early
nineteenth-century Irish immigrants whose primary concern was for the moral

---

4 See, for example, M. Mascuch, *Origins of the Individualist Self: Autobiography and Self-Identity
in England, 1591–1791* (Cambridge, 1997).   **5** S. Hall, 'Cultural Identity and Diaspora' in J.
Rutherford (ed.), *Identity: Community, Culture, Difference* (London, 1990), p. 222.   **6** K.
Ganguly, 'Migrant Identities: Personal Memory and the Construction of Selfhood', *Cultural
Studies*, 6: 1, 1992, p. 30.   **7** Mascuch, *Origins*, p. 9.

development of both author and reader. The second category contains works which are mainly preoccupied with documenting a way of life, while the third encompasses what is undoubtedly the most well-known type of immigrant self-writing, Fenian autobiography, as well as the memoirs of Irish parliamentarians. Although there are much fewer texts in the fourth category, two stand out as particularly fine examples of the self-betterment narrative, *My Struggle for Life* (1916) by Joseph Keating and *The Story of a Toiler's Life* (1921) by James Mullin. But it is with the moralists that I wish to begin, since their texts are among the earliest I have found from the nineteenth century.

The earliest nineteenth-century Irish immigrant autobiographers were artisans whose works were published in Victorian working-class journals or craft periodicals. In the mid-1850s two such workers published their abbreviated memoirs anonymously in the *Commonwealth*, a weekly Glasgow newspaper devoted to the moral and intellectual improvement of the working classes. The author of 'Life of a Cotton Spinner', published in 1856, was born in Glasgow of Irish parents in 1799, his family having left C. Antrim the previous year 'to avoid the troubles of that unhappy period'.[8] His memoir is in many respects a classic migrant worker's tale which chronicles his continual movement between between Glasgow and Belfast in search of regular employment. The central theme of the work is the author's relentless struggle with adverse fortune that, despite financial prudence and frugal living, thwarted his lifelong ambition to achieve a college education. Migrancy and adversity are also the defining themes of the 'Life of an Irish Tailor', published in the *Commonwealth* in April 1857.[9] The author, who identifies himself only by the initials 'J. E.', was born in Co. Antrim in 1816. Orphaned when very young, he was apprenticed at the age of twelve to a country tailor with whom he spent seven years. Following an unsatisfactory period of employment in Belfast, he moved to Liverpool, where the discriminatory work practices of the Tailors' Club hampered his progress. When 'a dullness in trade' led to redundancy, he embarked upon a ten-week tramp around the industrial centres of northern England in search of work. Unable to find any, he returned to Ireland and eventually found employment as a 'caretaker and watchman in a large establishment' in an unnamed town.

The third artisan autobiography of this period is 'Fifty Years' Experience of an Irish Shoemaker in London' by John O'Neil,[10] published serially between May 1869 and February 1870 in the weekly occupational journal, *St Crispin: A Magazine for the Leather Trade*. O'Neil was born in Waterford in 1777 and died in Drury Lane, London in 1858. In addition to being a shoemaker of some note, he is described as

---

8 'Life of a Cotton Spinner', *The Commonwealth*, 27 December 1856, p. 3. **9** 'Life of an Irish Tailor', *The Commonwealth*, 18 April 1857, p. 3. **10** The text contains no consistent spelling of the author's surname. 'John O'Neil' appears as the heading on each of the weekly instalments, yet the name appears variously as 'O'Neil', 'O'Neile', 'Neil' and 'Neill' in the narrative proper. This inconsistency may be a product of editorial carelessness, as the autobiography was serialised over a decade after the author's death.

'a Laureate of the Temperance Movement' who 'was always in the shade and on the brink of poverty'.[11] He was also remembered as the author of eight plays and several volumes of prose and verse, including a number of temperance poems. O'Neil's autobiography, which is a more sustained and more detailed narrative than the two *Commonwealth* memoirs, chronicles the vicissitudes of his professional and domestic life in London from his arrival in 1808 to the late 1840s.[12] The work is woven around two main narrative strands: his trials and triumphs as a shoemaker and his doomed attempts at writing, which was for him 'the chief consolation of life in every extremity'.[13] The autobiography provides a useful insight into the London shoemaking trade in the early part of the nineteenth century, as well as illuminating the material and normative forces operating within the metropolitan working-class community. As the father of a large impoverished family – his first wife bore him at least eleven children – O'Neil was prone to many physical and psychological privations. Starvation and pauperism were seldom far from his mind, and he was frequently out of work. As he succinctly puts it in chapter eleven, following another sacking: 'I had, as it was the common saying among the craft of that day, "three outs for the one in" – out of cash, out of credit, out of work, and in debt'.[14]

The shared desire of all three of these authors was to document a way of life and promote certain moral convictions, motives which place them firmly in the tradition of nineteenth-century British working-class autobiography. As David Vincent has observed, this tradition was founded upon 'the secularization of a long-established tradition of spiritual autobiography', much of which was written by Puritans and Quakers, in which pious experience was preserved in first-person discourse.[15] The influence of the spiritual tradition on working-class narratives, he claims, 'is to be found not in the structure but rather in the tone and general purpose of the works. The meaning of the past is now conceived in secular terms, but in spite of this fundamental change the autobiographers, on the whole, retained a desire to write respectable and above all morally improving pieces of work'.[16] This is certainly true of these three immigrant autobiographers, whose texts contain a blend of secular and spiritual influences. The secular element is evident in the titles of their works, which suggest that the authors' occupation and the social status they derived from it acted as the master narrative that shaped the way they saw their

---

11 Details of O'Neil's life are given in 'Biographies of Noted Shoemakers' in the edition of *St Crispin* of 20 February 1869, p. 100. **12** One of the most conspicuous features of O'Neil's autobiography is the almost total absence of any reference to his earlier life in Waterford or Liverpool, where he first settled on coming to England. The emphasis throughout is on his London experiences, as if what went before was of no consequence. **13** J. O'Neil, 'Fifty Years' Experience as an Irish Shoemaker in London', *St Crispin*, 2: 48, 27 November 1869, p. 263. **14** Ibid., *St Crispin*, 2: 39, 25 September 1869, p. 147. **15** D. Vincent, *Bread, Knowledge and Freedom: A Study of Nineteenth-Century Working Class Autobiography* (London, 1981), p. 36. For a more recent analysis of this tradition, see Mascuch, *Origins*. **16** Ibid., p. 17.

lives. This aspect aligns them with many nineteenth-century working-class autobiographers who defined themselves in terms of their occupational or political identity, thereby signalling their belief in the pre-eminence of the relationship between self and society over that between self and God.[17]

In the case of these immigrant autobiographers, however, occupational self-definition is not a reliable indicator of a wholly secular, let alone a political, worldview. None of them shows any signs of political radicalism, though O'Neil refers to, but did not take part in, trade union activism. Nor did they see themselves as part of an evolving working-class movement; O'Neil, for example, makes no reference to the rise of the Chartists, despite the fact that a contemporary of his, the radical tailor Francis Place, was one of the authors of the 1838 People's Charter. On the contrary, all three tend to see the meaning of their lives in moral rather than political terms, their narratives being closer in tone and purpose to Puritan self-writing rather than to the memoirs of political radicals. In each of these three texts the testimonial impulse is underpinned, if not actually overridden, by a moral seriousness and a desire to encourage good behaviour in others, so that the reader is offered an improving tale for imitation rather than an expression of unique individuality or a testament of political activism.

The eponymous cotton spinner's main autobiographical objective – to affirm the efficacy of religious faith in the face of doubt and despair – is expressed through a central epiphanic experience in which he recalls how he was spiritually rescued from the depths of depression by a profound intuition of God's goodness as revealed in the natural world. Any lingering doubts abut the author's Christian probity are dispelled by an editorial coda, which recommends the autobiography to working-class readers as a moral exemplum: 'This narrative of a good man's struggles with adversity, is worthy of the special attention of working men. We have seen numerous first-class testimonials in his favour, and believe that, up till the present time, he has maintained an unsullied reputation'. 'J. E.', the Irish tailor, was exercised by the evils of alcohol, tobacco and gambling. Having succumbed to the temptations of all three at various times in his life, he concludes his narrative on a morally improving note by extolling the benefits of temperance. His sentiments are echoed by John O'Neil, whose desire to promote the virtues of sobriety and industry among the working classes is clearly stated in the closing chapter of his autobiography, where he expresses the hope that 'by giving my experience from the first time I entered the Metropolis, in the triple character of shoemaker, author and Teetotaller' his memoir will 'serve as a landmark to steer the future adventurer on this mighty ocean of good and evil, that by perseverance, industry, and sobriety, he may ride securely, avoiding many of the rocks and quicksands that threaten him on every side'.[18]

But if these three autobiographers' preoccupation with moral instruction aligns

---

17 Ibid., p. 18. **18** O'Neil, 'Fifty Years' Experience as an Irish Shoemaker in London', *St Crispin*, 3: 60, 19 February 1870, p. 87

them with the British tradition of self-writing, they can also be read in another discursive context, namely, the racial construction of the Irish in Victorian Britain. As
several historians have pointed out, Victorian racist discourse constructed Irish
immigrants as an alien, inferior and potentially traitorous people who were not entitled to a place within 'respectable' British society, thereby relegating them to the
discrete world of the ethnic ghetto.[19] This discourse stressed a number of characteristics which rendered the immigrant Irish as degenerate 'others': backwardness,
irrationality, rootlessness, gregariousness, dirtiness and, of course, drunkenness. By
promoting two of the most cherished ideals of Victorian Britain – temperance and
self-improvement – these three autobiographers can be seen to be implicitly challenging negative stereotypes of the immigrant Irish, and in the process revealing
their interpellation as moral, self-improving subjects by bourgeois Victorian society.

The subversion of cultural stereotypes of the immigrant Irish is also a feature
of *At Scotland Yard* by John Sweeney, a classic testimonial autobiography of the late
Victorian period. Sweeney was born into a small farming family in Co. Kerry in
1857. His autobiography reveals little about his early life in Ireland, except that his
family suffered eviction when he was two years old and emigrated to London in
1875. In that year Sweeney joined the London Metropolitan Police and was posted
to Hammersmith. In 1884 he joined the Criminal Investigation Department at
Scotland Yard, where he was assigned to the Special Branch division, formed in
1881 as a 'Fenian Office' to deal with militant Irish republicans. In his role as sergeant Sweeney was directly involved in countering the violent threat posed by
Fenian and Clan na Gael activists in London, as well as curbing the frequently disruptive public clashes between Irish nationalists and unionists over Home Rule. He
eventually rose to the rank of detective-inspector before leaving the force in 1902,
aged forty-five.

Sweeney's autobiography consists of an extensive chronicle of his varied professional experiences during twenty-seven years of police service. As befits a retired
detective-sergeant, he is primarily concerned with factual accuracy and verisimil-
itude: 'I am confident that I have in no way romanced, and that nowhere have I
been guilty of any misrepresentation of fact that should do harm or injustice to
anyone'.[20] He represents himself throughout as a public guardian of the peace and
an enforcer of law and order, roles in which he took a manifest degree of pride and
satisfaction: 'I "shadowed" suspects; I guarded public men; I watched by royal resi-
dences; I helped to keep the public peace; I tracked the perpetrators of outrages. I
was one of the cogs in the machine, the workings of which are felt in continents
other than ours and across other seas'.[21] The mixture of individuation and self-

19 For a cogent analysis of this phenomenon, see J. MacLaughlin, '"Pestilence on their
backs, famine in their stomachs": the Racial Construction of Irishness and the Irish in
Victorian Britain' in C. Graham and R. Kirkland (eds), *Ireland and Cultural Theory*
(Basingstoke, 1999), pp. 50–76. 20 J. Sweeney, *At Scotland Yard* (London, 1904), p. vi.
21 Ibid., p. 19.

effacement that characterises this statement is typical of the autobiography as a whole. Although Sweeney uses the subjective 'I' throughout, there is little overt self-revelation or personal introspection in his narrative. Despite having a wife and family, he makes no attempt to connect his public, professional life with his private, emotional life. Nor does he discuss his social activities, apart from passing references to his interests in athletics and rowing. It is as if the private sphere did not exist for him, or that he did not attach any significance to it, or that his private self was inseparable from his professional role. Even more than the cotton spinner, tailor and shoemaker discussed above, this London-Irish policeman defines his subjectivity exclusively in relation to his work.

It is not only his inner life that Sweeney keeps hidden from view; he is also conspicuously reticent about his experience of being an Irishman in the Metropolitan Police during this most turbulent period in Anglo-Irish relations. One of his few explicit allusions to his Irishness occurs in chapter four, where he proudly recalls being selected for the special police protection unit which accompanied Queen Victoria to Ireland during her extended visit in April 1900. He writes of this, one of his 'most honourable calls of duty': 'Being alike an Irishman and an English police officer, I shared the responsibility of the important duties involved in the protection of Queen Victoria, in the capital of my own country, and I felt, as it were, a sort of double responsibility'.[22] In general, however, Sweeney adopts an unreflective attitude towards his ethnicity, which does not appear to have been an issue for him in his professional career. Only once does he allude to an occasion on which his Irishness was the subject of prejudicial comment by a fellow officer. It occurred while he was assigned to the protection of Lord Salisbury at Hatfield House in Hertfordshire, and arose out of what Sweeney calls 'the excessive ignorance of a certain local constable'.[23]

Sweeney's benevolent view of those who would offend him on racial grounds is largely attributable to his underlying regard for the British people and nation with which he strongly identified. He saw himself as a loyal imperial subject whose deferential respect for monarchy and the institutions of the state was accompanied by a corresponding disdain for those who sought to undermine them, not least 'the seditious Irish, particularly the Irish-Americans'. Chapter two of his autobiography contains a detailed account of the series of 'dynamite outrages' that shook London between March 1883 and January 1885, masterminded by republican activists. Sweeney's Irish background meant that he was a natural choice for the task of shadowing suspected Clan na Gael agents and attending their meetings: 'Being an Irishman born and bred, I knew quite as much of the Irish language as did the people whom I had to watch, and so was specially selected for this work'.[24] This work evidently caused him no ambivalence; indeed it is clear from his account of his undercover activities that he had nothing but contempt for extra-parliamentary Irish agitation, whether it emanated from the militant spirit of Fenianism or the

22 Ibid., p. 89. **23** Ibid., pp. 122–3. **24** Ibid., p. 49.

social grievances of the Land League. To him, both groups were made up of 'seditious revolutionaries', and while he evinces some respect for the constitutional nationalism of Parnell, his political sympathies were firmly unionist, loyalist and pro-Establishment.

Sweeney's socio-political conservatism and his whole-hearted identification with British values and attitudes make him, at first sight, a rather unusual Victorian Irish immigrant. Yet, as Elizabeth Malcolm suggests elsewhere in this volume, his views may be more representative than one might think, given the relative popularity of police work among nineteenth-century Irish immigrants. That he was certainly not the only Anglophile immigrant autobiographer is confirmed by James Mullin's *The Story of a Toiler's Life* (1921), an exemplary narrative of self-improvement. Born in Cookstown in 1846, Mullin became an apprentice carpenter to a cartmaker in his early teens and remained in the trade for nine years, 'under circumstances as adverse and with prospect as gloomy as Fate could inflict on any man outside a prison'.[25] Despite such hardship, he was characteristically keen to emphasise the self-improving aspect of these years and the fact that they left his 'passion for books' undiminished. His intellectual perseverance eventually led him to Cookstown Academy and from there to Queen's College, Galway on a scholarship. After many struggles with economic and academic adversity, he graduated with a degree in medicine in 1880 and emigrated to Wales, where he established himself as a general practitioner in Cardiff.

In his youth, Mullin had been a member of the Fenians and was briefly an agent for the *Irish People*, to which he also contributed nationalist verse. He abandoned the movement after the debâcle of 1867, however, and maintained a contemptuous attitude towards politics thereafter, until he read the biased coverage of Irish affairs in the London press in the early 1880s. This prompted him to join the Cardiff branch of the Irish National League, of which he served as chairman for twenty-five years. During this time Mullin developed strong Home Rule sympathies, and while he was reluctant to dismiss his youthful republican militancy, it is clear from his autobiography that it had long since been supplanted by a rather complacent bourgeois imperialism:

> I often smile at the irony of Fate which has made a staunch supporter of the British Connection out of such an uncompromising rebel as I considered myself. But I attribute this fact to the changed attitude of British people, my better knowledge of their character, and my complete confidence in their sense of justice.[26]

---

25 J. Mullin, *The Story of a Toiler's Life* (Dublin, 1921), p. 44. **26** Ibid., p. 79. His imperialist views are again evident in the closing chapter, where he uses such phrases as 'our Empire' and 'our tropical possessions' when recalling his travel experiences in Jamaica and the West Indies during his retirement years.

The autobiographies of John Sweeney and James Mullin serve to highlight the heterogeneity of Irish immigrant culture in Victorian Britain and qualify received notions about the political radicalism of Irish immigrants and their resistance to cultural assimilation and integration. Together they constitute a significant counterpoint to the tradition of nineteenth-century Fenian autobiography which, as Seamus Deane has noted, almost constitutes a genre in itself.[27] One of the defining features of this tradition is the unequivocal identification of the individual with the nation. In works that are often as much history as autobiography, the private self is effectively subsumed into the political narrative of the nation. This central trope of Irish nationalist autobiography has been effectively summarised by Sean Ryder:

> In its presentation of the lives of national 'heroes', the genre produces inspirational, idealized versions of national subjectivity, linking the life of the individual with the larger political collective which nationalism aims to establish. It is conventional for such narratives to suggest the absolute identification of the individual with the nation itself – the historical, contingent subject, in other words, appears to achieve authenticity and completion – its heroic realisation – through identification with the transcendent, impersonal entity known as 'the nation,' or 'national destiny.' The hero becomes, literally, the embodiment of the 'spirit' of the nation.[28]

While the achievement of this discursive association of subject and nation proved relatively straightforward for Irish nationalist autobiographers at home, their emigrant counterparts in Britain struggled to create a satisfactory version of national subjectivity. In the remainder of this essay I want to examine the difficulties and dilemmas of self-identification evinced in the autobiographies of two Victorian Irishmen, John Denvir and Tom Barclay, both of whom exploit the potential of autobiography to be 'the text of the oppressed and the culturally displaced, forging a right to speak both for and beyond the individual'.[29]

Denvir was born in 1834 into an immigrant Antrim family, which had settled in Liverpool in the early part of the century. He followed his father into the building trade, and eventually established his own business in Liverpool. His publishing activities began in the late 1850s with his managership of the *Catholic Times*, of

---

27 See Deane's preface to the extract from Thomas Clarke's *Glimpses of an Irish Felon's Prison Life* in *The Field Day Anthology of Irish Writing*, ii, pp. 280–1. Sweeney may well have encountered Clarke in the course of his professional duties during the early 1880s. Another Fenian autobiographer, Jeremiah O'Donovan Rossa, was certainly known to him; his notoriety earned him a special mention in chapter seven of *At Scotland Yard*. **28** S. Ryder, 'Male Autobiography and Irish Cultural Nationalism: John Mitchel and James Clarence Mangan', *Irish Review*, 13, Winter 1992/93, p. 70. **29** J. Swindells makes this point in relation to female, black and working-class autobiography in her introduction to *The Uses of Autobiography*, (London, 1995), p. 7.

which he later became editor, and continued throughout the rest of his life. In 1870 he launched the popular *Illustrated Irish Penny Library* series which consisted of cheap volumes of biography, fiction and poetry, and later wrote a major survey of the Irish in Britain, as well several novels. He was a founder member of the Home Rule Confederation and later became its national agent and organiser. His autobiography, *The Life Story of an Old Rebel* (1910), comprises his recollections of the politics and personalities of Irish nationalism in Britain from the 1840s to the early 1900s, with particular emphasis on Liverpool.

Like Sweeney, Denvir reveals little about his private or emotional life, focusing instead on his youthful association with Fenianism and subsequent involvement with the Home Rule movement. The implicit purpose of the narrative is to stress the need for individual and collective perseverance in the face of oppression and persecution in order to bring about the deeply desired goal of national independence. Irish nationalism, whether in its parliamentary or physical-force form, is represented throughout as an elevating and energising force which, rooted in the cultural landscape of rural Catholic Ireland, unites Irish people at home and abroad in a common bond. The author's personal experience serves as the embodiment and vindication of nationalist resolution, and the autobiography ends in vatic mode, with Denvir issuing a spirited appeal to the youth of Ireland to remain true to God and nation in anticipation of the imminent victory of nationalism over imperialism.

One of Denvir's main autobiographical motives was to bear accurate historical witness to the growth and development of Irish nationalism in Britain from O'Connell to Redmond, and thereby assert its moral authority. Like Mullin, he was keenly sensitive to the distortions of British press coverage of Irish affairs and strove to provide a nationalist corrective to anglocentric accounts of Irish history in his writings. His autobiography is not simply a recapitulation of an agreed past, therefore; it is a strategic intervention in a contested historical narrative. We see an example of his method in chapter seven, when he digresses from his account of the 'breaking of the van' in Manchester to criticise previous descriptions of the 1867 Fenian rescue attempt, claiming that 'it is important that the information given in books for the benefit of the present and future generations of Irishmen should be correct'.[30] The meticulous, almost pedantic, nature of Denvir's historical amendments – he clarifies the precise location of the rescue attempt and the direction in which the police van was travelling – reveals much about his view of the past and about his sense of autobiographical duty to act as a literary custodian of vital national truths. In particular, it bears out the truth of Julia Swindells' observation that:

> In making a claim to a political voice, the autobiographer is often also in the process of contesting, explicitly or implicitly, what the authority of the

30 J. Denvir, *The Life Story of an Old Rebel* (Dublin, 1910; repr. Shannon, 1972), p. 99.

'educated' account has to offer. Certain experiences, particularly those associated with systematic oppression, have not been recorded, or have been
represented partially, in stereotype or with flagrant bias. In this context,
autobiography can appear the most direct and accessible way of countering
silence and misrepresentation.[31]

As Denvir's scrupulous attention to historical detail suggests, the testimonial
purpose of his text is itself a function of his use of autobiography to establish a uni-
fied, coherent national identity for himself and the immigrant community to
which he belonged. He was keen to bring emigrant and second-generation identities, which were marginalised in revivalist and nationalist ideals of Irishness, into
the centre of contemporary debates about culture and ethnicity. This desire is
apparent in the opening chapter, in which he eulogises the patriotic identity of the
Irish community in Britain:

> Anyone who has mixed much among our fellow-countrymen in England,
> Scotland and Wales knows that, generally, the children and grandchildren of
> Irish-born parents consider themselves just as much Irish as those born on
> 'the old sod' itself. No part of our race has shown more determination and
> enthusiasm in the cause of Irish nationality.[32]

His own life story then becomes a paradigm of exilic patriotism in which personal
contact with Irish political leaders and activists becomes a substitute for personal
experience of Ireland.[33]

Denvir's emigrant status, however, problematises his self-identification with the
nation. Despite Leon Ó Broin's assertion that 'Physical dissociation took nothing
. . . from his essential Irishness',[34] the text suggests an underlying insecurity about
the author's cultural identity. In chapter three, for example, in the course of his recollection of the time he spent as a child with his relatives in Co. Down in 1846, he
recalls how friends and neighbours would gather in the evening for '"a cailey"'.
His anglicised phonetic rendering of the word causes him such unease as to prompt
an immediate apology to his Irish audience: 'I hope my Gaelic League friends will
forgive me if I don't give the correct sound of this word, but that is my remem-
brance of how they pronounced it some sixty years ago in Co. Down'. As if to
compensate for any perceived lack of 'authentic' Irishness, he immediately goes on
to recall his enthusiastic public readings of speeches by O'Connell, while simultaneously betraying a latent anxiety about his nationality which is registered in his

---

31 Swindells, *Uses of Autobiography*, p. 7.   **32** Denvir, *Old Rebel*, p. 2.   **33** There is a certain
symbolic aptness in the fact that his first impression of Ireland was in representational form
– a map on the back of one of O'Connell's Repeal cards – since the country existed for
him as an imaginary homeland for much of his life.   **34** L. Ó Broin, 'Introduction', *The Life
Story of an Old Rebel*, p. v.

memory of being referred to by neighbours as the "wee boy from England".[35]
Denvir's later involvement with a company of travelling players and musicians
called the Emerald Minstrels, whose primary aim was to cultivate 'Irish
Nationality', suggests a continuing need for cultural self-definition, a need to have
his Irishness publicly demonstrated and endorsed. His autobiography can therefore
be read as the final, *textual* expression of this need, an attempt to persuade his Irish
audience to sanction the self-identity manifest in the story of his lifelong devotion
to the cause of Irish nationalism. Read thus, his text is an act of imaginary recu-
peration, an assertion of his right to belong to what Benedict Anderson terms the
'imagined political community' of the nation.[36]

Denvir's preoccupation with issues of cultural and national identity is replicated
in Tom Barclay's *Memoirs and Medleys: The Autobiography of a Bottle Washer* (1934).
Written over a period of seven years (1924–31) when the author was in his seven-
ties, *Memoirs and Medleys* is a compelling account of the material and mental struggles of a self-taught 'proletarian working man'[37] of the mid-Victorian era. Born in
Leicester in 1852 to parents who fled Ireland during the Famine, Barclay's early
years were spent moving from one cramped, disease-infested slum dwelling to
another, shadowed by hunger, ill-health and his father's alcoholism. At the age of
eight he was sent to a rope factory where he worked a seventy-hour week for a
shilling and sixpence. This was the first of Barclay's many menial jobs in as many
as twenty factories in the Leicester area where, apart from short periods in London
and Ireland, he lived and worked until his death in 1933.

Despite the book's subtitle, Barclay's narrative is structured around his intellectual rather than his occupational development. Vivid early descriptions of the material poverty of the Leicester-Irish immigrant community are followed by a detailed
and lively account of the author's intellectual and political progress. His autobiographical motives were twofold: to testify to a life dedicated to self-learning and
the pursuit of knowledge, and to justify his ideological evolution from pious young
Catholic to freethinking secularist and socialist activist. Thus, his autobiography is
an expression of individualist self-identity, the antithesis of the spiritual autobiography which sought to promote piety, supplication and the abnegation of the individual personality. His text, moreover, is highly polemical and often openly
propagandistic on behalf of socialism and the writings of his great hero, George
Bernard Shaw, to whose works and ideas he refers throughout. His style of conversational intimacy is reminiscent of the Irish oral tradition, and he shows a highly
self-conscious awareness of his putative audience. Digressions from the main narrative are frequent; he apostrophises his mother, conducts an imaginary debate with
the reader and harangues the politically apathetic masses. The most revealing

---

35 Denvir, *Old Rebel,* p. 37.   **36** Anderson's celebrated definition of the nation occurs in
his *Imagined Communities: Reflections on the Origin and Spread of Nationalism* (London, 1991),
p. 6.   **37** T. Barclay, *Memoirs and Medleys: The Autobiography of a Bottle Washer* (Leicester, 1934;
repr. Coalville, 1995), p. 82.

digression of all occurs in chapter six where he frankly admits to a calculated violation of the autobiographer's unspoken pact with the reader to remain true to his or her subjective response and give a truthful account of the individual 'life': 'Let no one who may happen to see these things I write imagine that I am telling the whole truth and nothing but the truth about myself. I'm omitting to turn my worse side towards you, and why not?'[38] This flagrant confession of selectivity, couched in a typically conversational idiom, reveals Barclay's sophisticated – one might almost say postmodern – awareness of the artful, self-conscious nature of autobiography, and of its function as calculated self-portraiture.

As David Nash has observed in his Introduction to the 1995 edition, *Memoirs and Medleys* is 'a unique document for the study of the Irish diaspora in England', not least because of the insights it offers into the formation and expression of a second-generation Irishman's cultural identity.[39] Catholicism, that most distinctive social marker of the Irish in Victorian Britain, was central to Barclay's childhood identity. Like thousands of other nineteenth-century Irish immigrants, the Barclay family relied upon Catholicism, which in their case was made up of an amalgam of orthodox devotionalism, folk religion and peasant superstition, to sustain them in the face of grinding poverty. Young Tom received a thorough induction in the faith and developed an intense personal piety. As he matured, however, his faith, based as it was on ritualistic observance, could not withstand the weight of intellectual inquiry. Hungry for knowledge, he enrolled at the Leicester Working Men's College in the early 1870s and, with the zeal of the autodidact, began to renounce Catholicism for freethinking secularism, which led in turn to his adoption of the philosophy that became his new religion, socialism. Together with a group of likeminded individuals who 'believed in Heaven on Earth as fervently as ever the Religionist believes in a Blessed State of Immortality',[40] Barclay worked tirelessly for the socialist cause for the rest of his life, organising lectures, distributing bills and writing for the *Countryman*, a free Leicester socialist newspaper. Much of his autobiography comprises a trenchant exposition of his lifelong belief in the potential of socialism to ameliorate the harsh living and working conditions of the poor, tinged by an exasperation borne of the indifference with which his fellow workers responded to his advocacy.

If, as Nash claims, Barclay's postive rejection of religious faith makes him a rather exceptional Victorian Irish immigrant, then his dilemma of identity makes him a more representative second-generation Irishman. Growing up in the 1860s, Fenianism was as much a part of Barclay's childhood as Catholicism. He recalls how his parents cheered the rescue of James Stephens in 1865 and lamented the hanging of the Manchester Martyrs two years later, while their English neighbours 'danced and rejoiced'. As this statement suggests, the Barclays' reflexive anti-English sentiment was reinforced by a prevailing anti-Irish prejudice, the casual intimacy of which is graphically evoked in his recollection of being 'hounded and harrassed'

38 Ibid., p. 103.   **39** Nash's Introduction is not paginated.   **40** Barclay, *Memoirs*, p. 72

by the English children with whom he shared the slum. In such a politically charged atmosphere, local rows could easily assume mythic significance. Once, when besieged by a gang of local youths led by a boy named Billy, young Tom instantly transformed the confrontation into a miniature re-enactment of one of the defining contests of Irish history: 'My imagination went to work: Billy was King William and we were the Irish: it was the siege of Limerick being in some mysterious manner enacted over again'.[41]

Racial hostility eventually took its toll, however, and the boy's proto-Fenianism was soon replaced by its antithesis: a sense of shame at his Irish origins. His changing perception of his Irishness is recorded in a passage which vividly encapsulates the attenuation of his heritage under socio-cultural pressures, leading to psychological division.[42] It was several years before Barclay's Irishness reasserted itself, but when it did, it did so with compelling force.[43] Chapter six opens with a dramatic revelation: 'One day, somewhere in the [eighteen] nineties, I became impressed (I might say *obsessed*) with the thought that I couldn't be really Irish without a knowledge of the Irish language'(emphasis in original).[44] This essentialist conviction (which he subsequently rejected in favour of a more pluralist conception of Irishness) led him to attend Gaelic League classes in London and to establish a short-lived branch of the League in Leicester in 1902. It was shortly after this that he visited Ireland for the first time, to attend the annual Oireachtas festival. His lyrical recollection of this visit as a 'holy' event suggests that for him, as for many members of the second-generation Irish community, Ireland was not so much a physical place as a mythic realm of psychic wholeness, what Salman Rushdie terms an 'imaginary homeland',[45] forged from the symbols and narratives of Irish cultural nationalism.

Although disillusioned by his subsequent failed attempt to settle permanently in the country, Ireland remained his spiritual lodestar, never more so than during the revolutionary period. A diary entry from July 1919 records his desperate desire 'to *do* something – within three days of being sixty-seven . . . – for poor, distracted, ill-fated Ireland!' (emphasis in original).[46] Three years later, however, the Civil War had changed his mood to one of dismay. The social conservatism of independent Ireland was a great disappointment to him, and he railed against the restrictions

---

41 Ibid., p. 8.   **42** See *Memoirs*, pp. 23–4. Barclay's account of the socio-cultural influences that shaped his cultural inferiority complex about being second-generation Irish in England is replicated to a remarkable extent in the autobiographical trilogy of Bill Naughton, who grew up in Lancashire during the interwar years. See L. Harte, 'Migrant Memories: The recovery of self in the autobiography of Bill Naughton', *Critical Survey*, 8: 2, 1996, pp. 168–77.   **43** It would be wrong to assume that Barclay sublimated his ethnicity entirely during his early manhood. His continuing engagement with Ireland is evident from a letter he wrote to the *Leicester Chronicle and Mercury* in May 1882 in which he expressed his abhorrence at the Phoenix Park murders of that month. See *Memoirs*, p. 139.   **44** Barclay, *Memoirs*, p. 95.   **45** S. Rushdie, *Imaginary Homelands: Essays and Criticism, 1981–1991* (London, 1992), p. 10.   **46** Barclay, *Memoirs*, p. 138.

imposed on cultural and intellectual expression that were an affront to his liberal pluralism. Yet his patriotism prevailed throughout, though he could never escape entirely the feeling of being detached from his cultural moorings and remained prey to a lingering sense of ethnic longing, poignantly evoked by his description of himself as 'a would-be Irishman'.[47]

The autobiographies of John Denvir and Tom Barclay constitute an account of cultural otherness in which the immigrant subject represents himself as an interstitial figure, suspended in a stasis between two cultures, resisting full integration into the life of Britain yet unable to achieve 'authentic' selfhood through identification with the Irish nation. Both write from a problematic, indeterminate position outside essentialist definitions of Irishness, from where they endeavour to insinuate themselves into the nationalist version of subjectivity. Their negotiation of cultural identity, therefore, proceeds from, and is continually shadowed by, an awareness of identity loss and cultural amputation, as neither writer ultimately manages to overcome the debilitating contingencies of geographical and generational dislocation. As such, they bear out the truth of Stuart Hall's observation that 'Migration is a one way trip. There is no "home" to go back to'.[48] 'Home' was clearly a much more flexible identification for the likes of John Sweeney and James Mullin, both of whom evince a deep-seated regard for the ideologies and value-systems of late Victorian Britain in their autobiographies. Their early nineteenth-century antecedents seem equally reconciled to prevailing bourgeois values and show clear signs of their ideological incorporation within an overarching British identity. And yet, their ethnicity cannot be wholly erased, for it is possible to read their autobiographies as oppositional texts that challenge the negative construction of the immigrant Irish in Victorian discourse. For them, as for their fellow immigrant autobiographers, self-writing served as a subtle and effective means of constructing, performing and negotiating a complex self-identity in the public realm of discourse.

47 Ibid., p. 102.   **48** S. Hall, 'Minimal Selves' in L. Appignanesi (ed.), *Identity: The Real Me* (London, 1987), p. 44.

Two versions of home and abroad from the Peninsular Campaign: *Vandeleur* and 'The Burial of Sir John Moore'

PETER DENMAN

In Irish writing, the state of being abroad, and the encounter with foreign culture, are both frequently associated with ideas of deprivation and disadvantage. Emigration, exile, punitive transportation, offer the rubric under which the Irish are seen at a distance; and to these we might also add absentee landlordism. These became established as stereotypes in Irish writing in English during the nineteenth century, ranging from the popular level of verses such as those by Ada Lady Dufferin, author of 'The Emigrant's Farewell', through to the biographical depictions of the Irish modernists such as Joyce and Beckett as artists in exile.

But the idea of 'abroad' serves not just as a motif of deprivation but as one of imaginative resource – witness the case of Thomas Moore's orientalist poetic fantasy *Lalla Rookh* (1817) and James Clarence Mangan's poetic 'translations' a couple of decades later. Abroad can also provide a removed and neutral arena in which to situate narratives that want to avoid too much exposure to the tensions of the Irish-English relationship, as in some of Charles Lever's novels, such as *The Daltons* (1852), *The Dodd Family Abroad* (1854), and *One of Them* (1861). And in Gothic and vampire fiction by Irish writers, from Maturin's *Melmoth the Wanderer* (1817) to Le Fanu's 'Carmilla' (1872)[1] and Stoker's *Dracula* (1897), the Mediterranean world and central Europe serve as keys to a disturbingly exotic and uncanny condition in which to play out psychological situations with a bearing on political and cultural tensions at home. As a young nineteenth-century poet, Yeats commenced his career with *Mosada* (1886), a dramatic poem set among the Moors; much later in his career, of course, he famously envisaged an imagined expedition overseas in 'Sailing to Byzantium'.

I list these examples simply in order to suggest that the literary concept of 'abroad' can combine the conventional motif of exile with an enabling resource. Various questions might arise from consideration of these texts. When a nineteenth-century Irish writer imagines the expatriate condition, what is the corresponding concept of the home which is left behind, the 'this-ness' which defines the 'otherness' of abroad? What use is made of the notion of being abroad when defined with reference to Ireland, particularly in the period just after the Act of

---

1 A novella included with four other stories in J.S. Le Fanu *In a Glass Darkly* (London, 1872).

Union which gave a distinctly political cast to the concept of the homeland? This was also a period before the strong motif of exile had fully established itself in Irish writing in English, as the theme did not gain full prominence until the increase in mass emigration later in the century. Does the concept of going or being abroad differ in Irish literature from what is found in, say, English writing? I would suggest that it does, in that there is a distinct genre of travel writing in the nineteenth-century English tradition. This was fuelled by a mix of exploration, evangelism and exploitation, as is shown by works such as Frances Trollope's *Domestic Manners of the Americans* (1832), George Henry Borrow's *The Bible in Spain* (1843) – not really a work of evangelism – and Robert Louis Stevenson's *An Inland Voyage* (1878) and *Travels with a Donkey in the Cevennes* (1879). The genre is sufficiently prominent in nineteenth-century English writing to warrant a dedicated chapter in the *Oxford History of English Literature*.[2] Travel writing is characterised by an awareness of a materially secure home-based readership, whereas the literature of exile longs for a home that it creates in the imagination.

The answers to these various questions are outside the scope of this article. The concentration here is on just two early nineteenth-century Irish texts, each with a bearing on the Peninsular Wars. One is the poem by Charles Wolfe, 'The Burial of Sir John Moore at Corunna', famous throughout the nineteenth century and still known today. The other is *Vandeleur*, an anonymously-authored novel which merits rather better than the neglect in which it has languished since its publication.

The novel *Vandeleur* occupies two of the three volumes published as *Tales of Military Life* in 1829; its author is unknown, although it has been persistently but implausibly associated with William Maginn. The title page *Tales of Military Life* describes it as written by the author of *The Military Sketch Book*, which had appeared two years previously. The earlier, and therefore the later work also, has been tentatively but certainly erroneously attributed to Maginn.[3] Whoever the author was, and it is not certain that the author was Irish, the novel shows a sustained engagement with what was, at the time of publication in the 1820s, fairly recent Irish and European history. As an 'authorless text' telling a story that moves across national boundaries, the uncertainties in identifying the author throw into relief questions about how we categorise home and abroad.

Vandeleur takes Dublin as its starting point, and Dublin at a particular and crucial moment at the start of the nineteenth century. The Emmet rebellion is

---

2 P. Turner, *English Literature 1832–1890 Excluding the Novel* (Oxford, 1989). **3** The misattribution occurs in the *Cambridge Bibliography of English Literature*, ed. George Watson, 4 vols (Cambridge 1941), and various library catalogues. William Maginn, born in Cork in 1791, was one of the leading magazinists of the 1820s and 30s, writing for *Blackwood's*, and editing *The Representative, Fraser's*, and the *London Magazine*. Maginn's work – that which is identifiably his – has not yet had the considered treatment it deserves, although there have been various accounts of his progress, alternately lamenting his dissipation and admiring his liveliness. The most recent is T. Eagleton's essay 'Cork and the Carnivalesque' in *Crazy John and the Bishop and Other Essays on Irish Culture* (Cork, 1998).

described in its opening chapters, with a vivid description of the streets of the city on 23 July 1803. The Robert Emmet initiative is treated with a certain measure of sympathy, not through shading it with pro-Nationalist feelings but by treating it as a romantic frolic. The book steers a middle course on Irish politics, with strong anti-Orange sentiments expressed. After the first six chapters, the action moves to Bath, and then the army regiment with which most of the characters are associated sets sail for Lisbon and the Peninsular war. As Ostin, one of the protagonists, follows on a later vessel, he encounters the boat bringing back the body of Sarah Curran, Emmet's beloved, to Ireland.

Vandeleur anticipates the military novels of Charles Lever, *Charles O'Malley* (1841), *Jack Hinton the Guardsman* (1843), *Tom Burke of Ours* (1844), which began to appear the following decade. Lever's novels are told more episodically, and in the first person. They provided a voice for the exploration of Ireland, generally as seen by an outsider who is brought into contact with Ireland by his posting. Largely humorous in intent, they mix the military novel with travel writing, with Ireland becoming the territory travelled to and characterised. Arguably it was this tendency to treat Ireland as an exhibit, as much as the stage-Irishness of the humour, which irritated some Irish readers. *Vandeleur*, on the other hand, takes Ireland, and a number of Irish military characters, as its point of departure, and then moves the action abroad.

The Peninsular War, as the principal land action of the campaign against Napoleon, provided the major foreign theatre for military engagement at the beginning of the nineteenth century. Since the French revolution and the Napoleonic wars, opportunities for travel on the continent had been interrupted. While it is not suggested that they enlisted in the army with the object of seeing the world, military service offered the context in which Irishmen and Englishmen, real or fictional, might visit the European mainland in the early years of the century.

Vandeleur is a revealing exercise in literary development. The Preface tells how the narrator has spent the greater part of his life in military service and as a result has met a wide range of people of all moral states. This breadth of experience in human nature is the ostensible justification for his writing the stories – a justification that was to be used also by Samuel Warren for his much more popular *Passages from the Diary of a Late Physician* (1832), another career-based compendium of fictional tales. But it is equally the case that military service provided a sort of society in which the immediate demarcations are not those of class, property and ideology, so much as they are those of the ranks and duties peculiar to the army. With the large Irish presence among the personnel in all ranks, army society provided a restricted forum in which national differences, while still noticeable, were accidental rather than essential.

The peculiarities of dialect had recently been introduced into fiction in English, particularly by Walter Scott but starting perhaps with Maria Edgeworth's *Castle Rackrent*. Since then, it had been mostly speech patterns and accents that departed from the perceived standard that were shown in print, and Hiberno-English was a frequent feature. But in *Vandeleur* we get an instance of the Irish striking back, with southern English speech targeted. Raftery is an Irish groom who has Anglicised himself to the extent of changing his name to 'Rafty' and speaking with newly acquired vowels: 'Schoolmeastau, give us none of bog-launin heau'. 'Bog-learning' is, of course, a specific rejection of Irishness.[4] The brief phonetic transcription of a consciously affected English accent captures the dropping of the 'r's and the intrusive diphthongs on vowel sounds, with short [a] being rendered as [e]. It is a reminder that an Irishman going abroad might do more than simply change location; he might also change the mannerisms, idioms and characteristics which identify him as Irish. In fact, the main plot of *Vandeleur* reflects this, with its conventional plot of a displaced heir in which it emerges that the true Vandeleur has been supplanted by a rascally cousin. Redmond Allan, whom we met in the early chapters in the action surrounding Emmet's rebellion, and who subsequently turns up fighting on the French side in Spain, is the true Vandeleur. This kind of thing is the stock matter of fiction; nevertheless, questions regarding identity cluster around the actions of Redmond during the Peninsular campaign when, motivated by humanity rather than patriotism, he switches sides at will. They also serve to give a particular colouring to issues of allegiance and homeland, at a time when the Irish homeland had been constitutionally redefined.

The campaign of Sir John Moore's army is in the background of *Vandeleur*, as is also Wellington's campaign. The hardships endured by Moore's army on the retreat to Corunna are glossed over in the novel, but there is a description of his burial. This had become a famous episode, already memorialised in Charles Wolfe's earlier poem, 'The Burial of Sir John Moore at Corunna', and the description in *Vandeleur* closely parallels that of the poem. It may be written in imitation of the poem, or it may be that both shared a contemporary report of the event as a common source for their material.

Charles Wolfe himself was born in 1791, the son of Theobald Wolfe of Kildare, the same from whom Wolfe Tone took his name. Wolfe spent his teenage years in England, where he was schooled, and returned to Ireland in 1809 to study at Trinity College Dublin. He became a clergyman, had various livings in Ulster, and died in 1823, still in his early thirties. By 1842 there had been eight editions of his works, comprising his sermons and poetic compositions, but there is really little of interest other than 'The Burial of Sir John Moore'. While his memorialists and enthusiasts assert that he would have produced more and greater poems had he lived, this would appear to be a polite and pious aspiration. Anyway, one good poem is already more than most people achieve.

Charles Wolfe's poem is an instance of a specific moment and place abroad being imagined from a specific reference time and place in Ireland and it provided a defining literary image of that war. The piece belongs to that class of poems

---

4 The *1811 Dictionary of the Vulgar Tongue* confirms that the prefix 'bog' was a dismissive description of things Irish. *Lexicon Balatronicum. A Dictionary of Buckish Slang, University Wit, and Pickpocket Eloquence* (London, 1811), s.v. Bog Lander, Bog Trotter, Bog Latin.

which enjoyed immense popularity for a time, and constitute the single work for which its author is remembered, if at all. The poem was written in Ireland, and first published in the *Newry Telegraph* in 1817; it achieved prominence when taken up soon afterwards in one of the first numbers of *Blackwood's Edinburgh Magazine*. The poem was widely known from then right through until the end of the nineteenth century. It was translated, its authorship was variously claimed and disputed, it was parodied, spurious versions of it circulated, and it secured a firm place in both Irish and English anthologies. It was included in Samuel Lover's *Poems of Ireland* in 1858, and in F.T. Palgrave's canon-making *Golden Treasury of the Best Songs and Lyrical Poems in the English Language* in 1861. Later it appeared in the four-volume *Cabinet of Irish Literature* (1895) edited by Charles Read. It was also included by more pro-grammatic anthologists around the turn of the century, part of whose purpose was cultural definition. In 1900, as well as appearing in Quiller-Couch's *Oxford Book of English Verse*, it was also in Brooke and Rolleston's *Treasury of Irish Poetry*, and Yeats' *Book of Irish Verse*. Thereafter, however, its currency waned. The temper of both Irish poetry and war poetry changed dramatically during the second decade of the twentieth century. Nevertheless, the poem still enjoys a vigorous life in school texts and occasionally as a recitation; as such it probably ranks alongside Kipling's 'If', Milton Hayes' 'The Green Eye of the Yellow God', and Robert Service's 'The Shooting of Dan McGrue'. This is illustrious company, in that they have all entered a wider public consciousness than have most other poetical works. These last three were all written in the early twentieth century, a hundred years or so after 'The Burial of Sir John Moore', but it was at just about this time that Wolfe's poem exchanged respectability for popularity.

Because there was some early confusion about its authorship, which generated mild controversy and resulted in details being offered by witnesses, something is known of the background to the poem's composition. The central event occurred during the opening stages of the peninsular war, a decade earlier than its compo-sition. In the winter of 1808, troops under John Moore had retreated from Madrid to Corunna on the north-west coast of Spain. There they fought a holding action against the pursuing French forces before making an embarkation on to the wait-ing ships. In that last battle the commanding officer Moore was killed. He was buried just before the last of his troops embarked. The source text for the popular knowledge of the event is a description of his funeral, written by Robert Southey and printed soon after the event in the *Edinburgh Annual Register* for 1808:

> The body was removed at midnight . . . A grave was dug for him on the rampart there, by a body of the 9th regiment, the aides-du-camp attending by turns. No coffin could be procured; and the officers of his staff wrapped the body, dressed as it was, in a military coat and blankets. The interment was hastened; for about eight in the morning, some firing was heard, and the officers feared that, if a serious attack were made, they should be ordered away and not suffered to pay their last duty.[5]

Wolfe, while a student a Trinity some years later, came across the periodical passage and began versifying it almost immediately.

Many of the details of the poem self-evidently have their origins in the language of that short paragraph of prose description. The mention of the rampart, the haste, the shooting, all find their way into Wolfe's verses.

> Not a drum was heard, not a funeral note,
> As his corse to the rampart we hurried;
> Not a soldier discharged his farewell shot
> O'er the grave where our Hero we buried.
>
> We buried him darkly at dead of night,
> The sods with our bayonets turning;
> By the struggling moonbeam's misty light
> And the lantern dimly burning.
>
> No useless coffin enclosed his breast,
> Not in sheet nor in shroud we wound him;
> But he lay like a Warrior taking his rest
> With his martial cloak around him.
>
> Few and short were the prayers we said,
> And we spoke not a word of sorrow;
> But we steadfastly gazed on the face that was dead,
> And we bitterly thought of the morrow.
>
> We thought, as we hollowed his narrow bed
> And smoothed down his lonely pillow,
> That the Foe and the Stranger would tread o'er his head,
> And we far away on the billow!
>
> Lightly they'll talk of the Spirit that's gone
> And o'er his cold ashes upbraid him, -
> But little he'll reck, if they let him sleep on
> In the grave where a Briton has laid him.
>
> But half our heavy task was done
> When the clock struck the hour for retiring:
> And we heard the distant and random gun
> That the foe was sullenly firing.

5 *Edinburgh Annual Register,* 1808, p. 458.

> Slowly and sadly we laid him down,
> From the field of his fame fresh and gory;
> We carved not a line, we raised not a stone,
> But we left him alone in his glory.

A misunderstanding of the prose description contributed to one of the poem's most prominent details, that of the burial taking place at night. In fact, the body of Moore was taken to the citadel at midnight, to lie there while a grave was prepared. The actual burial did not take place until after daybreak.

The poetic version conjures up a scene that is composed of negatives and absences – no memorial cenotaph, no funeral music, and the prospect of his being left alone the next day as his troops are taken to the sea. This catalogue of negatives is given to lament the actual lack of ceremony, although, by mentioning them, the catalogue introduces retrospectively the images of honour due to the dead soldier. The motif of absence contributes also to the de-localisation of the poem. Were it not for the title, with its careful specifying of the name of the dead general and the place at which the scene is enacted, there would be nothing to situate the poem. Moore is referred to in generic terms of praise: 'Hero', 'warrior', 'Spirit that's gone'; the French appear as 'the enemy', 'the Foe' and 'the Stranger'. The poem is written largely in the first person plural ('We buried him darkly', 'Our Hero') but the nature of this community referred to is not specified. The voice of the poem could be aligned with the troops under Moore's command, or – with more dramatic immediacy – with those who were members of the burial party. On the other hand, the 'we' might extend to include all those in whose interests Moore was fighting and gave his life, and who participate imaginatively in the actual and poetic obsequies.

The one term of specificity in the poem occurs in the line where the burial party is implicitly described as composed of Britons: 'In the grave where a Briton has laid him'. The term 'Briton' was probably the most inclusive term available to Wolfe. Historically it referred to the pre-English Celtic inhabitants and, as the OED records, it came into vogue during the eighteenth century after the Act of Union of England and Scotland; when it was pressed into service as an inclusive term for Scots and English. In 1817, soon after the Irish Act of Union, it had an additional usefulness in eliding difference; although it would not be long before difference was reinstalled, and the term 'West Briton' for Irishman joined that of 'North Briton' for Scotsman – the latter without the pejorative Anglo-Irish shading that the former designation later acquired.

What we see in the publication history traced earlier is a negotiation between Britain and Ireland, which is quite familiar. There is an equivalent negotiation in the actual text between a here and a there – a lost homeland and a foreign abandonment. The poem was subsumed into a British consciousness. Arguably, this started when the poem was taken up by Scottish and English publications; it was attributed to Byron, and it eventually achieved the apotheosis of inclusion in

Palgrave's *Golden Treasury*. At one stage in the nineteenth century two spurious verses were added, in which there is an insistent Englishness which only points up the studied vagueness of Wolfe's writing.

> By Englishmen's feet when the turf is trod
> On the breast of their hero pressing,
> Let them offer a prayer to England's God –
> To him who was England's blessing.[6]

As against this English cast, the suggestion has been made that there is a distinctively Irish turn of phrase in the last line of the fifth stanza, 'And we far away on the billow', which reproduces an identifiably Irish construction (*Agus sinn i bhfad ar an fharraige*). To this could be added the observation that 'far away on the billow', equates to the Irish *thar lear* (over the sea, on the water) as an expression for 'abroad', and the term 'Stranger' for the enemy might also have an Irish provenance.

But these are no more than hints and turns of phrase, which suggest, not surprisingly, the ghost of an Irish diction in poetry in English. By suggesting and at the same time evading the particularities of allegiance, while imaginatively exploring an abroad which remains largely unopposed to and unrelated to a homeland, Wolfe's poem manages to be an Irish poem of expatriation which is universalist and inclusive, if not unionist, in effect. It suggests that individual worth transcends national placing, and that expatriation and death abroad are deprivations which can be redressed -at least partly – through poetic commemoration. As such 'The Burial of Sir John Moore at Corunna' has more in common with say, Rupert Brooke's sonnet 'The Soldier' ('If I should die, think only this of me . . . There is some corner of a foreign field that is for ever England') or Yeats' 'An Irish Airman Foresees His Death' than it has with the Irish Victorian poems and ballads of emigration and exile of the intervening period. And, as with the more popular pieces mentioned earlier, there seems to be an affinity with poems from the early twentieth century.

An echo of the peninsular campaign has persisted into modern Irish poetry. In Seamus Heaney's short sequence 'Singing School', at the end of the volume *North* (1975), his poem 'Summer 1969' describes spending that summer abroad in Madrid as the troubles break out in Belfast in his homeland. The painting he contemplates in the cool of the Prado Gallery is Goya's painting of the 'Shootings of the Third of May', showing the executions carried out by the occupying French troops. It serves as a reminder of the challenge to an artist's response in times of national

---

6 Quoted in 'Memoir and Remains of Charles Wolfe', *Dublin University Magazine*, 20: 120, November 1842, pp. 618–34.

crisis. But the comparison that the painting prompts is not a historical one with the Peninsular War but, as the poem's title suggests, a poetic one with Easter 1916 in Dublin and Yeats' poem of that name. That in itself is an indication of a distance travelled.

'Who is Kim?': Rudyard Kipling and the haunting of the colonial imagination

KATHLEEN COSTELLO-SULLIVAN

Rudyard Kipling's eponymous character, Kim, is often taken as a classic example of what Homi Bhabha calls colonial 'hybridity,' or a modified version of the 'not quite/not white' paradigm.[1] Such readings do not always interrogate the assumptions of *purity* that underlie Kim's supposed hybridity; however, as Gayatri Spivak notes, 'too uncritical a celebration of the 'hybrid' . . . inadvertently legitimizes the 'pure' by reversal.'[2] While Kipling's narrator insistently invokes Kim's whiteness and his 'Englishness' to counterbalance the character's threatening hybridity, that invocation is predicated on the erasure of a third ethnicity – Kim's Irish identity, a self neither 'English' nor, in contemporary usage, precisely 'white.' The elision of the problematic and disruptive presence of Kim's Irishness permits a false perception of purity, both racial and cultural, even in the face of hybridity. That impurity, in turn, is betrayed by what Derrida might call 'linguistic impurities' in the text.[3] While Kim's Irishness thus may reflect the fractured identity oft attributed to Kipling, its inclusion simultaneously highlights Kipling's concomitant struggle to counterbalance an imaginary Oriental(ist) identity with a uniform Western one. Kim's Irishness suggests Ireland's awkward place in the coloniser's imaginary, as a Western, white colony problematising racial schemas of difference. I will suggest that, like the Orientalist biases and assumptions that shape Kipling's characterizations, Kipling's introduction of Irish identity into the text betrays the uncertainty of a unitary *British* identity.[4]

While critics customarily note the threatening quality of Kim's hybridity, they often conclude that it symbolises and even reifies British imperial power/

---

1 For his well-known and oft-cited discussion of hybridity, see H. Bhabha, *The Location of Culture* (New York, 1994), esp. pp. 1–5, 33–6. While Kim is 'white' and therefore does not qualify as a 'mimic man' per Bhabha's discussion of 'black semblance', the threatening aspects of Kim's racial border-crossings are well-documented and speak to the same issues of colonial ambivalence (see Bhabha pp. 85–92). I will suggest, however, that this category of 'white' is far less monolithic than critical apprehension often suggests. **2** G.C. Spivak, *A Critique of Postcolonial Reason: Toward a History of the Vanishing Present* (Cambridge, 1999), p. 65. **3** J. Derrida, *Monolingualism of the Other; or, The Prosthesis of Origin*, trans. by P. Mensah (Stanford, CA, 1998). **4** A. Nandy argues that Rudyard Kipling 'could not be both Western and Indian' and so was obliged 'to redefine . . . the Indian as the antonym of the Western man . . .' See Nandy, *The Intimate Enemy: Loss and Recovery of Self under Colonialism* (Delhi, 1983), pp. 76, 79.

71

knowledge structures. Kim's 'hybrid' nature, as an 'English' child raised in and even *by* a monolithically Orientalised yet paradoxically heterogeneous India, is seen as symptomatic of the English need and ability to 'know' India in some fundamental respect in order to govern well. The suggestion that it is possible to *know* India, as well as the idea that India can be simultaneously foreign and entirely knowable at once, evokes Edward Said's concept of Orientalism and highlights Kim's hybridity as both an ideal and a tool of colonial domination.[5] Since his hybrid (i.e. English and Indian) background uniquely qualifies him for participation in the 'Great Game' of British imperialism, Kim is thus often considered to represent an idealised embodiment of British colonial rule.[6]

This is not to suggest that critics fail to recognise the complexity of Kim's positionality. Judith Plotz notes that, while '[i]n some ways he [Kim] is deeply Indian . . . of course, he is not Indian . . .'[7] While the narrator is at pains to establish Kim's 'Oriental' side, noting 'the Asiatic side of the boy's character' and 'the Oriental in him,' he also readily and repeatedly claims Kim as English and notes his destiny to 'command natives.'[8] Kim's alleged Englishness is also countermanded by his Irish heritage: Edward Said calls Kim 'an Irishman in India,' and Plotz notes that Kim 'is [not] exactly English either.'[9] The narrative does recognise the Irish element of Kim's character, by problematically attributing his covetousness, craftiness, sense of humour, and short fuse to his Irish heritage, and Kim himself denies any English identity: '[W]e walk *as though* we were mad – or English'.[10] The resulting difficulty in labeling Kim either Indian *or* English is thus often read as symptomatic of his hybridity.

In spite of these stipulations, critics often conclude that Kim's hybridity is ultimately contained and that he is, in the final analysis, English, as the narrator assures us. This acceptance seems to be predicated on a certain slippage in the use of that term. Primarily, 'English' and 'British' are often used interchangeably in critical readings that identify Kim. As Catherine Hall notes, however, 'Englishness is an ethnicity, just like any other', yet the claim that English equals British remains pervasive.[11] To conflate 'English' and 'British' is to perpetuate the privilege of Englishness over other ethnicities identified as 'British.'

At the same time, 'Britishness' itself ought not to be taken as a monolithic term:

5 E. Said, *Orientalism*, 1st ed (New York, 1978), pp. 31–73. See also Bhabha's discussion of the stereotype and the disavowal of difference, pp. 66–84. 6 Kipling's sympathies for the British colonial project are well known. For a discussion of Kipling's imperialist sympathies, see Said's 'Introduction' in *Kim*, pp. 7–46, esp. 7–10, 27–30, 43–6. 7 J. Plotz, 'The Empire of Youth: Crossing and Double-Crossing Cultural Barriers in Kipling's Kim.' *Children's Literature*, no. 20 (1992), pp. 111–31, esp. p. 112. 8 R. Kipling, *Kim*, ed. E. Said (New York, 1987), pp. 161, 268, 173. 9 See Said, 'Introduction,' p. 38; Plotz p. 112. 10 Kipling, *Kim*, p. 280, my emphasis. 11 C. Hall, *White, Male, and Middle-Class: Explorations in Feminism and History* (New York, 1992), pp. 205–6.

> . . .there is an important need to underscore the multiplicity of Britishness, for while the English proper might perhaps take their identity for granted, those who existed in the margins of this identity. . .could only be integrated into the emerging discourse of conquest and imperial expansion through the invention of a British identity . . .[12]

Just as English is one ethnicity under the blanket identity 'British,' so one must remember that 'British' can connote other identities.

This uncertainty in dealing with the distinction between Englishness and Britishness complicates Kim's alleged Englishness. While Plotz recognises that Kim is 'of course not Indian,' she demurs less securely that he is not 'exactly' English either. Given that the narrative indicates, albeit implicitly, that Kim is of entirely Irish descent, her uncertainty seems ill founded. Moreover, later in her reading Kim is unconditionally identified as both 'truly British' and as 'English Kim.'[13] Plotz's reading exemplifies the critical uncertainty in dealing with Kim's Irish heritage, as well as the conflation of English and British that places that Irishness under erasure.

It is clear that Kim's identity in the text is established less in relation to any particular *national* identification than by his *racial* identification as white. 'The boy's true nature and identity are secured . . . by the invocation of an essentially racialist notion . . . As the narrator assures his readers on the first page of *Kim*, Kim is 'English' and 'white.'[14] The alignment of Kim's whiteness with an implicit Englishness follows a lengthy pattern of imperial racial thought, and assertions of Kim's whiteness, not assertions of his Englishness, riddle the text. The narrator suggests that Kim suffers from 'the white man's horror of the Serpent'; he flatly asserts that he is 'white'; and, interestingly, in stating that Kim will be sent to St Xavier's for schooling and training for imperial service, Father Victor conflates the racial with the cultural: 'They'll make a man o' you, O'Hara, at St Xavier's – a white man . . .'[15] It is his whiteness that will ultimately validate and underscore Kim's imperial authority.

In his study, *White*, Richard Dyer notes that whiteness has a long history in relation to colonialism, 'since colonialism is one of the elements that subtends the construction of white identity.'[16] In order to differentiate between colonisers and the colonised, race became a privileged signifier of difference, in which black and

---

12 S. Gikandi, *Maps of Englishness: Writing Identity in the Culture of Colonialism* (New York, 1996), p. 29. Gikandi's assertion that the 'Celtic fringe . . . came to have a greater emotional investment in an invented British nationalism' (29) requires some clarification, in that neither this assertion nor the general taxonomy of 'Celtic fringe' seems adequately to capture long-standing resistance to British imperial hegemony, at least for the Irish. **13** See Plotz pp. 112; 115; 118. **14** D. Randall, in 'Ethnography and the Hybrid Boy in Rudyard Kipling's Kim,' in *Ariel: A Review of International Literature*, no. 27:3 (July 1996), pp. 80–103. **15** Kipling, *Kim*, pp. 91, 49, 143, 165. **16** R. Dyer, *White* (New York, 1997), pp. 14, 79–104.

white were fundamentally and essentially juxtaposed.[17] Satya Mohanty notes that this differentiation – what he calls 'racialisation' – exerts considerable political and cultural influence:

> The analytical concept of 'racialisation' suggests . . . that the color line does not merely divide and separate; it also involves a dynamic process through which social groups can be bound, defined, shaped. This process not only creates stereotypes of the colonized as 'other' and inferior; . . . the colonizer too develops a cultural identity that survives well past the formal context of colonial rule.

The question of hybridity in *Kim* is ultimately resolved, then, through the assertion of Kim's racial identity. While his cultural hybridity evokes challenges to his identity as a Sahib (and therefore as an Englishman and a white man), Kim's ultimate adoption of the role of a 'white male colonial ruler' seems to align him with the English imperial project and to secure his white, English identity.[18]

In spite of this alliance, however, Kim's 'nature' and/or hybridity are far from resolved. The narrative's insistence on Kim's whiteness betrays an anxiety over the question of *purity*, which Kim's hybridity threatens even as his racial and cultural classifications proffer it. Dyer explains that, while '[e]ighteenth- and nineteenth-century philosophers and politicians . . .[had] no compunction about detailing the innate quality of white people,' such categorization simultaneously 'creates a category of . . . peoples who may be let in to whiteness under particular historical circumstances.'[19] When whiteness is aligned specifically with colonial privilege, it must be selectively applied, and its purity becomes relevant in order to maintain illusory distinctions between the colonisers and the colonised. For this reason, '[r]acialization involves not just the denigration of "black" . . . but also in crucial ways a less obvious definition of "white".'[20] L. Perry Curtis' ground-breaking book, *Apes and Angels: The Irishman in Victorian Caricature,* has sufficiently traced how selective the apportioning of Irish whiteness could be.[21]

The monolithic use of whiteness in *Kim* parallels textual efforts to place Kim's Irishness under erasure. Kipling can thereby posit a homogenous image of

---

17 There are multiple analyses that consider the racialization of colonialism. For a discussion of the oppositional construction of whiteness, see Dyer pp. 11–13. For a discussion of the racial stereotype in colonial discourse, see Bhabha pp. 66–84.   18 S.P. Mohanty, pp. 314–15, in 'Drawing the Color Line: Kipling and the Culture of Colonial Rule,' in *The Bounds of Race: Perspectives on Hegemony and Resistance.* ed. D. LaCapra (Ithaca, 1991), pp. 311–43. 19 Dyer pp. 18–19.   20 Mohanty, p. 314. On degrees of whiteness, see Dyer p. 51. Carlyle's infamous comparison between West Indians and the Irish in 'The Nigger Question' illustrates the selective racialisation of the Irish. See Thomas Carlyle, pp. 350–6, 378, 'The Nigger Question,' in *Critical and Miscellaneous Essays in Five Volumes.* Vol. iv: *The Works of Thomas Carlyle in Thirty Volumes,* vol. 29 (New York, 1980), pp. 348–83.   21 L.P. Curtis, *Apes and Angels: The Irishman in Victorian Caricature* (Washington, 1971).

Britishness based on race, which supercedes national distinctions, and counter Kim's threatening hybridity. Interestingly, all explicit allusions made to Kim's Irish heritage are derogatory: his father is a drunkard and opium addict, and the several references to his 'Irish character' all adhere to fundamental stereotypes of 'the' Irish personality.[22] Rather than recognising and interrogating these stereotypes, many critics even apply the very labels that Kipling exploits. Andre Viola accepts that 'Kim's Irish descent . . . may explain his ebullience and versatility,' and Plotz, after recognising Kim's Irishness, cites that heritage as an indicator of potential sunburn: '[Kim] almost moves in and out of his own skin, sometimes as pale as his Irish genes dictate . . .'[23] Aside from the obvious fact that such stereotypes are fundamental to the colonial process, as Bhabha has shown, they are common colonial generalisations and their presence undermines the narrative insistence on Kim's fundamentally pure Englishness.

Kim's Irishness is also repressed in the minimalist way in which it is presented. The narrator's initial insistence that Kim is 'English' is undermined instantly when we learn his father's clearly ethnic name and of his membership in an Irish regiment: 'Kimball O'Hara [was] a young colour-sergeant of the Mavericks, an Irish regiment'.[24] Perhaps, in keeping with other stereotypes that Kipling employs, O'Hara Sr's drunkenness was intended for another indication. Either way, the reader is left to infer that Kim's father was Irish.

Interestingly, the same device that is employed with Kim's father is used in introducing Fr Victor, whose name, dialect, and religious persuasion all suggest that he is Irish. It is notable that, while he is identified as 'the Roman Catholic Chaplain of the Irish contingent' and speaks with a phonetically stereotypical Irish accent – 'they'll make a man o' you' – he is claimed as English shortly thereafter: 'The two Englishmen sat overwhelmed'.[25] While the relationship between the two priests highlights Kipling's implicit suggestion that neither creed nor nationality are as significant as racial identification, and by association their joint cooperation in British colonialism, I would argue that the author's refusal to identify Fr Victor as Irish explicitly – and his immediate disavowal of that Irishness in identifying the character as an 'Englishm[a]n' – reflects the ambivalence and uncertainty of this endeavor.

A similar repression of Kim's Irishness is emphasised through the remarkable way that Kim's mother's heritage is introduced: 'Kim followed like a shadow. What

---

22 Kipling, *Kim*, p. 49. For a classic delineation of stereotypes on the Irish, including some that Kipling employs, see M. Arnold's priceless exposition in 'On the Study of Celtic Literature', in *On the Study of Celtic Literature and Other Essays* (London, 1882), pp. 13–136, esp. on Irish energy (p. 78), temperament (p. 86), and sentimentality (pp. 80–4). For a reading that traces such stereotypes in action, see E. Michie, 'From Simianized Irish to Oriental Despots: Heathcliff, Rochester and Racial Difference,' in *Novel* 25 (Winter 1992), pp. 125–40. **23** See p. 162, A. Viola, 'Empire of the Senses or a Sense of Empire? The Imaginary and the Symbolic in Kipling's "Kim",' in *Ariel: A Review of International Literature* 28: 2 (April 1997), pp. 159–72; Plotz p. 115. **24** Kipling, *Kim*, p. 49. **25** Ibid, pp. 133, 139.

he had overheard excited him wildly. [. . .] The lama was his trove, and he purposed to take possession. Kim's mother had been Irish too'.[26] While the 'too' in this sentence admits to what the narrative only suggests earlier – that his father was in fact Irish – the inclusion of Kim's mother's heritage seems sudden and out of place in its introduction into the narrative. With this information, the paragraph ends abruptly and the narrative continues as if uninterrupted: 'The old man halted by Zam-Zammah and looked round till his eye fell on Kim'. Annie O'Hara's heritage is thus thrust forward even as it is practically retracted. The unsettling manner in which her heritage is presented, as well as the textual separation of Kim's parents' ethnicity, together rupture a clear apprehension of Kim's heritage and suggest textual resistance to it.

Even when Kim's heritage *is* explicitly noted, it is left unhelpfully vague, as when the narrator compliments Kim for a bit of witty repartee: 'The retort was a swift and brilliant sketch of Kim's pedigree for three generations'.[27] Given the reader's poverty of knowledge regarding Kim's pedigree, the compliment is hardly enlightening, and his Irishness is thus offered and obscured in the same sleight of hand.

Perhaps predictably, a textual interrogation of Kim's whiteness recurs whenever Kim encounters an Anglicised or English context. The manner in which race and ethnicity complicate and even contradict each other in *Kim* is then evident. Fr Victor needs to validate Kim's whiteness by resorting to a memory of Kim's parents' whiteness, which only marginally evokes an Irish context: 'Kimball O'Hara! And his son! But then he's a native, and I saw Kimball married myself to Annie Shott'. With Fr Victor's corroboration, Kim seems to both whiten and Anglicise before our eyes: '"You see, Bennett, he's not very black"'. It is only when Kim admits that his father was '*Eye*-rishti' – Irish – that Fr Bennett, the Anglican clergyman, admits that Kim is white: '"It is possible I have done the boy an injustice. He is certainly white. . ."'. Yet that identification is almost immediately put under erasure and transmogrified into Englishness: 'We cannot allow an English boy – Assuming that he is the son of a Mason, the sooner he goes to the Masonic Orphanage the better'.[28] The English priest cannot finish his assertions on Kim's Englishness, and is forced instead to resort to Kim's Masonic heritage as a means of reintegrating Kim into a European community.[29] It is as if Bennett and the narrative would have us forget Kim's Irishness as soon as we learn of it.[30] While Kim's Irishness confirms his whiteness and lessens his Otherness by separating him from

26 Ibid., p. 60. **27** Ibid., p. 114. **28** Ibid., pp. 133, 134, 136. **29** The implications of Kimball O'Hara Sr's association with the Irish Masons could, itself, provide an interesting avenue for consideration but is beyond the scope of this paper. **30** Of course, 'forgetting' is fundamental to the illusion of national purity. See p. 11, E. Renan, 'What is a Nation?', in H. Bhabha (ed.), *Nation and Narration*, trans. M. Thom (London: 1990), pp. 8–22.

the 'natives', then, his religious and ethnic marginality strain his identification as 'purely' English, thereby straining his identification as white.[31]

In spite of the narrator's initial insistence that Kim is both 'English' and 'white', the undermining of one often parallels the other. Notably, when Kim is lonely in the army barracks, a reference to his alienation from 'white men' is framed with references to England: 'Kim of course disbelieved every word the drummer-boy spoke about the Liverpool suburb which was his England . . .[T]his strong loneliness among white men preyed on him'. Similarly, the conflation of Irish and English allows Kim a similar disavowal of whiteness in relation to those who are technically of his own ethnicity. When Kim observes the Irish regiment from a distance, he clearly sees himself as distinct, focusing on their whiteness: ' "White soldiers!" [. . .]: Let us see." '[32] Like the narrator, Kim here fails to distinguish between English and Irish, and race serves as the nodal point of erasure.

One final instance betrays the instability of Kim's identification as English, and the tenuous erasure of Irishness under a broader, whiter Britishness. When Kim is in the midst of a delicate and deceptive plot, the narrator notes that '[t]he humour of the situation tickled the Irish and the Oriental in his soul'.[33] This alliance of Irish with the radically Other Oriental undermines the narrative insistence on Irish/English homogeneity and the racial delineation upon which it seeks to rest. Rather than elaborating a greater sense of pure units composing the whole, then, *Kim* illustrates the instability of such categorizations even independent of hybridity.

I have suggested that Kim's identification with Englishness is predicated on the textual erasure of his Irish identity and the alignment of whiteness with Englishness. While Irishness is problematically positioned, in a nineteenth-century context, against whiteness, this is clearly an instance in which one ethnicity – here, Irishness – is utilised as a ' "buffer" between the white and the black or indigenous.'[34] Kipling's decision to complicate Kim's ethnicity by rendering him Irish, only to undermine it repeatedly, suggests the type of fetishisation of the stereotype that Bhabha has elaborated. By proffering an *Irish* Kim who is readily assimilated under a broader Britishness – itself a conflation with the category of Englishness – Kipling recognises and yet disavows the distinction between English and Irish, based on an imaginary 'purity' represented by whiteness. As Bhabha notes, 'the stereotype is a complex, ambivalent, contradictory mode of representation, as anxious as it is assertive . . . The myth of historical origination – racial purity, cultural priority – . . . functions to 'normalize' the multiple beliefs and split subjects that constitute colonial discourse as a consequence of its process of disavowal.'[35] Yet, while this conflation can be seen to reassert Kim's alleged Britishness and to celebrate a model of contained hybridity, the ambivalence of that representation ought

31 Not surprisingly, 'white' of itself carries a specific connotation of purity: 'white. . . signifies and represents innocence, purity.' See Sloan cited in Dyer p. 73. **32** Kipling, *Kim*, pp. 151, 127. **33** Ibid., p. 297. **34** See Dyer p. 19. **35** Bhabha pp. 70, 74. For Bhabha's elaboration on fetishism and the racial signifier/stereotype, see pp. 75–84.

not to be undervalued. The dubious success of the alignment of Kim's whiteness
with Englishness is evidenced by Kim's refusal of, alternatingly, white and/or
English identity, his cultural unlocatability, and the inconsistency with which
Kipling treats Kim's ethnicity in the narrative, as we have seen. All of these factors
serve to challenge the illusion of purity that the text seeks to promote.

The tremendous linguistic variation in *Kim* serves as a final indicator of resistance to any textual suggestion of purity. Randall notes that 'Kipling's text, as it
develops, registers a multiplicity of competing codes – English, Urdu, Hindi,
Punjabi, Pushtu – none of which is clearly constituted as definitive and authoritative'.[36] At the same time, there seems to be difficulty in tying down Kim's mother
tongue. This linguistic indeterminability parallels the ethnic and racial indetermi-
nacies that riddle the text. If Kipling seeks to assert Kim's fundamental Englishness,
one would expect *Kim* to show the protagonist's linguistic flexibility subsumed
under the rubric of beneficial colonial flexibility. And indeed, when endangered, it
is through thinking in the English language that Kim is able to find relief: '[H]is
mind leaped up from a darkness that was swallowing it and took refuge in – the
multiplication-table in English!'.[37] Such instances seem to suggest some innate
alliance to English as a mother tongue and to reinforce the suggestion that Kim's
other linguistic dalliances are merely practical. In his study, *Monolingualism of the
Other*, however, Derrida notes that such a belief in a natural language is merely an
illusion:

> For contrary to what one is often most tempted to believe, the master is
> nothing . . . Because the master does not possess exclusively, and *naturally*,
> what he calls his language, because, whatever he wants or does, he cannot
> maintain any relations of property or identity that are natural, national, con-
> genital, or ontological, with it, . . . he can . . . pretend historically . . .[38]

Since language is not a 'given,' Derrida explains that a colonial culture can and
often does 'pretend' to some façade of cultural purity for legitimisation: 'this last
will [of language], in its imperative and categorical purity, does not coincide with
anything that is given . . .'[39] In Kipling's *Kim*, the falsity of linguistic purity parallels the illusion of racial purity. Critics have widely noted Kim's 'sing–song' English
– what Said calls 'a superbly funny, but gentle, mockery of the boy's stilted Anglo-
Indian' – and Plotz notes 'the "native English" ("oah yess") of Kim before his St
Xavier's training . . .'[40] The plurality of languages works insistently to counter and
undermine Kim's identification as English.

Along with Kim's lack of proficiency in English, we must consider the narrator's own hybrid language. Randall has noted that the narrator identifies with Kim
in his alienation from the English – '[he] speaks of "the English" . . . as if referring

36 Randall p. 92.   **37** Kipling, *Kim*, p. 202.   **38** Derrida p. 23, emphasis in original.
39 Derrida p. 47.   **40** See Said's 'Introduction,' p. 41, and Plotz p. 116.

to an alien group' – and that alienation is paralleled by the use of linguistic indeterminability, a sense that the narrator, too, is alienated from the language and culture of the English:

> The language of *Kim* is necessarily hybrid; yet – this must be stressed – it is
> *more hybrid than it needs to be* . . . By mimicking the forms and figures of sub-
> continental languages, the dialogue recalls that English is very rarely the
> spoken language of the world of *Kim*.[41]

While Randall reads the narrator's comments as highlighting his Anglo-Indian
sympathies, I think rightly, I would suggest that the linguistic indeterminability also
highlights *cultural* dislocation. As an Anglo-Indian himself, Kipling would have been
well familiar with the marginal place an Anglo-Indian held in relation to an
Englishman.[42] This marginality highlights Derrida's discussion of individuals who
are isolated from their presumed mother tongue: '[It is] a language supposed to be
maternal, but one whose source, norms, rules, and law were situated elsewhere.'
Like England – 'the Metropole . . . at once a strong fortress and an entirely other
place' – English is familiar and yet strange, purely the narrator's and yet never his.[43]
Thus, rather than the language of the narrator being 'more hybrid than it needs to
be', as Randall asserts, I would suggest that the language merely represents the
text's hybridity – not in excess, but in impurity.

If the narrator betrays signs of cultural impurity and hybridity, Kim is even
more alienated. Although Kim's hybridity is frequently used in attempts to categorise him, Derrida notes that 'as soon as one is dealing with questions of culture,
language, or writing, the concept of group or class can no longer give rise to a simple topic of exclusion, inclusion, or belonging.'[44] Kim's alienation from English,
culturally, linguistically, and even racially, can be traced not only to his residence in
India as an 'Indian' or his membership in a community of Anglo-Indians, but also
to the erasure of his Irishness, and to the Irish language itself. The expectation that
Kim will resort ultimately to English is itself a displacement that places his 'own'
mother tongue – Gaelic Irish – under erasure.[45]

Understanding that Kim is radically displaced – as an Anglo-(Irish-) Indian,
deepens our understanding of his linguistic, racial, and ethnic indeterminability. His

41 See Randall, pp. 94; 92–3, my emphasis.   **42** I am reminded here of Benedict
Anderson's discussion of the Creole and his perceived inferiority. See pp. 47–65, esp. 58–60,
in B. Anderson, *Imagined Communities: Reflections on the Origin and Spread of Nationalism*,
Revised edition (London, 1991).   **43** See Derrida pp. 41–2.   **44** Derrida p. 52.   **45** Of
course, the concept of the 'naturalness' of any mother tongue is itself a misnomer, as '[t]he
language called maternal is never purely natural, nor proper, nor inhabitable' (58). Thus the
expectation that Irish would be his 'natural' tongue is also false. While I recognise that Irish
had been eradicated in many parts of Ireland through English colonialism by the nineteenth
century, a Derridean reading suggests that even those who are dislocated from birth from
their 'own' culture are subject to a 'negative heritage' (53).

linguistic fluency and his radical unlocatability highlight his dislocation: 'a new-comer without assignable origin, would make the said language come to him, forc-ing the language then to speak itself by itself, in another way, in his language.'[46] There are multiple instances of Kim shifting language positions in order to make himself understood, such as in the scolding of the rude taxi-driver who disrespects his whiteness.[47] Kim literally speaks 'for *the other*' as there is no place from which to speak for himself.[48]

Kim's insistent and oft-cited questioning – 'Who is Kim?' – also reflects his cul-tural and linguistic dislocation. Derrida notes that cultural dislocation is married to linguistic disruption:

> For him, there are only target languages [*langues d'arrivée*], if you will, the remarkable experience being, however, that these languages just cannot manage to reach themselves because they no longer know where they are coming from, what they are speaking *from* and what the sense of their jour-ney is.[49]

It is just this sense of dislocation, culturally and linguistically, that leads Sara Suleri to call Kim aphasic.[50] The multiplicity and hybridity of his language position leaves no stable, 'pure' ground from which to speak.

The thickness of Kim's Indian accent is a final indicator of his linguistic and cultural impurity. While critics have read Kim's accent as a sign of Anglo-Irish pres-encing in the text (Randall) or even as a delightful narrative device (Said), it is important to note that accents, too, reflect linguistic impurity. 'The accent indicates a hand-to-hand combat with language in general; it says more than accentuation.'[51] Far from a mere rhetorical device, Kim's accent, like his polylingualism, betrays his radical unlocatability, both culturally and linguistically, and the narrative's inability to contain him under the pure label of 'English.' We are never able to 'hear' either of Kim's parents, but rather only hear the echo of their Irish accents through the identification and reassurances of the implicitly Irish Fr Victor. Similarly, Kim's accent obscures his heritage and displaces his Irishness with an Indianness that can be explained away. His accent thus highlights the obscurity of Kim's Irish identity, even as it betrays the impurity of his Englishness.

The narrative attempt in *Kim* to identify the protagonist as English is ultimately doomed to failure. The effort to erase Kim's Irishness in favour of a whitened and monolithic Britishness is undermined by eruptions of Irishness and its stereotypes in the text, which highlight the constructedness of Britishness in relation to the identities it sought to dominate.[52] That Kipling includes Irishness, only repeatedly

46 Derrida p. 51.   **47** Kipling, *Kim*, p. 168.   **48** Derrida pp. 40, emphasis in original. **49** Derrida p. 61.   **50** S. Suleri, pp. 116–17, in The Rhetoric of English India (Chicago, 1992).   **51** Derrida p. 46.   **52** For a discussion of the oppositional construction of Britishness against Irishness, see D. Kiberd, *Inventing Ireland* (London, 1995), esp. p. 15; for a

to undermine it, suggests the type of fetishism of the stereotype that Bhabha has elaborated and perhaps highlights the particular difficulty Ireland posed for the nineteenth-century colonial imagination in seeking to classify the colonised Irish as white. The uncomfortable resonances raised by the introduction of Irishness into the text reminds the reader that, just as Kim's 'Oriental side' cannot be dismissed on the basis of race or pleas to some innate purity, so too must the text's ultimate reassertion of Britishness be suspect. Rather than supporting a hierarchised but containable hybridity, Kipling's inclusion of Irishness renders Kim's supposed Britishness all the more illusory and ironically undermines the appeal to racial superiority it is tacitly meant to reinforce. This failure is exasperated by the collapse of linguistic purity in the text: Kim's heteroglossia, his lack of a mother tongue, and his cultural displacement from English and Englishness emphasise the very impurity that the text seeks to repress and countermands the suggestions that Kim will ultimately, always resort to English under duress.

Kipling's appeals to Anglo-Indianness and a British India based on harmonious heterogeneity falter because the premise is unstable: linguistic and ethnic indeterminability collapse the racial distinction he hopes will buffer the Oriental/English divide. Perhaps readings of hybridity in *Kim* will be more effective when we realise that the combinations which constitute hybridity cannot be hyphenated into categories of purity. When Kim agonisingly asks, 'And what is Kim?', his answer is not a categorisation, but an echo of the uncertainty that haunts Kipling's text and the imperial project he supports.[53] It is that echo which attunes Kim to his entire world, in all its multiplicity and impurity.

more general discussion of the construction of the coloniser in opposition to the colonised, see A. Memmi, *The Colonizer and the Colonized* (Boston, 1965), esp. pp. 70–87; F. Fanon, *The Wretched of the Earth* (New York, 1963), esp. pp. 35–6; or Nandy, esp. pp. 30–5.   **53** Kipling, *Kim*, p. 331.

'The heroic Irish doctor'? Irish immigrants in the medical profession in nineteenth-century Wales[1]

LOUISE MISKELL

Since the late twentieth century the historiography of the Irish in Britain has become more inclusive. Second generation migrants, women as well as men, those in small towns and in regions previously omitted from the picture of immigrant destinations, have all been incorporated into a widening picture of Irish migrant life in Britain.[2] Greater attention to middle-class migrants, or 'Micks on the Make' as Roy Foster called them,[3] has also been part of this widening agenda, but the role of the Irish middle class in the cultural, political and social life of migrant communities is still largely obscure and has been identified in one recent study as an area requiring further detailed research.[4]

A key issue confronting any historian attempting to address this dearth of work on middle-class Irish migrants is the question of 'ethnic fade'. Did migrants who attained better paid work, in higher status occupations and who lived in superior housing to the majority of their countrymen, become less 'Irish' as a consequence of their upward mobility? Contemporary accounts exist which suggest that this was the case. Hugh Heinrick's survey of the Irish in England for the *Nation* newspaper in 1872, for example, observed that some Irish migrants, 'having attained to comparative prosperity, wish to forget their nativity and in all things conform to English thought and English habit.'[5] Historians have signalled the difficulty of reconciling notions of assimilation and integration with the survival of a distinct Irish ethnicity by employing phrases like 'an awkward minority' and 'a curious middle

1 I am grateful to Dr P. O'Leary of the University of Wales, Aberystwyth and to Bryn Jones of Cardiff Central Library for their help and advice during the research for this chapter. I also benefited from a number of suggestions made to me informally by delegates at the Ireland Abroad conference in Aberdeen (April 2000) where an earlier version of this paper was presented.   2 See for example, D.M. MacRaild, *Culture, Conflict and Migration. The Irish in Victorian Cumbria* (Liverpool, 1998); J. Herson, 'Irish Migration and Settlement in Victorian England: a small-town perspective', in R. Swift and S. Gilley (eds), *The Irish in Britain, 1815–1939* (London, 1989), pp. 84–103; M. Kanya-Forstner, 'Defining Womanhood: Irish Women and the Catholic Church in Victorian Liverpool', in D.M. MacRaild (ed.), *The Great Famine and Beyond. Irish Migrants in Britain in the Nineteenth and Twentieth Centuries* (Dublin, 2000), pp. 168–88.   3 R.F. Foster, *Paddy and Mr Punch. Connections in English and Irish History* (London, 1993) chapter 14.   4 MacRaild (ed.), *The Great Famine and Beyond*, p. 33.

place' to describe the position of the Irish in Britain by the late nineteenth century.[6] Recently, however, the whole notion of 'ethnic fade' has undergone revision, particularly in relation to Irish shopkeepers and publicans. In Liverpool, these service-providers, operating in a highly competitive environment, actively promoted their Irishness as a means of attracting custom.[7] This commercial use of ethnicity has also been shown to extend to other sections of the Irish middle classes. A number of Irish journalists found a successful niche market in catering specifically for a Catholic readership.[8] But what of Irish doctors?

Very little research has been done on the Irish in the medical profession.[9] In studies of nineteenth-century urban Britain they are often identified as the receivers but rarely the providers of medical services, reflecting the 'classic British perspective' on the Irish as a problem group.[10] They were the people who, 'more than any other suffered the deprivations of urban crisis and were the most vulnerable to its ravages'.[11] Nevertheless, they were sufficiently prominent on the other side of the medical fence, working as doctors, to attract the notice of contemporaries. They were commonplace enough in south Wales to receive comment from John Denvir in his 1892 survey of the Irish in Britain. Denvir visited south Wales prior to writing his survey and found that Irish doctors were a common sight in Welsh towns where they often encountered dangerous work at the scenes of colliery accidents. 'You never miss the heroic Irish doctor, if there be one in the neighbourhood, as there generally is, with his ready skill and tenderness for the unhappy victims.'[12]

It is difficult to be precise about how many Irish doctors there were in south Wales at any one time. Practitioners tended to move around, especially in the early years of their careers. Moreover trade directories tended only to list surgeons and physicians, omitting the many who worked as medical assistants. Incomplete though the directory lists are for these purposes, they still bear out Denvir's claim that it was common to find one or more Irish doctors in Welsh industrial towns. They were to be found in a variety of positions. In Bridgend there was Michael Leahy, born in Waterford, qualified in Edinburgh and working as the physician and surgeon to the Llynfi and Tondu Iron Works.[13] In the Rhondda valley there was

5 A. O'Day (ed.), *A Survey of the Irish in England (1872)* (London, 1990), p. 127. 6 See D. Fitzpatrick, 'A Curious Middle Place: the Irish in Britain 1871–1921' in Swift and Gilley (eds), *The Irish in Britain*, pp. 10–59; S.J. Fielding, *Class and Ethnicity. Irish Catholics in England, 1880–1939* (Buckingham, 1993), pp. 13–18. 7 J. Belchem, 'The Liverpool-Irish Enclave' in MacRaild (ed.), *The Great Famine and Beyond*, pp. 130–36. 8 Foster, *Paddy and Mr Punch*, p. 290. 9 A notable exception to this is L.M. Geary, 'Australian Felix: Irish Doctors in Nineteenth Century Victoria', in P. O'Sullivan (ed.), *The Irish Worldwide: History Heritage and Identity. Volume 2, The Irish in the New Communities* (Leicester, 1992). 10 G. Davis, 'The Irish in Britain, 1815–1939', in A. Bielenberg (ed.), *The Irish Diaspora* (Harlow, 2000), p. 19. 11 See for example, D. Porter, *Health, Civilisation and the State. A History of Public Health from Ancient to Modern Times* (London, 1999), p. 90. 12 J. Denvir, *The Irish in Britain from the earliest times to the fall of Parnell* (London, 1892), p. 407. 13 *Kelly's Directory of Monmouthshire and the*

William Cuthbertson, born in Dublin and working as a surgeon in the rapidly growing industrial village of Ton Pentre.[14] At Ynys Hafod, meanwhile, there was Ernest Hackett, born in Blackrock, Cork, educated at Queen's College Cork and the College of Surgeons in Edinburgh, who became chief surgeon to HM Prison, Usk.[15]

This aim of this study, however, is not to attempt to enumerate the Irish medical presence in south Wales in the last quarter of the nineteenth century, but rather to follow up Denvir's observation with an examination of the experience of Irish doctors in Welsh towns. This is possible thanks to the existence of a number of autobiographical accounts by Irish doctors who spent all or part of their careers in Wales in this period,[16] along with supplementary evidence from newspapers, trade directories and the census. It will be shown that the kind of medical work on offer in south Wales had a particular appeal for doctors with limited financial means in the early stages of their careers. Many Irish doctors qualifying in the second half of the nineteenth century fitted this description. It will also be argued that, for a number of these doctors, their Irish contacts and networks were important in helping them to gain a foothold in the highly competitive world of nineteenth-century medical provision. As such this study has a contribution to make to the revision of the notion of 'ethnic fade' among migrants of middle-class status as well as to the broadening of the picture of Irish life in nineteenth-century south Wales.

To explain the presence of Irish doctors in Wales and indeed throughout Britain in the second half of the nineteenth century, some account needs to be taken of the position of the medical profession in Ireland. Joseph Lee has shown that the medical and legal professions provided an accessible and popular avenue to social advancement in Ireland in the second half of the nineteenth century. For men of modest means a career as a doctor was a goal within their reaches. There was potential for earning while still training, either as a medical assistant in a practice, or as a tutor to younger medical students. Even for those with greater capital it was often a more attractive option than a career in business or industry because it promised status as well as potentially high earnings. The result was a high entry rate into both medicine and the law, to the extent that Lee argues that 'a surfeit of the professional middle class' was produced.[17]

In medicine, the establishment in 1845 of Queen's University with its constituent colleges in Belfast, Cork and Galway broadened opportunities for entry to those who could not afford the high fees for courses in Dublin.[18] The result was

Principal Towns and Places of South Wales, 1884 (London, 1884), p. 704; 1881 Census, Newcastle Higher Parish.   **14** Ibid., p. 704; 1881 Census, Ystradyfodwg Parish.   **15** J.A. Jenkins, *South Wales and Monmouthshire at the Opening of the Twentieth Century*. W.T. Pike (ed.), *Contemporary Biographies* (Brighton, 1907), p. 278.   **16** M.F. Ryan, *Fenian Memories* (Dublin, 1945); J. Mullin, *The Story of a Toiler's Life* (Dublin, 1921), second edition, edited by P. Maume, (Dublin, 2000); F. O'Sullivan, *Return to Wales* (Tenby, 1974).   **17** J.J. Lee, *The Modernisation of Irish Society, 1848–1918* (Dublin, 1973), p. 18.   **18** This is discussed in Geary, 'Australian Felix', pp. 166–7.

an increase in the numbers achieving medical qualifications in Ireland, but no corresponding rise in demand for their work. Opportunities for private practise in Ireland were limited and public posts, with the Poor Law for example, were fiercely competitive and not well paid. The Irish Medical Association, meeting in Dublin in 1863, lamented the 'paltry remuneration granted to medical officers for their important and laborious services.'[19] Given these difficulties, leaving Ireland and commencing a medical career elsewhere was the best option for many newly qualified doctors.

For those who arrived in Britain, however, the situation was far from easy. In England and Wales the medical profession was highly competitive in the late nineteenth century. This was despite the fact that the ratio of doctors to patients had widened considerably in the period from 1850 to 1880.[20] The profession itself was highly stratified with a world of difference separating the graduate from one of the top London medical schools, perhaps with hospital connections, from the product of a Queen's University medical course whose reputation was never high and whose degrees carried much less kudos.[21] The educational and social backgrounds of doctors had a direct impact on the kind of jobs they could expect to obtain. Starting out on a medical career in this period was especially difficult for those who lacked the capital to purchase a practice outright, or the family or social connections to help them build up a patient list of their own. To a newly qualified doctor who found himself in this position, choices were limited, but it was in precisely these circumstances that south Wales attracted medical men from Ireland and elsewhere.

There were significant regional variations in levels of medical provision in Britain. London was particularly well served with doctors, as were seaside resorts and market towns, but Wales as a whole was not well supplied.[22] In 1881 Wales had 1,769 inhabitants per doctor, compared to a corresponding figure of 1,071 for England and Wales as a whole.[23] In growing industrial areas, medical provision was particularly sparse. Burgeoning towns like Cardiff, which almost doubled in population after 1881 as docks and rail links were developed,[24] presented fertile territory for doctors anxious to avoid competition from more experienced and established rivals. It was for this reason that James Mullin, a native of Cookstown, Co. Tyrone and a product of medical school in Galway, found his way to Cardiff. Having made up his mind to set up his own GP's practice from scratch, he left as little as possible to chance and tried to choose a location where his chances of success seemed most assured. To this end, he consulted the *Medical Directory* to compare doctor-patient ratios in towns throughout Britain. It is likely that, in adopting

19 *Times*, 2 January 1863. 20 A Digby, *Making a Medical Living. Doctors and Patients in the English Market for Medicine, 1720–1911* (Cambridge, 1994), pp. 13–19. 21 Geary, 'Australian Felix', p. 167. 22 Digby, *Making a Medical Living*, p. 20. 23 *Times*, 7 April 1864. 24 In the two decades after 1881 Cardiff's population grew from 83,000 to 164,000. P. Jenkins, *A History of Modern Wales, 1536–1990* (London, 1992), p. 239.

this approach, Mullin was following the advice of Charles Bell Keetley, who published extensively in the mid-Victorian period offering guidance for new GPs. He urged them to survey possible sites for establishing a practice and to take into account factors such as the size of the population and the number of other medics located there.[25] Mullin's researches revealed that Cardiff was one of the five towns with the lowest doctor to patient ratios and, on visiting the place Mullin says, 'I saw its possibilities and concluded that I could find no better sphere for my future labours.' Having settled on a town, he then had to decide on the exact site for his surgery. Again, Mullin adopted a pragmatic approach:

> I got a map of the town, as it was then, and marked the most central spot which the penny tram fare rendered accessible from all other parts. Taking a small shop there, I turned it into a surgery . . . It was a smart stroke of business in which I stole a march on a Bristol doctor who was on the point of coming and doing the very same thing.[26]

The fledgling town of Barry offered similar possibilities. In 1884 the decision was taken to build new docks there to relieve the pressure on Cardiff as the principal port serving the south Wales coalfield. There was an immediate influx of some 3,000 labourers employed on the construction of the first dock, which opened in 1889. It was an instant success, exporting 3 million tons of coal in its first year. The growth of the town was dramatic and by 1921 Barry had almost 40,000 inhabitants.[27] Irishman Peter O'Donnell established his medical practice in Barry in 1888 at the very beginning of this dramatic phase of growth.[28] In doing so it is likely that he, too, side-stepped much of the competition he would have encountered in a more established town where doctor-patient relations were already in place and where competition from local doctors would have been more intense. It is also likely that, as in Mullin's case, this was more than just a stroke of good fortune. After qualifying in Dublin in 1882, O'Donnell spent a short time in Cardiff where he would have been well aware of the major developments underway at Barry Dock and the possible advantages to be gained.[29]

Wales' rapidly growing industrial towns were not only a safe bet for doctors seeking to establish their own practices, they also afforded abundant opportunities for work as assistants to over-burdened GPs with heavy workloads. These medical assistantships were not regarded as an attractive option. 'Arduous and poorly paid "hack work"',[30] is how one recent commentator described them, and this assess-

25 C.B. Keetley, *The Student and Junior Practitioner's Guide to the Medical Profession* (2nd ed., 1885). **26** Mullin, *Toiler's Life*, p. 162. **27** See T. Ewbank, *The Geography and History of Barry* (Cardiff, 1920), pp. 49–50; B.C. Luxton, 'Barry', in S. Williams (ed.), *Glamorgan. A C. History* (1975) pp. 147–48; I.W. Prothero, 'The Port and Railways of Barry', in D. Moore (ed.), *Barry. The Centenary Book* (Barry, 1985 ed.), p. 232. **28** *Cardiff Times*, 14 August 1937, p. 15. **29** J.H. Williams, *General Practitioners of Barry, 1885–1979* (Barry Medical Society, 1979), p. 7; *Cardiff Times*, 14 August 1937, p. 15. **30** Geary, 'Australian Felix', p. 163.

ment is largely borne out by the experiences of Irish doctors in Wales who under-took such positions. James Mullin, prior to setting up his own practice in Cardiff, gained experience early in his career as an assistant to a colliery surgeon in Blaenavon for a salary of £120 a year. He was frequently required to do night work and found the demands of the job enormous. He later recalled, 'The two and a half years that I worked in Blaenavon were amongst the hardest in my life. I had known what hard physical work was, and I had known what hard mental work was, but here was a combination of the two such as I had never before experienced.'[31]

The ready availability of medical assistantships in Wales was partly a conse-quence of the popularity of contract practice there.[32] Friendly societies, dispen-saries, coal mining companies and other sick clubs all engaged salaried doctors to tend to the needs of their subscribers. This kind of work again held attractions for those who, perhaps for financial reasons, were unable to set themselves up inde-pendently as a GP. A doctor contracted by a colliery, for example, would not have to worry about competing with other GPs for patients – he had a ready-made client base. The rent on his house and the cost of medicines would also ordinarily be paid for out of membership funds. In addition, there was the lure of potentially high earnings. Some colliery sick clubs deducted a stipulated amount from mem-bers' salaries which was passed on in full to the doctor. In 1909, the two doctors employed by the Cambrian Navigation Colliery in the Rhondda grossed over £2,000 each from their work for the colliery medical fund.[33] In practice, many doctors who held these posts took on assistants to undertake their club work while they fulfilled other, more lucrative commitments. Mark Ryan's experience as a doctor in south Wales in the 1870s was as an assistant at the South Wales Colliery, Abertillery. A native of Kilconly, C. Galway and, like James Mullin, a product of medical school in Galway, his appointment in south Wales was nominally under the charge of a Dr Brewer. Brewer, however, was also the C. coroner and devoted lit-tle time to the colliery work, which left Ryan virtually in sole charge. Ryan does not state what his earnings were at Abertillery but the money he saved while at the colliery was sufficient for him to purchase a house in Galway for his parents to use in their retirement.[34]

Despite the potentially good earnings, the status of doctors who undertook contract work was low within the medical profession as a whole. This was because they were effectively employed and controlled by lay people and thus lacked the autonomy of the successful, independent GP.[35] James Mullin's account of his expe-rience as an over-worked assistant to a colliery doctor at Blaenavon was coloured

---

31 Mullin, *Toiler's Life*, p. 156. **32** Wales has been identified as an area where work clubs were particularly prevalent. See for example D.G. Green, *Working Class Patients and the Medical Establishment. Self Help in Britain from the mid-nineteenth century to 1948* (Aldershot, 1985), p. 9. **33** R. Earwicker, 'Miners' Medical Services before the First World War. The South Wales Coalfield', *Llafur*, 3, 2 (1989), p. 41. **34** Ryan, *Fenian Memories*, p. 51. **35** C. Lawrence, *Medicine in the Making of Modern Britain, 1700–1920* (London, 1994), p. 68; Digby, *Making a Medical Living*, p. 37.

by his frustration at the demands of his patients. He claimed that they regarded it as their right to call on the doctor however trivial the ailment:

> 'Are we not his master, do we not keep the roof over him, the clothes on his back, feed his family and provide him with a horse?' Such thoughts always seemed present in the minds of the colliers and were sometimes uttered in my presence.

At a later posting in Ogmore, Glamorganshire, he found his patients equally demanding.

> They claimed it was my duty to walk around every morning from house to house and inquire at each house if my services as a doctor were required, and thus save them the trouble of sending for me! It appears that my predecessor, a Scotsman named Robertson, did this – a Scotsman above all men![36]

Despite the hard work and the low status of medical assistants, especially those involved in contract work, such posts were often an essential first step towards the goal of independent medical practice.[37] Very few Irish doctors working in Wales found other routes to further their careers. One exception was Florance O'Sullivan, a second-generation Irishman who inherited his father's medical practice in Ebbw Vale in the early twentieth century.[38] Another, Dr Thomas Wallace who, at the age of thirty-two was working as a general practitioner in Crockherbtown, Cardiff in the 1880s, probably advanced his career significantly when he married Margaret J. Vachell, a member of an established Cardiff medical family.[39] His relationship by marriage to two other Cardiff medical practitioners, Herbert R. Vachell and C. T. Vachell, would have provided him with contacts in the wider Cardiff medical fraternity at a relatively early stage in his career.[40]

Few Irish doctors, however, had these sorts of family and social connections in south Wales to draw upon and, for them, it was their Irish contacts that provided essential early career support. Just as their countrymen in semi-skilled and unskilled occupations relied on Irish immigrant friends and neighbours for help with finding work and accommodation on arrival, so Irish doctors drew on ethnic support networks. It was the Irishman Thomas Wallace in Cardiff, for example, who provided Peter O'Donnell with his first medical assistantship in Wales prior to setting up his own practice in Barry.[41] In this case it is unclear whether O'Donnell and Wallace knew one another before working together in Cardiff, but in other

---

36 Mullin, *Toiler's Life*, pp. 151–6.   **37** Digby, *Making a Medical Living*, pp. 127–28.
38 O'Sullivan, *Return to Wales*.   **39** 1881 Census, Cardiff, St John's Parish.   **40** See *Kelly's Directory of Monmouthshire and South Wales 1884*, p. 705.   **41** J.H. Williams, *General Practitioners of Barry*, p. 7; *Cardiff Times*, 14 August 1937, p. 15.

instances evidence of networks developed at home or in medical school is much clearer. While at Abertillery Mark Ryan was assisted by his 'old friend' Dr Monaghan, practising in Tredegar, with his search for a better paid post elsewhere.[42] James Mullin's medical assistantship at Blaenavon was obtained as a result of an offer from an old classmate in Galway, Martin Quirk, who was chief surgeon at the local collieries.[43] On taking up the post Mullin lived as a lodger in Quirk's house, along with another Irish medical assistant, Michael O'Sullivan who worked as a dispenser.[44] Similarly in Ebbw Vale, Limerick-born physician and surgeon James Sheehy shared his home with two medical assistants, also born in Limerick. One was his eighteen-year-old nephew, John Daniel O'Sullivan who worked as a dispenser and the other was James Cleary who was Sheehy's assistant surgeon. The nephew, O'Sullivan, later established himself as a surgeon in his own right in the Monmouthshire village of Aberbeeg after completing his medical qualifications in Ireland.[45]

These examples indicate that 'ethnic fade' was not the norm for many Irishmen working in the medical profession in south Wales. Instead, reliance upon Irish support networks was often a vital part of their early career patterns. Use of this kind of support was especially important within a profession that was highly protective of some of its more coveted appointments. Key public positions were largely inaccessible to 'outsiders'. Posts as Poor Law medical officers, for example, were sought after by doctors throughout their careers as 'a means to consolidate their territory and a useful source of income.'[46] The desire to prevent outsiders becoming well known through such appointments extended not only to those from outside Wales, but also to doctors from neighbouring towns and villages. In Bridgend in 1870, attempts were made to block the appointment of a Maesteg doctor to a vacant public post by a 'cabal of medical men' who looked upon him as 'an intruder'.[47] In this protective climate few Irish doctors obtained public, salaried appointments. There were some exceptions such as John Mulligan of Tipperary, a product of Queen's University, Ireland, who was a general practitioner in Abersychan and medical officer of health to the local board.[48] Likewise, Martin Quirk at Blaenavon held the posts of medical officer of health to the urban sanitary authority and public vaccinator to the Blaenavon district in 1884.[49] Many others saw no route to significant professional advancement by staying in Wales. Those with particular skill or ambition tended to serve their time in medical assistantships and then move on to further their careers elsewhere. Mark Ryan, for example, spent only a few years

42 Ryan, *Fenian Memories*, p. 52. **43** Mullin, *Story of a Toiler's Life*, p. 149. **44** 1881 Census, 1 North St, Llanover, Monmouth. **45** See *Kelly's Directory of Monmouthshire and South Wales and the Principal Places of South Wales, 1895* (London, 1895), p. 240. **46** Digby, *Making a Medical Living*, pp. 117–18. **47** *Central Glamorgan Gazette*, 26 August 1870. I am grateful to Julie Light for this reference. **48** *Kelly's Directory of Monmouthshire and South Wales, 1895*, p. 226; 1881 Census, Trevethin Parish. **49** *Kelly's Directory of Monmouthshire and South Wales 1884*, p. 24.

at Abertillery before leaving to pursue his career in England. 'I had got tired of living in a valley between two mountains, and had no intention of spending my life
there.'[50] Dublin-born Walter Richardson gained experience as a GP's assistant first
in Wales and then in Kent before emigrating to the Australian goldfields.[51] Others
remained in Wales reluctantly. Florance O'Sullivan felt duty-bound to turn down
a hospital appointment to stay in Ebbw Vale and help his ailing father in the family medical practice, thereby resigning himself to 'what I knew would be hard
labour in the Valley'.[52]

For those who did stay, however, there is evidence of active involvement in Irish
community life in south Wales. One historian has identified doctors as the main
'secular counterpoint to clerical influence in Irish communities' in south Wales.[53]
Doctors not only participated in, but often played a leading role in organising Irish
social, political and religious activities. Mark Ryan, during his short time in
Abertillery, became a prominent member of the local Catholic congregation,
which heard Mass in Welsh in a room in a nearby public house, for lack of a
Catholic church. He also organised a meeting in Newport to discuss the organisation of Fenian activities.[54] James Mullin, meanwhile, became involved in a rather
different brand of Irish political activity. He found himself singled out for leadership duties when he attended the inaugural meeting of the Cardiff branch of the
Irish national league. He recalled that, 'Although I was a stranger and absolutely
unknown to any of my own country people, I suppose my position as a doctor gave
me some claim to recognition and I was unanimously elected vice chairman.'[55]
Soon afterwards he became chairman of the same body, a position he retained for
25 years during which time he chaired meetings and hosted visits of prominent
Irish politicians to Cardiff, including Michael Davitt and Charles Stewart Parnell.[56]
Dr Peter O'Donnell's role in Barry was similarly prominent. As there was no existing Catholic congregation, O'Donnell took it upon himself to secure the services
of a visiting priest from Cardiff. Masses were said in the doctor's own house in
Barry Road. Later, he was instrumental in bringing Barry its first resident Catholic
priest, a Fr Hyland.[57] He was also president of the local Catholic Young Men's
Society and his services to the Catholic church in this part of south Wales were formally recognised when he was awarded the Knighthood of St Sylvester by the
Pope in 1929.[58]

It has recently been argued that in performing such high-profile roles within
the Irish immigrant community, these middle-class 'culture brokers' succeeded in
constructing 'a self-enclosed, self-sufficient network which, to the eyes of the host

---

50 Ryan, *Fenian Memories*, pp. 49–51.   **51** Geary, 'Australian Felix', p. 163.   **52** O'Sullivan,
Return to Wales, p. 19.   **53** P. O'Leary, *Immigration and Integration. The Irish in Wales 1798–1922*
(Cardiff, 2000), p. 259.   **54** Ryan, *Fenian Memories*, pp. 49–51.   **55** Mullin, *Toiler's Life*, pp.
178–206.   **56** P. Maume, 'James Mullin, the poor scholar. A self-made man from Carleton's
country', *Irish Studies Review*, 7, 1 (1999).   **57** B.C. Luxton, 'Ambition, Vice and Virtue:
social life, 1884–1914', in D. Moore (ed.), *Barry. The Centenary Book* (Barry, 1984), p. 318.
58 *Barry and District News*, 5 Feb. 1932.

population served only to emphasize Irish-Catholic apartness.'[59] More research on middle-class migrants and Irish associational culture is needed before this stance can confidently be adopted in place of the idea of ethnic fade. Just one example from south Wales indicates that it was possible for middle-class Irish migrants to play a leading part in Irish community life and to attain positions of status and responsibility in the wider urban community. Dr Peter O'Donnell's influence in Barry extended far beyond the local Catholic Irish community. Almost from the time of his arrival in the rapidly growing town he played a central role in the establishment of civic institutions, and the development of cultural and social life for the population at large. He became a member of Barry Urban District Council in 1889 and served continuously until 1931, with three spells as chairman. His other public positions included membership of Barry School Board, Justice of the Peace, founder and captain of the local Cadoxton Cricket Club and chairman of the Cycling Club, founded in the town in the 1890s. His contribution to public life in Barry was formally recognised in 1932 when he was presented with his portrait in oils and an illuminated album address by the citizens of Barry which paid tribute both to, 'your loyalty to your religion and your faithful work on its behalf', and 'your unbroken membership of the authorities which have built up Barry to its present position.'[60] In local press reports he was portrayed first and foremost as a key public figure who played a vital role in building up the urban infrastructure of Barry as it developed into a sizeable town. His Irishness, although acknowledged, was of secondary importance to his identity as a pioneer of civic life.[61] Although O'Donnell's experience was probably untypical, it suggests that a greater degree of dual activity may have been possible in a new town where traditions of participation in the public life of the 'host' society had yet to be formed.

In general the available evidence points to largely harmonious relations between Irish doctors and local south Wales populations. Mark Ryan recalled that, 'I got along splendidly with the miners at Coomtillery [*sic*] and, when I left, an effort was made by Mrs Brewer, who travelled specially to London for the purpose, to get me back.'[62] Others who stayed longer built up loyal followings of patients. Florance O'Sullivan's father, who had emigrated from Cork and set up practice in the mining village of Cwm, near Ebbw Vale in 1892, received the backing of over 600 patients during a dispute with the Ebbw Vale Workmen's Medical Aid Society. O'Sullivan and fellow Irishman Dr Dwyer of Beaufort were dismissed by the Society after a dispute over the treatment of private patients but succeeded in rallying support from 676 of their old patients, who claimed repayment of their subscriptions to the Workmen's Aid Society and continued as patients of the two Irish doctors.[63] James Mullin's relations with the Welsh were also good. He claimed never to have experienced anti-Irish hostility in Wales, despite the fact that he was

59 Belchem, 'The Liverpool-Irish Enclave', p. 142. **60** *Barry and District News*, 5 February 1932. **61** See for example, *Barry and District News*, 13 and 20 Aug. 1937. **62** Ryan, *Fenian Memories*, pp. 49–51. **63** Earwicker, 'Miners' Medical Services', pp. 42–4.

there at the time of the Phoenix Park murders in 1882, which prompted a wave of disturbances and rioting in local Irish communities.[64] Mullin, however, found that he was generally exempt from the animosity, 'Whether I deserved it or no I was generally reckoned among the "good" [Irish], for I tried to assimilate myself to those I mixed with.'[65]

John Denvir's brief comments about Irish doctors in south Wales suggest that their good relations with local communities were forged as a result of their heroic work at the scene of mining disasters where they were 'united in a common sorrow' with the families of lost miners. A similar image was popularised in A.J. Cronin's semi-autobiographical novel *The Citadel*, featuring an immigrant doctor whose relations with his Welsh patients improve after he rescues a miner trapped by a pit explosion.[66] Two Irish doctors who gave accounts of this kind of work were Mark Ryan and Florence O'Sullivan who were both called to the scene of colliery explosions during their careers in Wales. The incident at Abertillery attended by Ryan involved the loss of twenty-seven lives and injury to a further seventy miners. In his account of the incident he recalls simply that, 'I had a very busy time attending to the injured and had to give evidence at the inquest on the victims of the disaster.'[67] O'Sullivan was called to a similar incident at Marine Colliery in Cwm. He was asked to go underground as part of a search and rescue party to locate two injured men. Aware of the possibility of further explosions, rock falls and gas build up, he recalls that he joined the rescue team 'in fear and trembling', only to find that after searching the mine and locating the two men, they were beyond medical help. His account of his work at the scene of the accident is more one of helplessness and frustration than heroism. 'My only contribution during all this time was to give morphia to the first of two dying men . . . I waited at the pit-top for 36 hours, but did little else, while other doctors better qualified administered oxygen and other treatment to survivors from other parts of the pit.'[68]

It is likely that Denvir's reference to the heroism of Irish doctors in south Wales owed more to the changing attitudes towards the medical profession at the time he was writing in the 1890s, than to the common experience of Irish medical men working in Welsh industrial towns. The late nineteenth century was a period of significant advance in the diagnosis and treatment of disease, which led to a greater reverence for the abilities of doctors to treat and cure their patients. According to one historian, it is to this era of medical advance that 'the image of the physician as a demi-god' can be dated.[69] Irish doctors in south Wales were rarely at the cutting edge of medical science but their occasional first-hand experience of mining

---

64 L. Miskell, 'Custom, Conflict and Community: a study of the Irish in south Wales and Cornwall, 1861–1891', unpublished Ph.D. thesis (University of Wales, 1996), pp. 191–227; J. Parry, 'The Tredegar anti-Irish riots of 1882', *Llafur*, 3, 4 (1983). **65** Mullin, *Toiler's Life*, p. 158. **66** A.J. Cronin, *The Citadel*, (London, 1939), p. 194. **67** Ryan, *Fenian Memories*, pp. 49–51. **68** O'Sullivan, *Return to Wales*, p. 29. **69** E. Shorter, 'The Doctor-Patient Relationship' in W.F. Bynum and R. Porter (eds), *Companion Encyclopaedia of the History of Medicine* (London, 1994) pp. 789–90.

disasters was an alternative form of medical heroism which a sympathetic commentator like Denvir could pick up on.

In reality it is likely that the harmonious relations experienced by Irish doctors
working in Wales, even at times of heightened anti-Irish sentiment, owed much to
their non-threatening position within the community. Much of the anti-Irish feeling evident in Wales was based on workplace rivalries and reflected financial inse-
curities among local industrial workers.[70] Hostility was usually directed at workers
who were deemed to pose a threat to the positions of skill and status ordinarily
obtained by native workers. It is likely that Irish doctors escaped much of the
resentment and suspicion directed at other Irish immigrants because they did not
affect the finely balanced divisions of skill and status within the workplace. Instead
many of them who carried out work for friendly societies, sick clubs, or other
medical societies, were subject to a large measure of wider communal control
through the committees that employed them. Moreover Irish medical men had a
reputation for being amongst the most hardworking in the profession,[71] a factor
which must have endeared them to the workers whose salary contributions made
up their pay.

The opportunities for medical work in the industrial towns of south Wales in
the second half of the nineteenth century would not have appealed to all sections
of the medical profession. The doctors they attracted were not from the upper
ranks of the profession but were the hard-working, newly qualified men who had
often strained their finances to the limit to complete their qualifications and
needed to start earning with as little capital outlay as possible. In these circumstances, the secure incomes available from contract practice or as a medical assistant were worth the hard graft and low status attached to such posts.[72] This much
is evident in the work of medical historians who have examined status divisions
within the profession. What this study, from the Irish immigrant perspective has
shown, is that although their standing within the medical profession as a whole
may have been low, within the migrant community Irish doctors were often highly
visible and active individuals who sometimes took on prominent leadership roles.
Moreover, their ethnic identity could prove a valuable asset in that it provided
access to an information-sharing network among Irish doctors through which
opportunities for career advancement were often gained. The active expression and
use of Irish identity by Irish doctors in south Wales, however, does not seem to have
been an attempt to cultivate a niche Irish market for medical services and did not
necessarily emphasise their 'difference' from the host population. The dependence
of many Irish medical men on employment by collieries, sick clubs, friendly societies and other, locally-based medical societies, and their large patient lists covering extensive geographical areas meant that their services could not realistically be
targeted at Irish-only recipients, even if this was deemed commercially viable. In

70 P. O'Leary, 'Anti-Irish Riots in Wales, 1826–1882' *Llafur*, 5, 4 (1991). **71** Digby, *Making a Medical Living*, p. 160. **72** Green, *Working-Class Patients*, pp. 21–3.

this respect they seem to have differed from their counterparts in the commercial and service sectors in Liverpool for whom the active expression of Irishness was part of a conscious business strategy. What this suggests is that the experience of middle-class migrants was as likely to vary according to factors such as occupation and regional location as that of their working-class counterparts. It gives a clear indication of the need for more research on Irish migrants in commerce, the professions and other middle-class sectors of the economy. It also illustrates that, without the inclusion of this often highly visible and active section of the population our picture of Irish immigrant life in south Wales and indeed throughout Britain will remain at best partial and incomplete.

'What would people say if I became a policeman'?: the Irish policeman abroad[1]

ELIZABETH MALCOLM

It is well known that the Irish were disproportionately represented in all ranks of the British army throughout the nineteenth century.[2] As most regiments were posted abroad, often for decades, joining the army could be interpreted as a form of emigration. But enlistment as a soldier was not the only way virtually to guarantee migration. Many Irish doctors and nurses emigrated, as did large numbers of priests and nuns, and also lawyers, teachers and civil servants.[3] Clearly, joining some professional groups in Ireland carried with it the strong possibility of migration; and perhaps a career abroad was one of the attractions of certain jobs. The literature on male emigrants' occupations has tended to be dominated by discussions of rural labourers. They formed the majority, but this focus on labourers has tended to obscure the fact that a diverse group left Ireland, and even those who left classified as labourers sometimes pursued very different careers overseas.[4] This article will look at another occupational group who were also noted for their propensity to emigrate – policemen.

In order to create a context for some of the following discussion, consideration needs to be given to the existing historiography of Irish policing abroad. This is not plentiful and tends to be fragmented and amateurish; nevertheless, there have been some valuable studies. Sir Charles Jeffries, in his influential general history of British colonial policing, published in 1952, identified the Royal Irish Constabulary

1 I would like to thank the Economic and Social Research Council, which helped fund this study, and also Mark Radford and Dr Dianne Hall for their research assistance. 2 E.M. Spiers, *The Late Victorian Army, 1868–1902* (Manchester, 1992), pp. 98, 131–2; K. Jeffery, 'The Irish Military Tradition and the British Empire' in K. Jeffery (ed.), *'An Irish Empire'? Aspects of Ireland and the British Empire* (Manchester, 1996), pp. 94–122. 3 L.M. Geary, 'Australia Felix: Irish Doctors in Nineteenth-Century Victoria' in Patrick O'Sullivan (ed.), *The Irish World Wide: History, Heritage, Identity. Volume Two. The Irish in the New Communities* (Leicester, 1992), pp. 162–79; Edmund Hogan, *The Irish Missionary Movement* (Dublin, 1992); S.B. Cook, 'The Irish Raj: Social Origins and Careers of Irishmen in the Indian Civil Service, 1855–1914', *Journal of Social History*, 20 (1987), pp. 507–29. 4 More work is needed on Irish professionals abroad, but, for some useful general comments, see D.H. Akenson, *The Irish Diaspora: a Primer* (Belfast, 1993), p. 124 and A. Bielenberg, 'Irish Emigration to the British Empire, 1700–1914' in A. Bielenberg (ed.), *The Irish Diaspora* (Harlow, 2000), pp. 225–6. For links between British professions and colonialism, see T. Johnson, 'The State and the Professions: Peculiarities of the British' in A. Giddens and G. MacKenzie (eds), *Social Class and the Division of Labour* (Cambridge, 1982) pp. 196–206.

(RIC) as 'the really effective influence upon the development of colonial forces during the nineteenth century'.[5] This interpretation was reinforced in 1988 by Stanley Palmer in his massive study of the origins of modern policing in England and Ireland. Palmer specifically argued that, while the London Metropolitan Police (the Met) was the model for urban policing throughout the empire, 'Ireland's constabulary was the more valuable because, by using it as their enforcing agent, British civil authorities could mould large, loosely governed areas into centrally administered colonies'.[6]

The theory that Ireland provided a model for British colonial policing has – perhaps inevitably – been challenged. In 1987 Mike Brogden argued that to characterise the influence of English, or indeed Irish, forces on colonial policing as a one-way process was misleading, since colonial experience had parallels to the metropolitan situation and exerted effects upon it.[7] He went on also to challenge the dichotomy usually set up between the RIC and the Met, pointing out that many colonial forces had combined elements of both models. The 'differences between mainland British police work and colonial and Irish policing practices were ones of degree rather than absolutes', Brogden suggested.[8]

The most influential critique of the so-called 'Irish model', however, was offered in 1991, in an article written by Richard Hawkins. Looking primarily at organisation and regulation, Hawkins identified the main characteristics of the Irish model as an armed, paramilitary force, housed in barracks and centrally controlled, with rigorously standardised procedures. But examining various nineteenth-century police forces in the empire – from Canada to the Caribbean, from the Sudan to the Cape, from India to Australia and New Zealand – Hawkins argued strongly that none of them exactly replicated the organisation of the RIC. He certainly did not deny that Irish police practices had been influential. They offered important 'precedents' he claimed, and especially so after 1907 when a colonial police training school was established at the RIC headquarters in Phoenix Park, Dublin. From then on, Hawkins conceded, 'the RIC undoubtedly held primacy among the police forces of the empire'.[9] Hawkins' essential argument that no British colonial police force was exactly the same as the RIC is undoubtedly true. But his approach to the issue was a rather narrow one. He only looked at struc-

5 C. Jeffries, *The Colonial Police* (London, 1952), p. 30. 6 S.H. Palmer, *Police and Protest in England and Ireland, 1780–1850* (Cambridge, 1988), p. 542. 7 This was certainly true of Ireland, where at times of crisis, as for instance during the Land War and the Anglo-Irish War, police officers with colonial experience were imported to bolster the RIC. For the career of one such policeman, see M. Silvestri, '"An Irishman is Specially Suited to be a Policeman": Sir Charles Tegart and Revolutionary Terrorism in Bengal', *History Ireland*, 8 (2000), pp. 40–4. 8 M. Brogden, 'An Act to Colonise the Internal Lands of the Island: Empire and the Origins of the Professional Police', *International Journal of the Sociology of Law*, 15 (1987), pp. 181, 187, 199. 9 R. Hawkins, 'The "Irish Model" and the Empire: a Case for Reassessment' in D.M. Anderson and D. Killingray (eds), *Policing the Empire: Government, Authority and Control, 1830–1940* (Manchester, 1991), pp. 24, 19.

tures, at the way forces were organised and controlled. He did not address how forces were composed, how they functioned and how composition may have influenced function. He did not examine why Irishmen joined the police, in what numbers, how they viewed this job, and how they in turn were viewed by the Irish immigrant communities that they policed. Nor did he deal with the experience of Irish-born policemen outside of the British colonial territories, although many men served in England[10] itself and also in the United States.

In this article I want to focus on composition: on the Irishmen who joined police forces abroad. And I want to make a basic point, but one I think that needs to be made in light of the fact that, due to Hawkins' article, the current trend seems to be towards downplaying Irish influence on policing abroad.[11] The point is just how many Irishmen we are talking about and, related to that, how widespread and lengthy was their influence. I also want to give some preliminary consideration to why Irishmen were so prone to join the police and to how they were viewed by their compatriots abroad. Irish policemen abroad fall into two major groups. There were serving policemen and ex-policemen, some of whom were recruited in Ireland by various English and colonial authorities, and others who emigrated in search of better pay and working conditions. In addition there were Irish immigrants, with no previous experience and who left Ireland classed mainly as rural labourers, but who joined police forces overseas. Both these groups will be considered, among others.

I

Irish policemen were not only found throughout the empire, but also in England itself to an extent that has not been fully appreciated. Not nearly enough study has been done of the recruitment of Irishmen and ex-RIC men into English forces and of their influence upon them. Yet we are talking about substantial numbers at all levels. For instance, of forty-seven English county chief constables appointed between 1856 and 1880, eleven or approximately one-quarter had previously served in Ireland.[12]

The Irish involvement in the setting up of the London Metropolitan Police in 1829 and of Special Branch in the early 1880s is fairly well known. The first two long-serving and influential commissioners of the Met were both Irishmen,[13]

10 Fewer Irish appear to have served in Scottish forces, but for the memoirs of an Irish-born policeman stationed in Edinburgh for some thirty years from 1830, see J. McLevy, *The Casebook of a Victorian Detective*, ed. G. Scott-Moncrieff (Edinburgh, 1975). 11 See, for example, the introduction to Jeffery (ed.), *'An Irish Empire'?*, pp. 10–11. 12 C. Steedman, *Policing the Victorian Community: the Formation of English Provincial Police Forces, 1856–80* (London, 1984), p. 48. 13 Colonel Sir Charles Rowan (*c.*1782–1852) was a Co. Antrim army officer who served as Met commissioner from 1829 to 1850; Sir Richard Mayne (1796–1868) was a Dublin barrister who served as commissioner from 1829 to 1868. D.

while Special Branch was established in response to Fenian bombings in England and initially contained a number of Irish officers[14]. Less well known, however, is the fact that many county and borough constabularies seem to have looked particularly to Ireland. Some are perhaps predictable, but others are not. Constabularies in Lancashire, Liverpool, Manchester, Birmingham, Hull and London had significant Irish involvement, at senior, as well as rank-and-file, level. But Hampshire, Gloucestershire, Buckinghamshire and Staffordshire, for instance, all had substantial Irish contingents. During the 1850s and 1860s some 8 to 10 per cent of the Buckinghamshire Constabulary were Irish born and most had served in the RIC. Interestingly, while Buckinghamshire's Irish policemen were largely catholic, those of Staffordshire were largely protestant. Why this was so is not altogether clear.[15] Gloucestershire's first chief constable, appointed in 1839, had served twenty years in Ireland and 'laid out his force on the Irish model'. Staffordshire's first chief constable, appointed in 1842, had served seventeen years in Ireland. His deputy, who eventually succeeded him in 1857, was also an Irishman, as were nearly half the officers of the force and over a quarter of constables. Of these constables, nearly half had served in the Irish constabulary.[16]

Moreover, this Irish representation was not just confined to the mid and late 19th century. It began earlier and lasted well into the twentieth century. Hull had an Irish-born chief constable from 1836 right through until 1866. When the Lancashire Constabulary was first recruiting in 1840–1, 28 per cent of those who joined were Irish born. Before the Famine influx of Irish into Lancashire, this figure was disproportionate.[17] Liverpool's first chief constable, appointed as early as 1836 was Irish born and, interestingly, was a journalist.[18] Palmer argued that Irish chief constables were appointed in Lancashire during the 1830s and 1840s as their paramilitary training was valued in the campaign to suppress Chartism.[19] But the Irish influence long outlasted Chartism. In the late 1860s still some 18 per cent of the Lancashire force were Irish born.[20] From 1881 to 1911 the Liverpool

Ascoli, *The Queen's Peace: the Origins and Development of the Metropolitan Police, 1829–1979* (London, 1979). **14** B. Porter, *Plots and Paranoia: a History of Political Espionage in Britain, 1790–1988* (London, 1989), pp. 96–113; R. Allason, *The Branch: a History of the Metropolitan Police Special Branch, 1883–1983* (London, 1983). **15** Steedman, *Policing the Victorian Community*, pp 73–5, 78–9, 83. Nottingham had an Irish-born chief constable, Major William Pontz, through most of the 1870s, who went on to serve in a similar capacity in Essex through most of the 1880s. J. Woodgate, *The Essex Police* (Lavenham, 1985), pp. 49–52. A sampling of local histories of county and borough forces suggests that the Irish were ubiquitous; and yet they have been virtually ignored by academic English police historians. Even Steedman, who recorded their substantial presence in her statistical tables, made no attempt to discuss their influence. **16** Palmer, who reported this information, used it somewhat perversely to argue that the Irish did not in fact have a strong influence on early English constabularies. Palmer, *Police and Protest in England and Ireland*, pp. 451–2. **17** B. Dobson, *Policing in Lancashire, 1839–1989* (Blackpool, 1991), pp. 52–3. **18** W.R. Cockcroft, *From Cutlasses to Computers: the Police Force in Liverpool, 1836–1989* (Market Drayton, 1991), pp. 52–3. **19** Palmer, *Police and Protest in England and Ireland*, pp. 452–3. **20** W.J. Lowe,

Constabulary was headed by two Englishmen, both of whom went on to more senior positions and served into the 1920s and 1930s: one in charge of the City of London police and the other as His Majesty's Inspector of Constabulary. Both had joined the police in Ireland and served there for a number of years before their English appointments.[21] A somewhat similar picture emerges as regards Birmingham and extends even later. The city's two chief constables between 1899 and 1941 were both Irishmen who had trained and served approximately sixteen years each in the RIC before their English appointments[22].

The example of Liverpool points up the fact that, as well as Irish policemen who emigrated and Irish emigrants who served as policemen abroad, we should not overlook non-Irish policemen who trained and served in Ireland before returning to their home countries. Well before the establishment of the international training school at the Phoenix Park depot and also long before the advent of the Black and Tans, significant numbers of Englishmen had joined the RIC, and some of these men took what they had learnt back to police forces in Britain. Brogden, in stressing the continuities between English, Irish and colonial policing, refers to the fact that English officers especially sometimes trained in Ireland and served in England, or vice versa, before moving on to serve in the empire.[23]

A number of historians – Roger Swift most prominently in terms of England[24] – have written about the Irish and crime. But this is clearly only one half of the equation. The topic of the Irish in the police, especially with regard to England, has largely been ignored. Also, if Irish-born and Irish-trained, and even English-born and Irish-trained, officers and men were influential in English forces, then the usual dichotomy recognised between the English-style of civil, de-centralised policing and the Irish-style of paramilitary, centralised policing starts to look a lot less clear cut. Brogden's somewhat cautious stress on continuities rather than discontinuities between the two is undoubtedly well placed.[25]

II

Some of the British colonies too offer interesting insights, not only into policing, but also into colonial attitudes and immigrant strategies. A striking example of the use of RIC men in the colonies is provided by Trinidad, for which some fifty RIC

'The Lancashire Constabulary, 1845–70: the Social and Occupational Function of a Victorian Police Force', *Criminal Justice History*, 4 (1983), p.46. **21** Cockcroft, *From Cutlasses to Computers*, pp. 59–65. **22** J.W. Reilly, *Policing Birmingham: an Account of 150 Years of Police in Birmingham* (Birmingham, [1989]), pp. 40, 90, 104. **23** Brogden, 'An Act to Colonise the Internal Lands of the Island', p.198. **24** Among a number of articles, see R. Swift, 'Crime and the Irish in Nineteenth-Century Britain' in R. Swift and S. Gilley (eds), *The Irish in Britain, 1815–1939* (London, 1989), pp. 163–82. I would like to thank Dr Swift for providing me with copies of some of his articles. **25** Brogden, 'An Act to Colonise the Internal Lands of the Island', p. 187.

men were recruited in the early 1880s, when there was a high resignation rate from the RIC due to the pressures of policing the Land War. The fact that the colony's governor, Sir Henry Blake, was a former RIC officer also doubtless had something to do with the recruitment of Irish policemen at this time. By 1885 the Trinidad police force had a little over 400 members. The two senior officers were English; the two sergeant majors next in seniority were Irish; of five sergeant superintendents four were Irish; of nearly fifty sergeants and corporals most were white, probably Irish, although there were some blacks; of 350 constables all were black and the vast majority were from Barbados. Barbadians were considered to make good policemen, unlike Trinidadians.[26] So the Irish police were slotted into the middle ranks, controlled by Englishman, but themselves in control of black policemen. Most of these black policemen, however, were also externally recruited. This reflects the widespread belief at the time that certain groups were better fitted to military or police service than others. The Irish, like the Barbadians, were considered to make 'good policemen', just as they were considered to make good soldiers. But, as Joanna Bourke has pointed out in her recent, controversial book on modern warfare, while viewed as aggressive and brave, Irish soldiers were also seen as reckless and unreliable, and thus in need of strong, that is English, leadership.[27] The personnel structure of the Trinidad Police suggests that, in some colonies at least, a similar attitude was taken to Irish policemen serving abroad.

Irish policemen were also particularly well represented in Australia in the late nineteenth century: in New South Wales (NSW), Queensland, Western Australia and, most especially, in Victoria.[28] In the mid 1860s 67 per cent of the recruits joining the NSW police were Irish born, as were 22 per cent of the officers and 62 per cent of the sergeants. Some 45 per cent of recruits in 1865 had previously served in a police force, the vast majority in the RIC. As NSW training at the time was perfunctory, while RIC training was lengthy and rigorous, whatever the regulations laid down, ex-RIC men must have drawn heavily upon their Irish experi-

---

26 H. Johnson, 'Patterns of Policing in the Post-emancipation British Caribbean, 1835–95' in Anderson and Killingray (eds), *Policing the Empire*, pp 83–4. Policing by strangers was a common colonial strategy: thus Sikhs, perceived as a 'martial race', were used to police Ceylon, Hong Kong, Singapore and even Rhodesia; Indians and Somalis, as well as the Irish, were employed in Kenya; while in the Gold Coast, not only the Irish, but also Nigerians and Sierra Leonians were used. Brogden, 'An Act to Colonise the Internal Lands of the Island', pp. 196–7. **27** J. Bourke, *An Intimate History of Killing* (London, 1999), p. 127. **28** For the substantial Irish involvement in New Zealand policing, see R.S. Hill, *Policing the Colonial Frontier: the Theory and Practice of Coercive Social Control in New Zealand, 1767–1867* (Wellington, 1986) and *idem*, 'The Policing of Colonial New Zealand: from Informal to Formal Control, 1840–1907' in Anderson and Killingray (eds), *Policing the Empire*, pp. 56, 59–61; for Canada, see W.R. Morrison, 'Imposing the British Way: the Canadian Mounted Police and the Klondike Gold Rush' in ibid., p. 94; and for South Africa, where the Irish were also much in evidence, see B. Nasson, 'Bobbies to Boers: Police, People and Social Control in Cape Town' in ibid., pp. 240–1, 247–9 and D.P. McCracken, 'Odd Man Out: the South African Experience' in Bielenberg (ed.), *The Irish Diaspora*, pp. 258, 260, 262–3.

ence. In 1871 the whole force was 60 per cent Irish and about a third of these were protestants. So police service attracted significant numbers of protestant, as well as catholic, Irish. By 1889, however, the Irish proportion had declined to 29 per cent in the face of a deliberate attempt to boost non-Irish recruitment. In 1882 the force's non-Irish commander had complained to the colonial secretary that 'newly arrived Irish apply, but no others' and had wished for thirty or forty recruits from the London Met.[29] Nevertheless, during the third quarter of the nineteenth century the NSW police were nearly two-thirds Irish born, and about half of these Irishmen had previously served in the RIC. The way the force was organised was certainly not exactly the same as the RIC, although contemporary critics worried that NSW had followed too closely the Irish model. In fact, the NSW case gives support to Palmer's suggestion that the RIC model was more influential in rural areas. In rural NSW police were armed and lived in barracks, while in urban NSW they lived in the community and were not ordinarily armed before the 1890s. The force wore English-style uniforms, officers were promoted from the ranks after 1864 and the regulations emphasised that this was a civil not a military body. Nevertheless, like the RIC, they were a 'national' force and were commanded by an inspector general.

Western Australia and Queensland also had strongly Irish police forces. In the early 1870s some 30 per cent of the West Australian force were Irish born, while in 1897 a Perth magazine bluntly defined a policeman as 'a man with a uniform, a brogue, and a big free thirst'.[30] In the mid 1860s 84 per cent of the Queensland police were Irish born, with 44 per cent having previously served in the RIC. However these proportions fell rapidly and were down to 23 per cent and 1 per cent respectively by the early 1890s.[31] The situation in Victoria was perhaps even more striking: although commanded by an Englishman, in 1874 fully 82 per cent of the Victorian police force were Irish born. At the time only 12 per cent of the male population of the colony were from Ireland. Furthermore, 46 per cent of the force had seen previous service in the RIC.[32] So nearly half the force had been trained in Ireland and undoubtedly brought their Irish experience to bear, particularly as, like NSW, there was little police training on offer in the colony. Another third, although not serving as policemen in Ireland, were Irish born. I think it is fair to say that Victoria had an Irish police force, in almost all but name, during the

29 R. Walker, 'The New South Wales Police Force, 1862–1900', *Journal of Australian Studies*, 15 (1984), pp. 30–1. **30** R. Haldane, *The People's Force: a History of the Victorian Police* (Melbourne, 1986), pp. 81–2. **31** Yet, even after 1900, the force was still relying on RIC manuals and in 1911 was considering recruiting men from the Belfast RIC. W.R. Johnston, *The Long Blue Line: a History of the Queensland Police Force* (Brisbane, 1992), pp. 25–6, 104, 115. **32** Haldane, *The People's Force*, pp 81–2; J. McQuilton, 'Police in Rural Victoria: a Regional Example' in M. Finnane (ed.), *Policing in Australia: Historical Perspectives* (Sydney, 1987), pp 40–1. For the vivid autobiography of a senior Irish-born policeman of this period, see J. Sadleir, *Recollections of a Victorian Police Officer* (Melbourne, 1913; reprinted, London, 1973).

mid and late nineteenth century. The force may not have followed RIC regulations to the letter, as Hawkins noted, but its composition and the training of its members must surely have had a substantial impact upon its practices. To downplay RIC influence in these circumstances is not credible. In addition, from the early 1870s, when imperial troops were withdrawn from the colony, the Victorian police also had a role in external defence, which must have reinforced their military character along RIC paramilitary lines.

One of the leading historians of the Kelly gang, John McQuilton, has argued that the heavy-handed policing of small farmers in north-east Victoria by an unrepresentative force employing RIC tactics, including intensive surveillance, spying and intimidation, helped contribute to an upsurge in bushranging that occurred in the late 1870s, culminating in the exploits of Ned Kelly. It is frequently remarked that Kelly was of Irish parentage; less often remembered is that most of the policemen he killed and most of those who pursued him were Irish born, as indeed was the judge who sentenced him to death.[33] The Kelly outbreak could well be interpreted as a clash between different groups of Irish, on opposite sides of English law. This incident was well documented at the time and has been closely studied since, but in England and the United States, as well as Australia, other less well-known conflicts between police and working-class communities during the nineteenth century and later must have essentially pitted Irish against Irish.

Kelly himself certainly recognised that he was up against, not just policemen, but specifically Irish policemen. His contempt for authority was undoubtedly fuelled by the fact that so many of those he perceived as oppressors were in fact fellow Irishmen. In his personal manifesto, the so-called 'Jerilderie Letter', he reserved his harshest rhetoric for Irish policemen whom he saw, not just as persecuting his family and friends, but as betraying their country. They were, he ranted, 'brutal and cowardly', 'lazy' and 'loafing', 'big ugly fat-necked wombat headed', 'magpie legged', 'splay-footed sons of Irish bailiffs or English landlords'. They had 'deserted the shamrock, the emblem of true wit and beauty to serve under the flag' of the country that had 'murdered their fore-fathers', transported large numbers of their countrymen to Van Diemen's Land 'to pine their young lives away in starvation and misery' and driven many others to America, although there they would 'bloom again another day'. It would appear that when he was younger the police had actually sought to recruit Kelly himself. Now he flung this back at them. 'What would people say if I became a policeman' he asked, 'and took an oath to arrest my brothers and sisters and relations and convict them by fair or foul means . . . Would they say I was a decent gentleman?' Labelling Irish policemen as gorillas and

---

33 McQuilton in Finnane (ed.), *Policing in Australia*, pp 42, 50, 52. The official enquiry into the Kelly outbreak, chaired by an Irish-born politician, was very critical of the police; their English chief commissioner was replaced by an Irishman who occupied the position until 1902, when he was succeeded by a man of Irish parentage. Haldane, *The People's Force*, pp 93, 95–6, 122–4.

baboons, Kelly commented sarcastically that 'the Queen must surely be proud of such heroic men . . .'[34]

When Kelly dictated this letter, he was an outlaw on the run, attempting to justify to his community the fact that he had recently shot to death three Irish policemen. Thus he had to blacken their reputations, and indeed the reputations of all Irish policemen who made up the majority of the force then pursuing him. Kelly's hostility to Irish policemen is doubtless an extreme case. Nevertheless, it is probable that at times of tension and crisis Irish communities in different countries also railed against the Irishmen employed in such large numbers to police them. From Ireland to England to the Australian colonies and, as we shall see, also the United States, governments relied upon the Irish to police the Irish. That some Irish despised such men as traitors is understandable. Unfortunately, it is much less clear how Irish policemen perceived their native communities abroad, especially when they came into violent conflict with them.[35]

III

Why did Irish policemen emigrate? I have already indicated that at times of discontent within the RIC, as for instance in the early 1880s when duties were onerous and pay was low, resignations mounted. The 1850s and 1860s were also years of discontent over pay. In addition, they were the decades in which many English, Australian and American forces were being established and were actively recruiting. Thus it is perhaps not surprising that Irish involvement in policing abroad reached heights during these decades. Chain migration was also a factor. It would seem that officers who had worked in the RIC, when appointed to senior positions abroad, looked to Ireland for staff. Constables who had emigrated wrote to former colleagues and to relatives – and many Irish families had a tradition of police service – encouraging them to follow their example. The surgeon of the RIC, giving evidence before a select committee in 1872 in support of demands for higher pay, noted that the men often received letters from friends and family abroad enticing them to leave with information on the better pay and working conditions available for policemen outside of Ireland.[36] And in Australia certainly pay and conditions were in many respects superior to Ireland. Marriage, for

34 Quoted in I. Jones and G. Tomasetti, 'Kelly – the Folk-Hero' in Manning Clark et al., *Ned Kelly: Man and Myth* (Melbourne, 1968), pp. 77–8. **35** Gordon, in his study of the major Irish riots that occurred in New York in 1870–1, noted in passing that some Irish policemen were dismissed for refusing 'to fight fellow Irishmen'. But, while he discussed the attitudes and actions of the rioters in some detail, he did not pay similar attention to the police involved. M.A. Gordon, *The Orange Riots: Irish Political Violence in New York City, 1870 and 1871* (Ithaca, 1993), p. 101. **36** *Report of the Commissioner . . . to Enquire into the Condition of the Civil Service in Ireland on the Royal Irish Constabulary . . .* [C-831] H.C., 1873, xxii, pp. 45, 55.

instance, was much easier. In the RIC men usually had to serve at least seven years before they were permitted to marry, and even then permission might not be forthcoming. In Victoria a superior's permission was required, but this was usually given freely.[37]

That a family history of police service could be a determining factor in an immigrant's choice of career abroad is especially clear in the case of Detective Inspector Jeremiah Lynch (1889–1953). Lynch was an Irish speaker from Co. Kerry, who trained as a teacher in Dublin, but emigrated to England in 1912 where he joined the Met. He served in Special Branch and retired in 1937 as deputy head of the Flying Squad. Lynch is an interesting example of an Irishman who became a senior London policeman during the early twentieth century. However, there is more to his story than this. Although he did not train and serve in the RIC, a glance at his family tree shows that it is full of men who did, related both by blood and marriage. Indeed, Lynch's older brother served in the RIC from about 1908 until disbandment in 1922, when, like many ex-RIC men, he left Ireland for a time fearing retribution. He contemplated joining the Kenyan or Rhodesian police forces, before finally opting for a job as a security guard in the House of Commons and resuming life on the family farm in Kerry at the end of the decade. Lynch came from a policing family background which doubtless influenced his choice of career abroad.[38]

But what of men who had not trained or served as policemen in Ireland and who lacked family policing connections: why did large numbers of them too join various overseas police forces? Government service, whether as a policeman, a soldier, a fireman, a clerk or a teacher, did offer secure, reasonably paid, pensionable employment for young, literate, male immigrants, who aspired to more than labouring or factory work. One young Irishman arriving in Brisbane, Queensland, in the early 1880s noted down the various work opportunities available, presumably advised by fellow travellers:

> Apply for employment at the undermentioned places. Surveyor general's office, commissioner of water works, commissioner of public works, commissioner of police. At Brisbane all these resides [*sic*]. Make separate applications. Doant [*sic*] make it known at one place that you applied at another.[39]

Obviously this young immigrant had concluded that some sort of government employment was his best option. And police service had strong attractions. When

37 Haldane, *The People's Force*, pp. 85–6.   38 I would like to thank Dr Donal Lowry of Oxford Brookes University for providing me with information on the career of Inspector Lynch who was his great uncle. Lynch apparently took early retirement in 1937 because he was unhappy with the influence of the freemasons in the Met, whom he believed were blocking his chances of further promotion.   39 Quoted in M. Finnane, *Police and Government: Histories of Policing in Australia* (Melbourne, 1994), p. 137.

Victoria decided to expand its force by fifty men in 1888, over 500 applications were received for these positions. Generally recruits were not in short supply, with at least ten men applying for every vacancy even after 1900.[40] How many of these applicants were Irish immigrants is unclear, but it is probable that many were. Being English speaking and literate, though unskilled, the Irish were well suited for work as policemen.

For the immigrant police service offered, over and above security, a degree of status and power. A recent historian of the Irish in New York has characterised Irish policemen as an 'elite' among their fellow immigrants.[41] It is probable that the camaraderie of working with and for fellow Irishmen generated a sense of solidarity and pride. Perhaps also the concept of a 'critical mass' is relevant here. Once enough Irishmen had joined a police force, something like a 'chain reaction' was initiated. Studies of the Victorian police and also of some American forces certainly suggest that police service became identified with the Irish. Irish immigrants looked to the police because they knew that so many of their fellow Irishmen were serving and, in turn, the police authorities, often Irish themselves, looked favourably upon Irish applicants for police jobs.

Finnane has claimed that in the eastern Australian colonies during the 1860s and 1870s immigrants from Britain and Ireland with military or police backgrounds were actively recruited for the police.[42] This was especially evident in Victoria where there was an explicit policy of favouring ex-RIC men in particular and Irishmen in general for police service. Sir John O'Shanassy, an Irishman, was the government minister in charge of the police during the late 1850s and early 1860s, and under his administration Irishmen were put on a fast track to police appointment.[43] Similarly in New York, from the 1840s large numbers of Irishmen began to join the police force. By the mid 1850s, when nearly a quarter of the city's population were Irish born, it has been estimated that perhaps as many as half of all policemen were of Irish birth or descent.[44] Again, as in Victoria, police appointments were highly politicised and, as the Irish became increasingly powerful in Democratic politics in New York, so their control of the police department tightened.[45] And, again, one is struck by how long this lasted, for it was not until perhaps the last quarter of the twentieth century that Irish control of New York policing largely came to an end.

But the politicisation of policing could cut two ways: while it could lead to a favouring of the Irish, it could also lead to their exclusion. We have already seen

40 G. Davison, J.W. McCarty and A. McLeary (eds), *Australians, 1888* (Sydney, 1987), p. 240; Haldane, *The People's Force*, p. 122.   **41** H.R. Diner, '"The Most Irish City in the Union": the Era of the Great Migration, 1844–77' in R.H. Bayor and T.J. Meagher (eds), *The New York Irish* (Baltimore, 1996), p. 97.   **42** Finnane, *Police and Government*, p. 136.   **43** McQuilton in Finnane (ed.), *Policing in Australia*, p. 39.   **44** For the debate over the exact numbers of Irish in the New York police during the 1850s, see J.E. Richardson, *The New York Police: Colonial Times to 1901* (New York, 1970), pp. 70–1.   **45** Diner in Bayor and Meagher (eds), *The New York Irish*, p. 97.

that the NSW authorities sought successfully to reduce the numbers of Irish policemen in the 1880s. An even more striking example of a deliberate policy of removing the Irish from the police is provided by New Orleans. The first Irish policeman seems to have been appointed there in 1830. Just twenty years later, in 1850, 32 per cent of the force were Irish born, while the Irish made up only 20 per cent of the white adult male population. Yet, by 1860, when the Irish had risen to about a quarter of the male population, they comprised just 11 per cent of the police. This dramatic decline in the numbers of Irish policemen had occurred in 1855 when the nativist party, popularly called the 'Know Nothings', gained control of the city and reorganised policing with the specific intention of getting rid of immigrants. However, the decline of the Know Nothings and the revival of the Democratic Party saw the Irish reassert themselves: by 1870, 37 per cent of New Orleans' policemen were Irish born, while the Irish made up only 14 per cent of the white adult male population.[46]

IV

Any student of the Irish abroad is inevitably struck by how large a topic this is and by how much of it remains to be explored. This is hardly surprising when we are talking about millions of people who spread themselves throughout the world over a considerable period of time. The Irish historian, used to dealing with a small country and a small population, can find the diaspora somewhat intimidating. Understandably, there has been a tendency to focus on certain groups and certain places, which has generated a dramatic, though somewhat one-dimensional, portrait of the typical Irish immigrant. But the diaspora was, and is, enormously varied. In recent years research has extended to unlikely places and to unlikely occupations; and this has shown that Irish experience and influence were far more complex and widespread than earlier historians often realised. A study of Irish policemen abroad fits into this new migration historiography. It challenges the traditional view of the Irish migrant as a misfit and an outcast, prone to drunkenness and crime, discriminated against and struggling to survive at the very bottom of society. Doubtless this was the experience of many, but far from all. Irishmen were considered to make good policemen, not only by British and British colonial authorities, but by American ones as well. The RIC was widely regarded as a

---

46 While Irish involvement in policing in New York and Boston is generally well known, Irish involvement in the south has been largely overlooked. Yet there were other southern cities with even more Irish policemen than New Orleans. In 1860, for instance, 62 per cent of the Savannah, Georgia, police were Irish born, 58 per cent of those of Charleston, South Carolina, 41 per cent of those of St Louis, Missouri, and 34 per cent of those of Mobile, Alabama. In 1880 some eleven large southern cities had police forces that were at least a quarter Irish; and four of these had forces that were around a half Irish. D.C. Rousey, *Policing the Southern City: New Orleans, 1805–89* (Baton Rouge, 1996), pp. 58–9, 72–5, 145–6.

highly-trained and extremely effective force. Thus when, in the mid-nineteenth century, governments in various English-speaking countries and colonies were seeking to extend and consolidate their power through the establishment of police forces, it is not surprising that many turned to the Irish – especially as, in some instances, those perceived as their most unruly and lawless citizens were Irish immigrants.[47] Why the Irish were thought to make good policemen and why the Irish were often employed to police the Irish are issues that demand further research.

British colonial forces certainly did not adhere rigidly to an 'Irish model' of policing, but this should not detract from the fact that Irish-born and Irish-trained men formed large groups, sometimes even the majority, in police forces throughout the world. How their Irish backgrounds and training informed their policing is still little understood. On occasion Irish policemen found themselves in the front line confronting their fellow Irish. How they negotiated their complex and sometimes conflicting roles and identities awaits further study. Ned Kelly may have laughed at the idea of becoming a policeman, but tens of thousands of Irishmen followed this career abroad. If many Irish ended up behind bars or, like Kelly, on the scaffold, equally large numbers of Irish were responsible for putting some of them there.[48] These numbers alone should command far more serious attention than they have so far received.

[47] The influence of the RIC abroad did not end with the force's disbandment in 1922, as, in addition to joining the Garda Siochana in the south and the Royal Ulster Constabulary in the north, hundreds of men took up further service overseas. The Palestine police, for instance, actively recruited ex-RIC men and they remained influential within the force into the 1940s. E. Horne, *A Job Well Done: a History of the Palestine Police Force, 1920–48* (Tiptree, 1982), pp. 76–9, 90–2.   [48] The complexities of Irish policemen dealing with Irish criminals has been illustrated graphically in a recent scandal in Boston, where the two chose to cooperate. Dick Lehr and Gerard O'Neill, *Black Mass: the Irish Mob, the FBI and a Devil's Deal* (New York, 2000).

Moral maids and materialistic mistresses: Irish domestic servants and their American employers, 1850–1920

DIANE M. HOTTEN-SOMERS

During the last half of the nineteenth century, Ireland's once fertile green fields gave way to a deadly famine, leaving the country in economic and political ruin and forcing her starving people to emigrate. Between the years of 1840 and 1850 well over two million people emigrated from Ireland to countries around the globe. During these same years, America was enjoying the profits of an industrial revolution, making the United States a favourite destination for almost one million Irish immigrants. Of these, around half were women and they, like their male counterparts, came in search of gainful employment.[1] Irish women emigrated to America at a particularly opportune time. Due to the country's rapidly developing consumer culture, Irish women were highly employable, as America's cultural transformation from a producer to a consumer society created a plethora of domestic servant positions. American middle-class women suddenly turned to hired domestic help to maintain their homes, rather than maintaining them themselves, and the flood of Irish immigrant women provided the necessary population to fulfill this collective consumer desire.

Yet America's cultural morphing into a consumer society not only heavily influenced Irish womens employment opportunities, but also created whole new definitions of public and private space and reshaped middle-class mistresses' domestic duties.[2] When goods had been produced in the home, women stayed strictly within the domestic sphere, working constantly to provide for their families' needs. However, when the commodities of the home became purchasable items, women left that arena and entered the public sphere as shoppers. In a sense, the consumer culture widened the domestic sphere to include the public, or consumer, space. Middle-class women's new identities as 'shoppers' created quite a domestic predicament. Taking on the responsibility of household shopping did not free middle-class women from their more traditional roles as mother, wife, and maintainer of harmonious domesticity. Rather, her role as 'shopper' became an addendum to her

---

1 K.A. Miller, *Emigrants and Exiles: Ireland and the Irish Exodus to North America* (Oxford, 1985). 2 See E.S Abelson, *When Ladies Go A-Thieving: Middle-Class Shoplifters in the Victorian Department Store* (Oxford, 1989), and S.A. Cordery, 'Women in Industrialising America' in C. W. Calhoun (ed.), *The Gilded Age: Essays on the origins of Modern America* Delaware, 1996), p. 112 & ff, for discussion on the entry of women to the public sphere.

already long list of domestic duties. For many middle-class women, they found the demands of having to work in two places at once, both the home and the public sphere, too taxing. To create more time for themselves, middle-class women turned to domestic servants.

The flood of Irish female immigrants throughout the nineteenth century and into the twentieth provided the perfect means of fulfilling middle-class women's need for domestic servants. Irish women headed out of Ireland literally starving for work and, realising the economic potential of America, chose this country over all others as their new home of financial opportunity. It is estimated that between 1851 and 1920 about 1.2 million Irish women emigrated to America, and the majority found employment there as domestic servants.[3] Between the years of 1860 and 1920 female workers claiming domestic service as their occupation climbed from 559,908 to 1,012,133.[4] Additionally, the Women's Education and Industrial Union, a Boston-based organisation whose work for the advancement of women made them one of the nineteenth century's most successful and influential social reformist groups, conducted an investigation of the number and nationality of women in domestic service. The results of this study showed that Irish women held close to fifteen percent of all domestic servant positions nationwide. And, in areas as densely populated by Irish immigrants like Massachusetts, the Irish made up more than half of the domestic service work force.[5] When the sheer volume of Irish immigrant women is combined with their desire to earn wages and the cultural shift to buy domestic services, these women positioned themselves and were positioned by the needs of middle-class women as one of the hottest commodities of the nineteenth century.

But it soon became apparent that employee and employer held rather different perspectives on the responsibilities of the domestic servant. The average Irish female immigrant came not only as an unskilled worker, but with little experience of any of the modern cleaning, cooking, or laundry techniques that were the backbone of the middle-class home. Within a short time after the influx of Irish domestics, middle-class women across the country realized what their 'Irish commodity' truly needed was a means of standardisation. Middle class women, and particularly social reformists of the time, called for domestic service to be shaped into an industry with the means to produce a perfectly standardised product. Thus, during the 1890s a proliferation of books and periodical literature addressed this issue in an attempt to metaphorically create a domestic servant factory line.[6] Mrs C.H.

3 A.J. Fitzpatrick and W.E. Vaughan (eds) *Irish Historical Statistics, Population 1821–1971* (Dublin, 1978), pp. 261–66. **4** J.C.G. Kennedy, *Population of the United States in 1860* (Washington, 1864), p. 675; W.C. Hunt, *Fourteenth Census of the United states Taken in the Year 1920, Vol. IV: Occupations* (Washington, 1923), p. 358. **5** 'Number and Nationality of Women in Domestic Service' in *Bulletin of the Domestic Reform League*, 3: 1, October 1908. **6** For a discussion of the standardisation of domestic training, see L.M. Salmon, 'Domestic Service from the Standpoint of the Employee' in *Cosmopolitan*, July 1893, pp. 347–353; K.G. Wells, 'the Servant Girl of the Future' in *North American Review*, July 1893, pp. 716–721;

Stone, a concerned mistress and dedicated advocate of social reform, set forth in *The Problems of Domestic Service* the deficiencies of these domestic servants and the means through which to create the model maid.[7] Stone claimed that many of the problems within domestic service arose because mistresses have merely viewed their girls as purchased housekeeping machines and have overlooked that these servants were mere human beings with needs and failings. Stone recognised the humanity of these servants and realised that the remedy to resolve the frustrating relationship that existed between mistress and maid was to create a standardised training regime for new domestic servants. Thus, towards the end of her book, Stone proposed that each and every city nationwide open a 'Training Home' to instruct these domestic servants in such tasks as 'the proper way of sweeping stairs, with a brush and dust pan, into which the dust from each step is swept, so spreading it as little as possible.'[8] These 'Training Homes' would ultimately produce pre-packaged model maids who could not fail to satisfy the most exacting mistress. Training homes would, therefore, produce the ultimate in standardized domestic commodities.

The Domestic Reform League of Boston, one of the Women's Educational and Industrial Union's most active departments, answered Stone's call. On 25 August 1897, Ada M. Child, chairman of the Committee to form the School of Housekeeping, wrote a letter to the members of the Domestic Reform League proposing the establishment of a School of Housekeeping. In this letter, she indicated how this school would enable both mistress and maid to obtain training in domestic service: '[it will] furnish an opportunity to both employer and employee, to study the science of housekeeping; its practical application to housework; and the principles which govern the domestic machinery.'[9] The Domestic Reform League quickly responded to Child's suggestion, and by the fall of 1897 the School of Housekeeping officially opened its doors for instruction, promising to remedy 'the servant girl problem' by helping to train both mistress and maid in the proper way to tend house'.[10]

The difference in the course programmes offered to mistresses and maids further shows how this standardization process 'commodified' Irish domestics. The classes for the mistresses helped to enhance their understanding and skills of the art of housekeeping. They were invited to the school twice a week to listen leisurely to lectures whose topics ranged from house sanitation to the art of housekeeping to domestic service and its relation to the industrial problem. It was as much of a chance to socialise with the leaders in the trade of domestic service as it was to learn about housekeeping.[11] The programme for the maids, however, had

---

J.M. Parker, 'Profit Sharing and Domestic Services as discussed at a Women's Club' in *North American Review*, May 1898, pp. 639–40.   **7** Mrs C.H. Stone, *The Problems of Domestic Service* (St Louis, 1892).   **8** Ibid, p. 28.   **9** Ada M. Child, 'A Letter to the Domestic Reform League' (1897).   **10** *School of Housekeeping Bulletin*, 1897.   **11** *Course Bulletin for Employers, November 1898*, School of Housekeeping.

none of these leisurely aspects. Theirs was a regime with the sole purpose of rigorously shaping these domestics into model maids. Girls who signed up for this training committed themselves to an eight-month-long programme that was split between a five-month classroom stint and a three month probationary training period in the home of a potential employer. Within the classroom programme standardisation reached its peak as its goal was not only to instruct future servants on how to complete such obvious duties as caring for the fire or the bedrooms and preparing the three main meals, but also became as specific as 'care of parlor and halls, and answering the door-bell properly.'[12] All aspects of a general domestic's duties were covered, ensuring that School of Housekeeping graduates would each be identically trained, and therefore practically interchangeable, as far as employers were concerned.

Yet, the standardisation of these Irish maids proved problematic. Training schools seemed like the perfect answer to a middle-class American culture that enjoyed the fruits of an industrial revolution. The modern factory produced a plethora of new and purchasable goods that helped to create the social standards for the middle-class home and family, so what impeded such a system from producing an Irish domestic servant who upheld these same standards within her work? The problem was a consequence of America's own Gilded Age. Most of these Irish maids arrived in the United States during the emergence of the culture of consumption and, like many Americans, were overwhelmed by the mass of material wealth. In a letter to her family back in Ireland, one Irish girl ecstatically describes the opportunity for materialistic gain in America, 'I can have here as many gold rings and diamonds and silk dresses as I like!!!'[13] And many Irish women had for the first time the prospect of a disposable income that would enable them to purchase such items. By 1893, Lucy Salmon, an expert on domestic service and professor of home economics at Vassar College, calculated that, at a lowest approximate estimate, employers paid $160,000,000 annually in cash wages to domestic servants.[14] A survey of servant wages in Boston at the turn of the century indicated that the weekly average wage of an Irish domestic servant was $4.13, making her total monthly income close to $20.00.[15] In comparison, factory workers, the second largest occupational group amongst immigrant women, averaged a weekly wage of $6.22, giving a total monthly wage of almost $25.00.[16] At first glance the factory girl appears to be the more advantaged, but it must be noted that she, unlike the domestic servant, had to pay for all her own living expenses from this salary. The domestic servant's whole salary, on the other hand, was hers to spend as

12 *Course Bulletin for Employees, 1899–1900*. 13 R.A.M. Harris and B.E. O'Keffe (eds), *The Search for Missing Friends: Irish Immigrant Advertisements placed in the Boston Pilot, Vol. 4: 1857–1860* (Boston, 1995), xxviii. 14 Salmon, 'Domestic Service', p. 346. 15 Report of an Investigation of 500 Immigrant Women in Boston (Boston, 1907). 16 C.D. Wright, 'The Working Girls of Boston' in The Fifteenth Annual Report of the Massachusetts Bureau of Statistics of Labour for 1884 (Boston, 1889), reprint L. Stein and P. Taft (eds), *American Labor: From Conspiracy to Collective Bargaining* (New York), p. 81.

she pleased since her employers paid for not merely bed and board, but work clothing as well.

However, the Irish domestic servants' potential to become an active participant within the culture of consumption points to one of the most complex and contradictory aspects of the mistress-maid relationship. The mistress could not allow her servant to become a consumer simply because she could not afford for her servant to leave the home to fulfill her materialistic desires. Obviously there is an inherent contradiction within the mistress' need to deny her Irish servant access to the consumer culture. As I discussed earlier, the middle-class woman had herself become the most predominant and active member of the consumer culture. The question then is if the mistress herself enjoyed the freedom to consume, how and why did she deny this luxury to her servant?

The answer to this question lies in the complexity of the nineteenth-century middle-class female identity. Although the industrialisation of American society had allowed the middle-class woman to leave the home as a domestic consumer, this had not relieved her of her duty as the moral barometer of the household. As historian Stacy Cordery has argued, despite the fact that modern America had provided her with more leisure time to roam within the public sphere, she was still obliged to conform to the 'cult of true womanhood'.[17] Thus, the middle-class woman found herself in quite a predicament. On the one hand, society expected her to continue her role as both domestic moral and material barometer. Yet, on the other hand, the transformations within American society during the nineteenth century had provided women with both the responsibility and the opportunity to leave the house to become fully fledged members of the public, or consumer, sphere.

One of the ways that middle-class women attempted to solve their paradoxical positions was by training their domestic servants to perform as surrogates for themselves not only as household labourers, but as moral compasses as well. In a sense, these middle-class mistresses needed to assimilate the Irish domestic servant into American society and turn her into a woman who reflected the moral and ethical character of the mistress herself. In an article entitled 'Ireland's Daughters in Their New Home,' Harriet Beecher Stowe, the author of *Uncle Tom's Cabin* and advocate of the 'cult of true womanhood,' discussed the vulnerable nature of Irish women in America and the important role the mistress should play in her life: 'Thousands of young Irish girls have landed on our shores, utter strangers, far from advice and protection of fathers and mothers . . . a kind, consistent, watchful, careful mistress will keep her servants in the way of honesty; a careless or incompetent one tempts them to fall.'[18] Mistresses were, according to Stowe, responsible for ensuring the moral development of the Irish servant girl, and seeing that their Irish domestics adopted their mistresses' middle class value system. And, this value system emphasised,

17 Cordery, 'Women in Industrialising America', p. 112. **18** H. Beecher Stowe, 'Ireland's Daughters in Their New Homes' in *Donahoe's Magazine*, January 1879, pp. 53–4.

above all else, the importance of good work, self-advancement through cultural activities, and, most crucially, high character.

Mistresses' attempts to assimilate their Irish maids into an American middle-class Protestant culture were assisted by several nineteenth-century domestic service instructional manuals and popular periodicals. These manuals and articles show the mistresses' desires to fully shape their Irish maids into model American women who were expressions of the 'culture of character,' and thus could be entrusted to maintain the moral as well as the material aspects of the household.[19] In both *Plain Talk and Friendly Advice to Domestics* (author unknown) and *Letters to Persons Who are Engaged in Domestic Service* by Catherine Beecher, sister of Harriet Beecher Stowe, both authors warned their servants of the evils of squandering their money on silken dresses and personal ornaments.[20] In the American middle-class spirit of using the dollar to get ahead, Beecher discouraged servants from buying 'showy dresses', and urged them to place the money thus saved into a savings account where interest would be earned. The thrifty servant could thus spend the time she would have squandered shopping, educating herself through reading daily to her mistress.

The suggestion of acceptable leisure activities also played a large role in persuading these women to adopt exemplary middle-class standards. Catherine Beecher indicated that attending religious meetings in the evenings was a perfectly acceptable activity if done to further one's understanding of and faith in Christ. Religious meetings were strictly for serious worship and she warned domestics against attending meetings for the purely social purpose of engaging members of the opposite sex in conversation.[21] Beecher's sister, Harriet Beecher Stowe, continued this line of advice by outlining some rules for leisure time:

> Rule the first is that no young servant should be out alone after dark giving reasons for this rule that are easily understood. Rule the second, that no one comes to the back door after a certain hour, because their friends are quite welcome to come to the front door; and once it is dark, bad characters are about, and young girls are easily frightened.[22]

19 Cultural historian W. Susman coined the phrase 'culture of character' in his book *Culture as History: the Transformation of American Society in the Twentieth Century* (New York, 1989). Susman argues that nineteenth-century America was obsessed with obtaining and developing citizens who had a high character, expressed through strict adherence to the protestant work ethic, and morally acceptable recreational activities. 20 C.E. Beecher, *Letters to Persons Who are Engaged in Domestic Service* (New York, 1842), and (author unknown) *Plain Talk and Friendly Advice to Domestics with Counsel on Home Matters* (Boston, 1855). 21 Beecher, Letters, pp. 122–5. 22 H. Beecher Stowe, 'Mistress and Maid' in *Donahoe's Magazine*, May 1885, p. 442.

Thus the mistresses' household standards stripped the servant of her freedom to choose when and how she would spend her leisure time, a time over which the employer should have had little control.

The question that begs to be asked is did these Irish maids heed their mistresses' advice? Was the mistress-maid relationship as truly influential as these mistresses hoped it would be? The answer to both of these questions seems to be an unqualified 'yes'. In several interviews, surveys, and articles written about the social activities of Irish maids, these domestics appeared to have assimilated the moral values of their 'concerned' mistresses. In an interview with Mary Meehan, an Irish woman who spent all her working years as a household cook, she described how she and the other maids only dressed as her mistress wanted, in the traditional black sturdy frock during working hours and in modest dresses with fashionable ribbons in their hair during hours of leisure.[23] In a survey conducted by the Women's Educational and Industrial Union on the social conditions in domestic service, 113 Irish servants in Boston claimed to have spent their leisure time and money just as Beecher, Stowe, and the other above mentioned mistresses had instructed them to do. These Irish servants used their leisure time to read, sew, or attend church services or socials and they diligently placed their money into secure savings accounts or sent it back to their families in Ireland.[24] An article in *Donahoe's Magazine,* one of the most widely read Irish-American monthlies, detailed the monetary support these Irish maids gave to their homeland:

> Mr. Patrick Donahoe furnishes us with a significant fact. There are numerous offices in Boston for the transmission of money orders . . . during the four weeks ending on Dec. 20, 1879, drafts of $2,250, and representing £5,736, passed through his hands. The senders were almost exclusively servant girls.[25]

Finally, in a letter home to Ireland, household servant Mary Harlon proudly explained that after only a few short months in New York city she was, 'happy in her present post, she now had a bank account of eighty dollars, and was putting aside money for a new silk dress.'[26] While Mary clearly did have consumer desires, her ability to prioritise saving over spending signifies her apparent adoption of a middle-class value system. Each of the above examples not only validates the mistresses' attempts to block their maids access to the consumer culture, but they also reveal that through living and working in American middle-class homes, these

23 M. Meehan, 'Irish Cook-Brookfield', interview by L. Bassett, in *American Life Histories: Manuscripts from the Federal Writers' Project, 1936–1940,* available at http://www.loc.wpaintro/wpahome. **24** *Social Conditions in Domestic Service,* prepared by the Massachusetts Bureau of Statistics of Labor in collaboration with the Women's Educational and industrial Union of Boston (Boston, 1900). **25** Unknown author, 'What is Thought of Our Irish Girls Abroad' in *Donahoe's Magazine,* May 1880, p. 437. **26** Harris and O'Keffe, *Search,* xxxii.

maids were successfully assimilated, shedding their Irish rural identities to become mirror images of their American middle-class mistresses.

The 'americanisation' of Irish maids accomplished its main goal: freeing the mistress from her domestic responsibilities. However, what these middle-class women gained – personal freedom – these Irish servants lost. Initially, Irish immigrant women were so economically desperate that sacrificing their personal freedom to provide monetary relief for their suffering families back home was but a small price to pay. However, as Ireland's economic recovery from years of famine relieved these Irish domestic servants from their financial responsibility to their kin, they began to realise what a high price they had paid to enter service. Irish women began to discover that they had given up their independence and their Irish identities to become servants.

This realisation by Irish domestics caused a crisis within the mistress-maid relationship. As Irish women began to recognise the sacrifices they made to be servants, they simultaneously began to realise the hypocritical nature of their mistresses. Servants observed their mistresses behaving exactly as they were trained not to. By the turn of the century, these maids began to voice their frustrations towards the paradox within which they lived. In an April 1912 edition of *Outlook* magazine one maid voiced her dissatisfaction with her mistress, 'Perhaps the lady goes downtown in the morning, has her own nice lunch at a restaurant, and tells me I can give the children a pick-up lunch, and I am lucky if I have enough in the pantry to give them fried bread.'[27] What domestic servants increasingly realised was not only the unfairness of their position, but also that they wanted personal time to enjoy the fruits of their labours. Irish domestics had worked hard for their money and finally were in a position where they could afford to spend on themselves, but both their working hours and the demands of their mistresses left them with little free time to do so. Thus, through the combination of the servants' realisations of their desire for personal freedom and the rise of women's social reformist groups, maids and social reformists from across the country began to call for a complete revamping of the domestic service industry.

Domestic service had traditionally been an industry that demanded extremely long hours from its maids. In an investigation conducted by the School of Housekeeping, the range of working hours for maids was between twelve and fifteen daily. In comparison, shop and factory workers' hours ranged between eight and ten hours per day.[28] As a result of this discrepancy, many maids began to leave their service jobs, claiming they would find shorter hours, more individual freedom, and more time for leisure in other industries. In an investigation of New York City women wage-workers entitled *Prisoners of Poverty: Women Wage-Workers, Their Trades and Their Lives,* Helen Campbell, one of America's most dedicated urban and

---

27 'The Experiences of a "Hired Girl"' in *The Outlook*, 6 April 1912, pp. 778–9. 28 *Social Statistics of Working Women*, prepared by the Massachusetts Bureau of Statistics of Labor with information collected by the School of Housekeeping (Boston, 1901).

social reformers, chronicled domestics' reasons for leaving the service industry.[29] The former maids' complaints ranged from loneliness to abominable living quarters to unruly children. Yet, what each ex-servant always mentioned in her interview was the lack of freedom involved in servantry. As one maid claimed, 'It's freedom that we want when the day's work is done . . . in service you're never sure that your soul's your own except when you are out of the house.'[30]

Articles written both by maids and social reformers within such popular periodicals amongst the middle-class population as *Harper's Bazaar, Ladies Home Journal,* the *Atlantic Monthly,* and the *Outlook* furthered this discussion on the need for a radical change within the domestic service industry.[31] In a March 1905 edition of *Ladies' Home Journal,* Annette Jaynes Miller claimed that she never had any trouble with her servants because she treated her maid as both a professional and a human being, standardising her work hours and duties while giving her time off to do such things as visit the dressmaker. Another article in this same magazine by Mrs Christine Broderick went as far as to suggest that the remedy to the servant girl problem was to have them 'live-out.' Broderick claimed that 'living-out' would give them ample time to socialise with friends, take in a movie, and even spend a whole day shopping, returning to their work at seven o'clock each morning refreshed after an evening of leisure. These articles call for and give evidence of the changes that occurred within the domestic service industry during the early twentieth century. Due to the work of such women's social reformist groups as the Domestic Reform League of Boston and the pressures that the flight of women workers from the service industry placed upon the middle-class woman and household, servants' hours and domestic responsibilities were standardised. Although these changes may appear as minor adjustments, they greatly and positively affected the life of the servant. With shorter hours, maids found themselves with the freedom to live their lives as they pleased. They were, for the first time in the history of domestic service, able to venture outside the home as independent individuals, free from the ever-observant eye of their mistresses' and able to participate as at least part-time members of the leisured class.

This freedom for the Irish domestic servant in particular allowed them to re-establish the Irish identity that they were forced to give up when they entered service during the nineteenth century. Domestic service had isolated these women from their ethnic communities that had, by the twentieth century, become a very large part of almost every major urban centre in America. Most of these Irish neighbourhoods were recreations of Irish cultural life as they were filled with pubs,

29 H. Campbell, *Prisoners of Poverty: Women Wage-Workers, Their Trades and Their Lives* (Boston, 1900). **30** Ibid, p. 224. **31** These include A.J. Miller, 'Why I Never Have Trouble with My Servants', *Ladies' Home Journal,* March 1905, pp. 4 and 52; author unknown, 'How My Wife Keeps Her Maids', in *Harper's Bazaar,* December 1909, p. 1231; author unknown, 'An Ideal Mistress', in *Outlook,* 10 August 1912, pp. 838–9; Mrs C. Broderick, 'Suppose Our Servants Didn't Live with Us' in *Ladies' Home Journal,* October 1914, p. 102.

dance halls, theatres, and homes with an open door policy that welcomed every-one Irish or non Irish to come in for a cup of tea and a long chat. To regain their identity, Irish domestic servants began to spend their free time in these communi-ties and reconnecting with their Irish roots, In many of the interviews with Irish domestic servants who emigrated to this country during the twentieth century, they often discussed how they spent their leisure time with their Irish relatives and friends. Both Katherine Donohghue and Catherine Keohane discussed how they and their sisters, who were also domestic servants, would spend their 'days out' vis-iting each other and their aunts, uncles, and other relatives who lived in the Boston area. Elizabeth Linehan remembers spending her leisure time taking fresh baked breads and soups over to a neighbours house for a friendly chat.[32] And Mrs John Wesst vividly recalls how her Sundays were spent reviving Irish culture through singing folk songs from home.[33] These kinds of leisure activities were not ones pre-scribed by their mistresses, but rather they reflected elements of how the Irish socialised in Ireland. There were no strict social observances that Irish people fol-lowed to see one another, and there was limited emphasis placed on self-advance-ment through studying. The modern Irish domestic, then, reflected her native culture by spending her leisure time as she would have in her homeland. And, by participating in such activities she seemed to be flatly rejecting any form of forced assimilation of specific American cultural practices.

By 1920, the mistress-maid relationship had almost reversed itself. Domestic servants had, for the most part, become 'live-out' employees. This change in the domestic service industry re-established a sense of personal freedom and ethnic identity, which was lost when the maid became a permanent part of the household as a 'live-in' servant. By having her own home to return to at the end of the work-ing day, the maid finally had her own place and time, free from the demands of the American middle-class home and mistress, to express her own individuality. And, surprisingly, with the onset of the live-out maid, middle-class women rediscovered the personal freedom she had once enjoyed through running her own household without having to attend to the needs and requests of her servant. In the words of one very insightful mistress, the household had become a site of independence for both the maid and the mistress:

> Freedom lies in that quarter, privacy and individuality for the maid; free-dom, too, for the household, to joke, to meddle, to be noisy, to have com-pany; freedom to lock the house and with a clear conscience prolong the motoring trip and sup at an inn.[34]

32 K. Donoghue, interviewd by E. Kaledin on 12/10/82, tape held at Schlessinger Library; C. Keohane and E. Linehan, interviewed by Ide O'Carroll.   **33** Mrs. J. Wesst, 'Pioneer life in Nebraska'. Interview with F.W. Kaul and L.A. Rollins, *American Life Histories*.
34 Author unknown, 'A Maid in the House', in *Atlantic Monthly*, May 1920, p. 715.

In a sense, as the age of social reform ushered the servant out of the house and the mistress back in with a redefined idea of domesticity, their comings and goings signalled that the mistress-maid relationship had evolved from one of interdependence to one of independence. And, with their new found sense of independence, both the American mistress and the Irish maid faced the twentieth century with the freedom to choose whether they would continue to create their identities within the domestic sphere, the consumer culture, or, most likely, a combination of both.

Richard Robert Madden: an Irish anti-slavery activist in the Americas

NINI RODGERS

Today R.R. Madden is remembered as an influential historian who shaped the popular consciousness. First published in 1842, his *United Irishmen, Their Lives and Times,* continued to make frequent and varied appearances over the next eighty years, extended, reorganised, pirated and abbreviated.[1] By the twentieth century its style and construction increasingly limited its appeal for the general reader, but it remained a rich quarry for the historian. Madden saw the '98 as 'the great Morgue of talent and enthusiasm',[2] a view reverberating through to the bi-centenary commemoration. It is not however generally remembered that this book was produced by an Irish emigrant earning his living as a writer and imperial official. The following essay will examine the nature of R.R. Madden's work as an anti-slavery activist and seek to explain the connection between such a career and his emergence as a nationalist historian.

In 1820, following an eighteenth-century pattern, R.R. Madden, twenty-one-year-old son of a Catholic silk manufacture and possessor of £30 capital, left Dublin for Bordeaux to seek his fortune. After travelling on the continent, he moved to London, where he worked as a newspaper reporter, attained a medical qualification from the College of Surgeons and acquired an ambition which was to remain with him the rest of his life: to be become a successful literary figure. In 1824, having considered his own aptitudes and experience and the current taste of the reading public, he set out for the East returning in 1828 with a travel book and a two volume novel, *The Mussulman,* which he sold for £300 each, a substantial amount for a first-time author. He married, set up practice in a promisingly fashionable area and in 1829 joined the burgeoning Anti-slavery Society.[3]

Anti-slavery, like Catholic emancipation, had first emerged in dynamic public

---

1 R.R. Madden, *The United Irishmen, their Lives and Times,* 2 vols (London, 1842); 2 vols (Philadelphia, 1842); 2 vols (London, 1843); 3 vols (Dublin, 1846); 3 vols (Dublin, 1858); *Address to the People of England on the Orange Regime in Ireland . . . reprinted from 'The United Irishmen, their Lives and Times'* (London, 1861); J.B. Daly (ed.), *Ireland in 98: Sketches of the principal men of the time, based upon the published volumes and some unpublished MSS of the late Dr. R.R. Madden* (London, 1888); V.F. O'Reilly (ed.), *The United Irishmen, their Lives and Times by R.R. Madden* (New York, 1910), reprinted 1916: J.J. O'Neill (ed.), *The United Irishmen, their Lives and Times by R.R. Madden* (Dublin, 1920). **2** R.R. Madden to Sir William Napier, 28 Aug. 1842, in T.M. Madden, *Memoirs from 1798–1886 of Richard Robert Madden* (London, 1891), p. 169. **3** Ibid., pp. 60–2.

form at the close of the eighteenth century, fed by enlightenment ideas and revolutionary hopes. But the connection of anti-slavery with growing evangelical enthusiasm in Britain, allowed that reform to prosper in a counter-revolutionary age. Thus 1806–7 saw the triumph of the campaign against the slave trade and in the 1820s the revived movement turned on slavery itself. As a cause seeking to cultivate the conscience and sensitivity of mankind, anti-slavery had always appealed to and welcomed literary people, making extensive use of their talents. Madden was therefore a valuable recruit and in 1833 when the reformed parliament abolished slavery within the British empire, he secured an official post as a stipendiary magistrate in Jamaica at £300 a year.

Madden was eager to escape from the strains of attempting to establish a fashionable practice and he would never again earn his living as a doctor. He was a man who throve on supporting a cause and saw the literary and historic potential of being present to record the beginnings of slave freedom, this 'mighty experiment'[4] as Lord Stanley, the Whig colonial secretary, had described it. But more personal reasons excited Madden's interest in Jamaica for he himself had possessed planter relatives, the Lyons of Roscommon. There was nothing particularly unusual about this. Throughout the eighteenth century Ireland's western gentry, Protestant and Catholic, Brownes, Kellys, Stauntons, O'Haras, Martins, Blakes, Frenchs, Lynchs, Tuites, and Bellews had invested in sugar estates. The Lyons plantations had been purchased in the 1780s when the granting of 'free trade' unleashed a spurt of enthusiasm in Ireland for West Indian ventures. Then Madden's maternal great uncle, always referred to as 'old Dr Lyons', appears to have developed two Jamaican plantations, Derry and Marly. Eventually he sold Derry and retired to Ireland, while the remaining, Marly, was managed and later inherited in succession by his brother, Theodosius Lyons, and his nephew, Garret Forde, who both died in Jamaica. (Garret Forde was R.R. Madden's mother's favourite brother.) Sometime in the first decade of the nineteenth century the Lyons plantation became absentee and eventually the subject of a long running chancery suit. Legal developments and a timely death in the early 30s, convinced Madden that now might be the moment to put in a claim of his own.[5] The Jamaican appointment gave him the opportunity to personally assess whether there was any future in embarking on the hazards of litigation. When eventually he reconnoitred Marly, early in 1834, he found it inaccessible and 'ruinate,' the sugar machinery all sold off years before, a dilapidated house inhabited only by what he at first took to be slaves abandoned due to age and illness. However, on closer investigation, it turned out that two of the women, a decade or so older than himself, were his cousins, the daughters of Mr Theodosius Lyons by his mulatto concubine. She was still alive, now very eld-

---

4 *Hansard's Parliamentary Debates*, third series, xvii, p. 1194.   **5** Madden, *Memoirs* p. 68. Marly had been mortgaged and then sold by the Irish Court of chancery, *c*. 1824. Madden seems to have envisaged making a claim on the current owners rather than actually acquiring the property.

erly and very suspicious at the appearance of Richard Robert. The two younger women were more informative, explaining that Madden could also have met a male cousin but he had been auctioned off in one of the court of chancery sales. On seeing the ruinate plantation, Madden perceived its hopelessness as a financial asset and its potential as literary copy. In his book on the West Indies his Jamaican family became a symbol of planterdom, drawn by the nature of the system into absenteeism, litigation and debt, leaving nothing behind but unacknowledged children, the remnants of an embittered and exploited work force and the forgotten grave of uncle Garret now sprouting someone else's sugar cane.[6]

It was relatively easy for R.R. Madden to turn from his old profession of travel writing to producing anti-slavery literature. But the job as stipendiary magistrate was a different matter: here he had no previous experience to draw upon and the remit in itself was daunting. He and his colleagues were stepping straight into the front line of a long-running quarrel. Since 1823 the government, under pressure from the anti-slavery lobby in parliament, had laid down an improved code of practice for the treatment of slaves. The planters were furious at the attempt to introduce these new metropolitan standards, humanitarian and evangelical, into their traditional plantation society, protesting that their rights as colonists and as property owners were being violated. Here Jamaica, the largest British island, with a forty-five man strong legislature, in existence since the mid-seventeenth century, was very much the leader of the protest. Reacting to disagreement among their rulers, the slaves rose in revolt at the very moment when the struggle for parliamentary reform in Britain was strengthening the electoral importance of the anti-slavery movement.[7] Under such pressures the Whigs moved unenthusiastically from amelioration to abolition, producing a compromise solution. The planters were to be given £20 million compensation and their work force was to be secured by a period of apprenticeship during which the ex-slaves would labour for their former owners without pay. Colonial secretary Stanley stressed that apprenticeship was to train the ex-slaves for freedom, while giving the planters time to adjust financially to new conditions.[8] The stipendiary magistrates were appointed to police apprenticeship and ensure that it worked fairly. On arrival in the West Indies they had to explain freedom to ex-slaves, who were going to have to remain on the plantations and work for their masters without remuneration, forty and a half hours a week for the next six years. Failure to carry out this labour would be punished by extra labour, discipline to be enforced if necessary by flogging (in the case of male apprentices) and imprisonment in the work house for all, regardless of gender. Erring overseers, agents and masters would be dealt with by fines, dismissal from post or a ban against holding apprentices. Hostile to the introduction of this new paid magistracy, the planters received the unwelcome newcomers with lavish

6 R.R. Madden, *A Twelvemonth's Residence in the West Indies during the Transition from Slavery to Apprenticeship*, 2 vols (London, 1835), i, pp. 160–71. **7** W.A. Green, *British Slave Emancipation* (Oxford, 1976), pp. 111–15. **8** *Hansard*, xvii, p. 1230.

colonial hospitality, while making it clear that difficulties would ensue if suitable co-operation did not follow.[9]

Thirty special magistrates took up positions in Jamaica in 1833–4. By the close of the year four of them had died, probably from yellow fever, and another four had given up their commissions and left.[10] Madden was one of the first to reach the island. He arrived some nine months before the Jamaican assembly, driven by the threat of loss of compensation, passed the hated abolition bill in August 1834. During those nine months Madden acted as an ordinary magistrate in St Andrew's parish in order to train for his future role. He got on well with the other special magistrates; most of whom were ex-naval or army officers, the kind of men he had met on shipboard during his eastern travels, and, like himself, professional, penurious, hanging on determinedly to their middle-class status. He set himself to learning Jamaican Creole so that he could understand what the slaves were saying.[11] When delivering judgement he sought to act fairly while displaying his concern for the maintenance of law and order.[12] He enjoyed planter hospitality, travelled round the island taking notes on everything of interest, including flora and fauna, for the book he planned to write was designed to appeal to his old audience, the armchair traveller, as well as to those concerned with the issue of slavery.

When it came time for him to take up his special magistracy he was moved from St Andrew's parish to Kingston. This meant that Madden was dealing with people who had been urban slaves, working as household servants, artisans, dockers and sailors. Many of the city's white households were economically dependent on such labour: spinsters, widows and retired people often lived by hiring out their slaves. Yet urban slavery, a condition for which the Caribbean institution had not been designed, had always presented severe problems of control, providing a high level of opportunity for private trading, theft, alternative employment, acquisition of literacy, scanting on set duties, even permanent escape.

Despite the obvious difficulties, Madden set about his task with enthusiasm. The cases brought before him fell mainly into two categories: complaints by masters against absconding apprentices and requests by apprentices for immediate manumission. In the first instance, Madden soon proved himself unsatisfactory to the white community. When he convicted apprentices for breach of labour dues and ill discipline he kept the sentences of flogging to a minimum. Frustrated masters, forbidden by law to whip recalcitrant apprentices and disappointed that Madden was not going to do it for them, extracted corporal punishment by manhandling their servants before him, under the pretext that they had to be physically forced to attend court. Madden refused to hear cases under such circumstances.[13] On the issue of manumission he preserved an equally determined front. The

9 'Report from Select Committees appointed to inquire into the makings of the Apprenticeship System in the Colonies with minutes and evidence' in *British Parliamentary Papers* (Shannon, 1968), Slave Trade, iii, p. 360.   **10** Madden, *West Indies,* ii, p. 266.   **11** Ibid., i, p. 129.   **12** Ibid., ii, p. 104.   **13** Ibid., ii, pp. 310–12.

Westminster government was eager to encourage this, seeing it as a school for wage labourers, suggesting that apprentices should exert themselves to earn money to buy immediate freedom. In setting the price of manumission, the special magistrate had to work with a regular magistrate and disagreements between the two, as Madden soon realised, could mean the complete failure of the apprentice's request. There were other cases of course in which the apprentice claimed that the original enslavement had been illegal so that free status should be immediately recognised. Madden actually encouraged applications on such grounds when he discovered that Jamaica contained Indians from the Mosquito coast enslaved by tradition not by law. In all, during his magistracy Madden received some three hundred applications for manumission of which eighty were carried through successfully, a success rate which proved to be dangerously high.[14] Once the pattern of his behaviour emerged he found himself harassed by the Kingston authorities, his office removed from the spacious court house into the squalor of an abandoned store. When he was assaulted in the street by an angry merchant and the police ignored his complaints, Madden decided that the protection of the apprentice was incompatible with his own personal safety and resigned his appointment.[15]

Giving up the magistracy, however, did not mean giving up anti-slavery activity. His book was ready for the press and published in Philadelphia, as well as London, lent strength to the American campaign to create a national anti-slavery society in the U.S.A. based on the British example.[16] Like all his writings, *A Twelvemonth's Residence in the West Indies* was a sprawling, verbose work but it included passages which were lively, perceptive, at times compelling. As a travel writer Madden had acquired skills enabling him to penetrate a strange society quickly. One of the most fruitful was his device of seeking out members of the medical profession. In Jamaica this led him to an elderly black doctor, whose repute as a healer under enslavement, had enabled him to earn enough to purchase his freedom and set up his own practice. In turn, the doctor introduced his friend, an intellectual and Islamic scholar who now, encouraged by Madden, wrote an account of his life and kidnapping in Africa and sent a letter home for the first time in thirty years.[17] Or again, drawing on his experiences as a magistrate, he revealed the struggles of Presant Pike, purchased as a child from a slave ship, working after her master's death to support his two children in England and, on their deaths, passed from trustee to trustee, to whom she handed over her wages, while she herself produced eleven children (seven dying in infancy, one of the remaining four sold by a trustee for £90). She then negotiated an agreement to buy herself and

14 'Select Committee' in *Parliamentary Papers*, p. 67.   **15** Madden, *West Indies,* ii, pp. 13–16. **16** Madden's *A Twelvemonth's Residence in the West Indies* was published in Philadelphia in 1835, by Carey, Lea and Blanchard, who also published *The United Irishmen* in 1842; R.W. Fogel, *Without Consent or Contract: the Rise and Fall of American Slavery* (London, 1991), pp. 265–7.   **17** Madden, *West Indies,* i, pp. 99–101; ii, pp. 183–9.

three children by instalments for £180. She had paid over £76 13s. 4d. ('I have all my receipts to show') for her personal manumission when apprenticeship arrived and the consequent legal investigations revealed that her children had no legal owner. Nevertheless, the trustees insisted that she should complete her payments as previously arranged so she wrote to the stipendiary magistrate asking him to confirm her family's freedom and, if possible, save her £103 6s. 8d.[18] Thus, through Madden's pen, the chained and kneeling African, the symbol of anti-slavery since 1787, was transformed into a series of real individuals ready and eager to enrich the nineteenth-century liberal world with their talents and endeavours as free citizens. A book, which had opened with wry musings on travellers' troubles and plaudits to planter hospitality, mounted into moral intensity and bitter condemnation of colonists who opposed the reforming intent of the imperial government.[19] In *A Twelvemonth's Residence in the West Indies* Madden served his apprenticeship and emerged a radical anti-slavery activist.

In his book and in a letter to the Colonial Office, he denounced apprenticeship as an unjust and unworkable system, which should be demolished immediately.[20] This confirmed the suspicions of many anti-slavery enthusiasts who had fought against the introduction of the institution in the first place. In an effort to silence growing criticism the government appointed a parliamentary committee to inquire into the working of the system at its most controversial – in Jamaica. Madden was called as a witness and, along with a number of more experienced colonial officials, supported its immediate ending. Opposed to the view of the officials was that of the proprietors and planters, who reported that after some initial confusions while the special magistrates settled into the job and the apprentices came to understand the true nature of the new system, it was working well. This was the finding which the government wanted to hear and which, on the whole, the Committee was prepared to endorse. But there was one failing which the Committee felt must be addressed. Conceived in the age of the 'Reform of Manners', and the definition of society as sharply gendered into separate spheres, anti-slavery had always drawn strength from the special position of women. Shocking revelations about the cruelties and 'improprieties' perpetrated against female slaves had attracted many to the cause and in 1823 the Westminster government had sought to ban the flogging of females. Now it appeared that, in the workhouse, apprentices lagging on the treadmill were flogged to make them amend their pace and that such groups included women.[21] On this emotive issue the government agreed to act, eventually producing a bill which removed the operation of Jamaican workhouses from local government control. The planters reacted with fury at this latest attempt to undermine their power over their workforce and the island's institutions. In a bid to emancipate themselves from

18 Royal Irish Academy (RIA), Madden Papers, MS. 24. 0. 11, fol. 233–7, To their Honours, the Special Magistrates, R.R. Madden etc. for the freedom of slaves.   **19** Madden, *West Indies,* ii, p. 296.   **20** 'Select Committee' in *Parliamentary Papers,* p. 49.   **21** Ibid., p. vii.

Westminster's surveillance, they passed a motion through the assembly abolishing apprenticeship.[22] Thus the radical wing of the anti-slavery cause, in which Madden had placed himself, triumphed. Apprenticeship ended two years early in 1838.

Anti-slavery was politically in the ascendant and with it Madden's reputation and career. In 1836 he was appointed to a new post, at the cutting edge of anti-slavery activity, as the first Commissioner for Liberated Africans in Cuba. At £800 a year it was much better paid than his Jamaican magistracy, while a temporary appointment as a judge on the Court of Mixed Commission in Havana brought his emoluments up to £1000.[23] Both posts were connected with the suppression of the international slave trade. When parliament banned the slave trade in 1806–7, the opponents of this measure had argued that, if Britain did so, other countries would simply expand their trading activities and replace her. This proved to be true. At the Congress of Vienna, Britain tried and failed to obtain support for an international ban. She then resorted to trying to make bilateral treaties with individual countries which committed them to banning their trade and allowing the British navy rights of search, should her West Africa squadron suspect their ships of slaving. The only countries prepared to take up such an ignominious position were those in need of Britain's friendship. Spain fell into this category, but her situation was complicated by the fact that her richest colony Cuba, on which the crown increasingly depended for revenue, was expanding its plantation system and was hungry for slaves. The Spanish solution was to sign the treaties that Britain proposed and then make no effort to fulfil them. In 1835, fifteen years after Spain had first signed a treaty completely renouncing the trade, Palmerston, who had become the watchdog of the anti-slavery lobby, pressed her into signing another more rigorously detailed version. Madden therefore arrived in Havana at a time when the anti-slavery lobby was hoping for a more aggressive policy towards illegal slaving. His post as protector of the liberated Africans meant that he had to supervise the future of Africans rescued from slave ships caught off the Cuban coast. There were no arrangements, of course, for those so liberated to be returned to their homelands, but under the new treaty Madden was to see that they were sent to the British colonies to serve as indentured labourers. The authorities in Cuba reacted with horror when they discovered that the new official was an abolitionist and did everything they could to hamper his activities, while, in return, Madden denounced them as hopelessly corrupt.[24] His experience on the Court of Mixed Commission reinforced this belief. Here he judged whether apprehended vessels were guilty of slaving, yet he knew that ships were successfully landing cargoes of slaves in the island's many inlets, or even sailing into Havana with forged papers,

22 Alan Burns, *History of the British West Indies* (2nd ed., New York, 1965), p. 641. **23** Leon Ó Broin, 'R.R. Madden, Historian of the United Irishmen,' in *Irish University Review*, 2: 1, Spring 1972, p. 21. **24** D.R. Murray, 'Richard Robert Madden: His Career as a Slavery Abolitionist' in *Studies: an Irish Quarterly Review of Letters, Philosophy and Science*, 61 (1972), pp. 48–50.

saying they were carrying plantation slaves from one part of Cuba to another. Once illegally imported Africans set foot on Cuban ground they were unfree, the Court of Mixed Commission could do nothing for them, as its powers applied only to those taken on captured vessels. The Cubans themselves resenting British interference with their commerce, set up the slave barracoons beside the British Consulate.[25]

As he came to know the island better Madden found himself both horrified and excited by Cuba. Here he discovered an intellectual and revolutionary life which he had not encountered in Jamaica. Below the Spanish administration was a Creole society, hankering after independence, inhibited from action by fear of slave revolt. But Madden felt he could discern groups ready to turn to rebellion if encouraged by promises of British aid. There were free coloureds, politically aware and frustrated by their restriction to artisan activities, and even a select group of rich and intellectual planters, critical of slavery, who encouraged a salon of young writers in the production of anti-slavery novels.[26] Among these was a poet and recently manumitted slave, Manzano, who produced the colony's first slave narrative, a genre which was currently taking anti-slavery circles in the U.S.A by storm. Madden translated Manzano's work into English and later in London arranged for its publication.[27] While on the island he continually pressed Palmerston to promise Cuba protection if she broke with Spain, co-operated in the banning of the slave trade, and introduced measures to ameliorate slavery.[28] The policy of encouraging anti-Spanish revolt was too forward even for the robust and ambitious Palmerston. But though the Foreign Office rejected his advice Madden passed on his ideas and personal contacts to the Glaswegian, David Turnbull, a free-booting, anti-slavery activist who had turned up in Cuba on a fact finding mission. Turnbull would later become British consul in Havana, a development which the Spanish authorities claimed had dire consequences. In 1843 several slave revolts broke out in Cuba and in 1844 the government claimed to have unmasked a widespread revolutionary conspiracy, La Escalera, led by the free coloured population and incited by British abolitionists, a conspiracy which they suppressed with torture, banishment and executions and the removal of Turnbull from the British consulate.[29] Whether or not the conspiracy was a real threat or an over-reaction by government (and today historians still argue bitterly over this issue) the violence of those years was the outcome of a slave society under abolitionist pressure. As in Jamaica in 1831, the existence of the anti-slavery movement encouraged hopes of freedom among the slaves and fear of resistance among their owners.

25 R.L. Paquette, *Sugar is Made with Blood: The Conspiracy of La Escalera and the Conflict between Empire over Slavery in Cuba* (Connecticut, 1988), p. 36, 149.   26 Ibid., p. 100.   27 J.F. Manzano, *Poems by a Slave on the Island of Cuba, translated from the Spanish by R.R. Madden with the History of the Early Life of the Negro Poet written by Himself* (London, 1840).   28 R.R. Madden, *Island of Cuba* (London, 1853), p. 84.   29 Paquette, *Sugar is Made with Blood,* pp. 138–53.

In 1839 Madden requested and received permission to return home on furlough but on this trip he was able to score another anti-slavery success, which reinforced his personal standing and increased the unease of Spanish slave traders and Cuban slave holders at the international forces gathering against them. Madden travelled by way of the United States, where he was met by the New York business man, Lewis Tappan, one of America's wealthiest and most prominent anti-slavery figures. Tappan had arranged that Madden should appear as a witness in the *Amistad* case. This case, now a Stephen Spielberg film, was in its own time a *cause célèbre*. A group of some forty-nine slaves on a Cuban vessel, the *Amistad*, had risen in revolt, taken over the ship and, in their attempt to sail back to Africa, had mistakenly landed in Connecticut. Arrested by the authorities and brought to trial, the Spanish claimed them as slaves from a Cuban plantation who had mutinied when they were being moved by sea from one part of the island to another. Madden appeared in court to provide telling evidence that the forty-nine were Africans being illegally imported by slavers.[30] Internal U.S. politics meant that it was some time before the legal wrangling resulted in the freeing of the *Amistad* captives, but the publicity given to Madden raised his profile in America and Britain.

Madden returned to London to take part, as the Cuban expert, in the first international Anti-slavery Convention in 1840. Over the past decades Spanish slavery had achieved a degree of sympathetic comment in Britain – like other Catholic colonies Cuba had a tradition of converting her slaves and a well-established system of manumission supervised by government functionaries. Madden denounced all this as a façade. Visitors to the island saw only the acceptable face of slavery, as they enjoyed planter hospitality in the attractive colonial towns and great houses of the wealthy, served by well-dressed slave servants apparently reared in a familial atmosphere. Behind this lay the horror of the swiftly expanding sugar plantations where newly imported Africans were subjected to brutal discipline and frequently worked to death.[31] Madden was an emotional man, both his sympathy and his temper were quick. A speedy and copious collector of evidence, he sometimes mixed hearsay with actual observation, but in the case of apprenticeship and Cuban slavery historical research has confirmed his conclusions. The role of apprenticeship in British emancipation was problematic rather than positive, while wide-ranging statistical studies have shown that regardless of the government or society involved, the worst slave conditions (highest death rate, lowest birth rate) existed on newly established sugar plantations, where the hard work required and the enormous profits to be made from cropping fresh soil encouraged continuous restocking and expansion of the work force.[32]

30 Howard Jones, *Mutiny on the Amistad: the Saga of a Slave Revolt and its Impact on American Abolition, Law and Diplomacy* (Oxford, 1987), pp. 99–110. **31** R.R. Madden, *Address on Slavery in Cuba presented to the General Anti-Slavery Convention* (London, 1840), pp. 1–31. **32** Fogel, *Without Consent or Contract*, p. 128, 132; R.B. Sheridan, "'Sweet Malefactor": the Social Costs of Slavery in Jamaica and Cuba, 1807–54' in *Economic History Review*, 2nd ser.: 29, May (1976) pp. 239–44.

At the anti-slavery convention Madden stressed the vital importance of continued international attack upon the trade in order to prevent the worst excesses of Cuban slavery. Increasingly by 1840 anti-slavery leaders in Britain were considering focusing their main emphasis not on ocean-wide arrest, which had proved so difficult, but on internal conditions in Africa, the source of the still-flourishing trade.[33] Madden could have returned to Cuba, but instead he accepted an appointment as Special Commissioner of Inquiry into the Administration of the British Settlements on the West Coast of Africa. Such a role seemed to fit well with his trouble-shooting reputation and fondness for tackling politically prominent issues. But this time everything went wrong, he took sick, almost died, saw very little of the areas he had been sent to investigate and returned home to find a Conservative government in office. Much less sympathetic to the anti-slavery lobby than the Whigs, the Conservatives disliked his report and offered him no further employment. His African post had paid him over £1000 a year, now he found himself dependent on journalism earning some £200 a year as special correspondent for the *Morning Chronicle* in Portugal.[34] The return of the Whigs to office in 1847 restored him to an official position, but anti-slavery had gone into decline, no longer expanding its official remit and bristling with assignments offering popular copy. So Madden became Secretary to the Colonial government of Western Australia where he spent only nine months beset by the problems of Aborigines and Orangemen. News that his nineteen-year-old son had been drowned while working as an engineer on the Shannon finally clinched his decision to return home.[35] His career, though varied and at times dramatic, was not what he had hoped for; literary fame in London and a prestigious administrative appointment abroad had eluded him. Eventually he succeeded in exchanging his Australian post with the Secretary to the Loan Fund in Dublin and, at the age of 51, settled down to live in Ireland after a thirty-year absence.[36]

The *United Irishmen* grew out of Madden's anti-slavery years; on occasion he attributed it to his anti-slavery experience.[37] By the time he left for Jamaica in 1833 he had experimented with a wide variety of literary forms, poetry, prose, fiction, non-fiction, but he had not considered becoming a historian. In 1834–5, resuming his role as a travel writer eager for copy, he had chosen to journey from Jamaica to London by way of the North American mainland, speedily covering ground from Philadelphia to Canada, seeking out and interviewing important and interesting figures – anti-slavery supporters, theatre people, medical men, prominent Irish emigrants. Of all those whom he encountered, the most hospitable were Ireland's political exiles or their descendants. The elderly William MacNeven, by now the

---

33 Howard Temperley, *White Dreams, Black Africa: the Anti-slavery expedition to the Niger 1841–2* (London, 1991) pp. 1–40.   **34** RIA, Madden Papers, MS. 24.0.9, fol. 129–41, R.R. Madden to Sir James Stephen, 5 Dec. 1843.   **35** Madden, *Memoirs*, p. 227.   **36** Ó Broin, 'Historian of the United Irishmen,' p. 30.   **37** R.R. Madden to Sir William Napier, 28 Aug. 1842 in Madden, *Memoirs*, p. 170 and Madden, *United Irishmen* (1846), i, p. 4.

sole survivor of the United Irishmen, proved particularly congenial as a doctor, a Catholic, and an intelligent commentator on anti-slavery. Back in 1807 MacNeven had published his own account of events leading up to '98 and he now encouraged Madden to become the historian of the United Irishmen.[38] After his return to London, Madden did visit Ireland for the first time in many years, more in the role of emigrant made good than historical researcher, but subsequent American experiences continued to kindle his nationalist feelings. Sailing from Liverpool via New York to take up his Cuban appointment, he discovered that most of the two hundred steerage passengers were Irish from the Farnham estate in Cavan, where the improving, evangelical landlord preferred Protestant tenants. He recorded that his blood boiled on hearing men say that they had been evicted because they were Catholics.[39] Once settled in Cuba, he sent back to Dublin for books and papers to enable him to start work on *The United Irishmen*.[40] By now other influences were causing him to contemplate his past. Despite the fact that he felt the church in Cuba was as much in need of reform as the slave system, the experience of living in a Catholic country revived his religious sensitivities. In the 1820s and early 30s Madden had been very much the liberal rationalist, marrying a Protestant and thinking little about his own personal faith. This had enabled him to work easily with the evangelicals who formed the back bone of the anti-slavery movement, but now he began to find their missionaries, whom he had formerly accepted as simple, good hearted men, as fanatical and importunate, pressurising him, as a British official, to gain admission from the Spanish authorities for bibles, which the church condemned as heretical. Conscience stricken and worried he wrote to the Catholic archbishop of Dublin suggesting that Ireland should launch a missionary initiative and supply the bible in the vernacular to Catholic colonies.[41] The difficulties of being a pious Catholic in a strongly evangelical Protestant movement increasingly crowded in on Madden. Yet most painful of all for him was the attitude of the Irish emigrants in America to anti-slavery and the Negro. The new arrivals from Ireland, who flooded into the worst jobs in the northern cities of the United States in the 1820s and 30s, were eager to take the advantages a white skin conferred and to boost membership of a party designed to protect the interests of northern labour and southern slavery. Committed to anti-slavery, growing in nationalist and Catholic ardour, Madden was 'surprized and shocked' to see his fellow countrymen showing no sympathy for a people suffering under a state apparatus which made them strangers in the land of their birth. So in 1840 when Madden lectured in London to reveal the horrors of Cuban slavery, he spoke in

---

38 Madden, *Memoirs*, pp. 86–99; William MacNeven, *Pieces of Irish History* (New York, 1807); Ó Broin, 'Historian of the United Irishmen', p. 23. **39** RIA, Madden Papers, MS. 24.0.9, fol. 377–93, Madden to William Murphy, Sept. 1836. **40** Leon Ó Broin, *An Maidíneach: Staraí na nÉirennach Aontaithe* (Baile Átha Cliath, 1971) p. 87. **41** Ibid. pp. 108–15; RIA, Madden Papers, MS. 24.0.9, fols. 451–63, Madden to Dr Wiley, 4 March, 1838; fols 43–50, Madden to Revd G. Thompson, 8 May 1838.

Dublin calling upon the Catholic church to educate 'the lower orders of our countrymen' to understand the incompatibility of slavery and Christianity so that, as
emigrants to America, they would put their 'extraordinary' political power to 'beneficial' use and support the anti-slavery cause.[42] Though it proved a formative force
on his life, Madden did not like the United States, seeing it as undermining much
that was best in the Irish character, love of family, love of God and causing his
transplanted countrymen to reject the principles of the United Irishmen.[43]

Schooled as an anti-slavery activist Madden believed that good government was
to be achieved through the exertion of a moral public opinion, the product of
enlightened and educated reformers, for he was a liberal not a democrat.[44] This was
how British anti-slavery had achieved its triumph and he saw the United Irishmen
in the same light. Reformers who sought to bring just government to their country, they had successfully created a moral public opinion in Ireland only to have it
flouted by a corrupt government, which drove them into rebellion, amply aided by
a selfish and manipulative France. Madden declared that such a scenario was a thing
of the past: in the nineteenth-century liberal world, the government would yield
to just demands.[45] Yet he was well aware that the politics of reform which he had
witnessed in the late 1820s and early '30s, all, to some extent, drew upon the threat
of violence: Catholic emancipation, parliamentary reform and abolition of slavery
were all adopted by governments seeking to avert the possibility of revolt and revolution. At the 1836 parliamentary committee, there were many voices urging that
apprenticeship was unworkable but only Madden pressed this argument by declar-
ing that if it were not immediately removed the tensions it was provoking could
produce another Jamaican revolt.[46] As his *United Irishmen* went to the press the
Repeal movement, to which he gave his support, was moving into similar
brinkmanship. Madden's critics accused his book of encouraging rebellion, an
accusation he always denied saying that he had journeyed widely and always
observed rebellion left the people worse off than before. His book was a warning,
not only to oppressive governments, but to the high minded and frustrated
reformer, that violent insurrection opened the floodgates of treachery and would
make him the victim of the most dishonourable among those he struggled to
free.[47] Yet the energy and diligence with which Madden researched and wrote up
the details of betrayal, the enthusiastic unmasking of scoundrels everywhere, suggested a fascination with rebellion. Here again such interests were fostered by slave
society, where rumours and discussions of past and possible conspiracy and revolt
were part of daily life. As Madden worked on his Irish books and papers in Cuba,

42 R. R. Madden, 'Address to the Hibernian Anti-slavery Society' Feb. 1840, printed as an
appendix to Manzano, *Poems by a Slave* pp. 135–7.   **43** RIA, Madden Papers, MS.
24.0.9.fols. 363–75, Madden to J. Weldon, Aug. 1847.   **44** Ibid., fols. 349–59, Madden to
Joseph Sturge, 12 Oct. 1845.   **45** Madden, *The United Irishmen* (Dublin, 1846), i, p. x.
46 'Select Committee' in *Parliamentary Papers*, p. 52.   **47** RIA, Madden Papers, MS. 24.0.9,
fols. 589–97, Madden to T.C. Mathieson, 1850; *The United Irishmen* (Dublin, 1846), i, p. ix.

the real world reinforced the literary one. Then the *Amistad* case re-enacted the themes of oppression, injustice, violence, forgery and deception.

The weaknesses of style and format which dogged Madden's historical work also owe much to anti-slavery. It trained him to take the moral high ground and defend it in a lengthy and disputatious manner disturbing to any piece requiring narrative flow. But above all, the demands of his professional career shaped the book's construction. Material was collected hurriedly on short visits to Ireland or by friends and put together quickly as he moved from place to place acquiring anti-slavery information and writing it up for official purposes, public lectures or general publication. Thus the format of individual biographies, which in the end produced a disjointed and repetitive history, was adopted and never abandoned. It is no accident that the 1998 commemoration did not produce a republication. Yet for later historians the book remains an exciting bran tub packed with hypotheses to confirm or deny, documents printed in their entirety, memoirs produced at Madden's behest which might otherwise have remained unwritten or unpublished. Meanwhile, time has matured *Twelvemonth's Residence in the West Indies* into a very similar resource, supplying not only detail on the well-recorded issue of apprenticeship but rarer material exploited by historians working on a wide range of subjects from attempts to reconstruct African memories of the Atlantic slave trade to the development of Creole speech in the Caribbean.[48]

48 Madden, *A Twelvemonth's Residence in the West Indies during the Transition from Slavery to Apprenticeship*, facsimile edition (Connecticut, 1970); Ivor Wilks, 'Abu Bakr Al-Siddiq of Timbuktu' in P.D. Curtin (ed.), *Narrative of West Africans from the Era of the Slave Trade* (London, 1967), pp. 152–69, where Madden, *West Indies*, ii, pp. 199–201 is reprinted and discussed; Barbara Lalla and Jean D'Costa, *Language in Exile: Three Hundred Years of Jamaican Creole* (London, 1990) pp. 163–4.

'Sketches of missionary life': Alexander Robert Crawford in Manchuria

OONAGH WALSH

'To have friends coming to one from distant parts – is not this a great pleasure?'[1]

Alexander Robert Crawford was always a wanderer. Born in Paris in 1868, he was educated as an adult in Belfast, graduating in classics from Queen's University Belfast in 1890, and spending the next two years in the Presbyterian General Assembly's theological college. He studied for a year at Princeton, returning to graduate M.A. from the Royal University of Ireland in 1894. During his 57 years he visited the United States, Russia, Canada, Japan, and China, as well as travelling extensively throughout Europe. A courageous individual, he was determined from an early age to devote his life to the conversion of China, a task that exacted a heavy personal toll. Crawford was based in Kirin Province in Manchuria, in the north-east of China, and spent much of his time in the Russian controlled town of Kirin. He arrived in 1895, but was forced to temporarily flee the country in 1900 as a result of the Boxer rebellion. He returned to China from Ireland in 1902 with his new wife, Anna Graham of Portadown, remaining there until 1913, working through a ferocious outbreak of plague in 1910 in addition to the more usual difficulties facing missionaries abroad. The Crawfords lost two infant sons in China, and their return to Ireland was prompted by his deteriorating health.[2] They lived in Belfast, where Robert worked as the editor of the children's religious magazine *Daybreak*, in addition to his responsibilities as dean of residence for Presbyterian students at Queen's University. He died in November, 1935.

In this essay I wish to examine certain aspects of Crawford's life and work in Manchuria, in particular his relationship with Chinese converts to Christianity, and his responses to other European workers in China. Although Crawford's primary purpose was to further Christian endeavour in China, he was aware of the often complex issues surrounding the position of expatriate Europeans. He was highly conscious of the impact, deliberate as well as incidental, of his residence in

---

1 Confucius, *The Analects*, chp. 1, quoted in C.C. Tan, *The Boxer Catastrophe* (New York, 1955), p. 3.   2 Before Crawford married he noted prophetically in a letter to his mother: 'Dr and Mrs Christie have lost their little baby of three months old, of infant cholera. There are very few of the Mission families who have not lost little ones in this country. Though the climate suits adults it doesn't seem to suit children.' A.R. Crawford, M.A., *Sketches of Missionary Life in Manchuria: being extracts from letters home of Rev. A.R. Crawford, M.A., Missionary of the Irish Presbyterian Church* (Belfast: 1899), p. 148.

Manchuria, and many of his early letters home were edited and published in 1899 in a volume entitled *Sketches of Missionary Life* (a text produced in the hope of raising interest in Presbyterian efforts abroad). The published letters attest to a curiosity about all aspects of Manchurian life, and a respect for the culture, yet also noted some anxiety regarding the erosion of that culture through European settlement. Crawford's other great passion was mapmaking; he was in fact elected a fellow of the Royal Geographical Society in 1914 for his work in mapping Manchuria. As he travelled to remote districts, distributing bibles, preaching, and testing those who wished to convert,[3] Crawford conducted a meticulous survey of uncharted territories, an action that placed him firmly within the ranks of secular Europeans in China.[4] His experiences in Manchuria, then, indicate how difficult it was for missionaries to maintain a single-minded approach to their work. Despite his best efforts, he became embroiled in civil disputes, when his privileged position as a European Christian was abused by converts in order to gain legal leverage. These issues were brought home with particular force by the Boxer Rebellion: race became the most important criteria in selecting just whom among the Christians would be removed to safety. Ethnicity also impacted upon relations with other Europeans: the assistance granted by the Russians during the missionaries flight from the Boxers both linked the 'foreign devils'[5] together in the minds of the Chinese, and put pressure upon the missionaries to publicly support the Russian military and economic presence in China. Finally, Crawford's passion for mapping further opened the interior for exploration by Europeans, and linked Crawford with individuals who had a purely exploitative intent in China. These, and other issues, made his role as missionary an ambiguous one.

Although at times uncomfortable, this was not an unusual position for missionaries to find themselves in. The association between missionary work and imperial advance has been well documented by scholars. Authors such as Brian Stanley and T.O. Beidelman have identified an explicit connection between the acquisition of a population's souls, and their material resources.[6] Although the association may not be as clear-cut as some have argued – in Africa for instance,

---

3 The distances involved were considerable, some 10,542 miles from 1895 to 1900, all by 'Chinese boat and cart'. D/2003/B/2/2/1. All manuscript references are to Crawford's papers in the Public Record office of Northern Ireland.   **4** In his early years, Crawford travelled with gold-diggers, quantity surveyors, and Russian soldiers, sharing both the cost of expeditions, and information about the interior. Although uncomfortable about his association with these individuals, who had a rather different purpose in China from his own, Crawford nevertheless rarely lost an opportunity to expand his knowledge of the terrain. See his *Sketches*, pp. 15 & 23, and letters D/2003/B/3/7/1 & D/2003/B/2/5/1.   **5** D/2003/B/3/2/53.   **6** B. Stanley, *The Bible and the Flag: Protestant missions and British imperialism in the nineteenth and twentieth centuries* (Leicester, 1990), and T.O. Beidelman, *Colonial Evangelism: a socio-historical study of an East African mission at the grassroots* (Bloomington, 1982); R.A. Bickers & R. Seaton (eds), *Missionary Encounters: Sources and Issues* (Surrey, 1996).

Figure 1. Crawford (front, in dark jacket) with unidentified mission workers, Kirin

Christian churches occasionally became the focal point for nationalist protest –
Christianity is nevertheless seen as one of the first, and most important, means of
alienating support from older practices and traditions, and creating a population
amenable to the value structures of the new rulers. In certain regions, especially
Africa and India, this model might be said to operate relatively straightforwardly.
In China however, the situation was far more complex, due to the great influx of
overseas settlers. The nineteenth century had seen an increase in the number of foreign residents, drawn by trade as well as religion, and there had been a series of
conflicts with various international powers.[7] The Opium and Arrow Wars of mid-
century had eroded Chinese trading rights, and by the 1870s Western traders had
established firm footholds in Chinese ports. The territorial ambitions of the West
also found explicit expression when China lost considerable portions of her own
empire: part of Turkestan fell to Russia in 1881, Tonkin to France in 1885, and
Upper Burma to Britain in 1886. At the same time, China was confronted by a
power much closer to home: Japan. In the early 1890s the two countries wrangled

7 China was of course herself an imperial power of some significance, continuing to contest
territorial rights in Korea and Manchuria throughout the nineteenth century.

over control of Korea, a conflict that erupted into the Sino-Japanese War of 1894–5, and ended in the humiliating defeat of China. The Western powers took swift advantage of China's weakened state to secure further concessions, with France, Russia, Britain and Germany negotiating favourable trading terms, access to resources such as coalfields and mines, and permission, in the case of Russia, to extend the Trans-Siberian Railroad across northern Manchuria to Vladivostok. Thus by the close of the century China was bound by treaties with the Western powers that significantly eroded domestic control, and she had to endure settlement by foreigners in increasing numbers. The various powers, furthermore, conducted a series of agreements between themselves, offering privileges to each other within China in return for support there and elsewhere, and even agreed separate spheres of influence, awarding great swathes of territory to each other in the event of the break-up of the country.[8] This concern to secure economic interests in China was underpinned by the so-called 'Open Door' doctrine of 1899. This American proposal called for 'equality of commercial opportunity among the powers in China irrespective of spheres of influence', and further distanced China from active intervention in her own economic affairs.[9] The final complicating factor by the end of the century was the make-up of China's rulers. Although the Manchus who conquered the country in the seventeenth century were in power, the majority of the population were Han.[10] Little wonder, then, that China in the late nineteenth century was a country ready for conflict.

Despite the tensions wrought by these developments, China was, from a European perspective, a land of opportunity. For the missionaries, the country was a vast territory of lost souls, ripe for the picking. For entrepreneurs, it held the promise of immense wealth, through trade and the exploitation of natural resources. But for imperial powers, it represented a prestigious challenge, a rich and cultured country whose possession, even partial, would reflect true world status.[11] These desires ensured a constant pressure upon the Chinese, creating an anxiety and resentment that was to find expression in the Boxer rebellion of 1900. As in many colonial or quasi-colonial relationships, however, some of the native population resigned themselves to the likelihood of a permanent European presence, and sought whatever advantage might accrue through association with them.[12] In particular, some Chinese intellectuals, students, traders, and elements in the military wanted selective modernisation that would enable China to engage with the Western powers on a more equal basis. On a basic level, Europeans enjoyed the legal privilege of 'extraterritoriality' (foreign exemption from Chinese jurisdic-

8 See C.C. Tan, *The Boxer Catastrophe*, pp. 3–14; P. Cohen, *History in Three Keys: The Boxers as Event, Experience an Myth* (New York, 1997), introduction. **9** P.J. Bailey, *China in the Twentieth Century* (Oxford, 2001), p. 123. **10** C. Mackerras, *China in Transformation, 1900–1949* (Essex, 1998), p. 5. **11** J. Osterhammel, 'Britain and China, 1842–1914' in A. Porter (ed.), *The Oxford History of the British Empire: the nineteenth-century* (Oxford, 1999), p. 146. **12** V.G. Kiernan, *The Lords of Humankind* (London, 1988).

Figure 2. Crawford and his wife (front right) and child, with
Elder Song, and unidentified female mission worker.

tion), a benefit that proved a significant attraction to some Chinese. Although
Christian missionaries were not especially prosperous, they nevertheless found
themselves the target of ambitious individuals, who sought their support in legal
disputes and quarrels. Crawford and his fellow workers were sensitive to accusations that they were being used in this manner, but frequently found themselves
embroiled in clashes between Chinese converts and the local governors. These
confrontations were often violent, and indicated the levels of resentment against
Christians in China. From the mid-nineteenth century onwards, there had devel-

oped a clear perception that Chinese Christians used their church contacts for material motives. This did have a basis in fact, so missionaries were continually on their guard to detect potentially untruthful applicants for admission to their churches. The first rule of Crawford's Presbyterian mission, for example, was to refuse to deal with those 'who come on account of law-suits . . . A similar prohibition against those whose motives are of material gain, or those who, being their own masters, do not abolish their idols.'[13] The missionaries therefore had a lengthy probationary period for intending converts, in order to weed out those who sought immediate benefit. But it was not always possible to identify such individuals, despite best efforts. The problem arose because Christians did indeed enjoy certain privileges in China. In 1858 Christian missionaries had been given permission to spread the gospel without molestation, and the rights of Christians were to be upheld in law. Because the obvious aim of missionary work was to replace an old system of worship with a new, converts were forbidden to take part in, or support, celebrations that honoured 'false gods'. These individuals were therefore exempt from contributing to community celebrations: this, and their implicit criticism of such events, caused great resentment in local areas. There was furthermore a perception that Christian missionaries interfered in legal disputes that involved converts, placing pressure on magistrates to find in the convert's favour even in the face of compelling evidence against him.[14] Although it was the Catholic Church that was most often accused of this practice, all of the Christian missionaries were presumed to act in a similar manner, to a greater or lesser extent.[15]

The perception was apparently held by converts as well as non-Christians. In 1898 Crawford bemoaned the fact that he could not get on with work because of constant appeals for justice from converts. 'Several things have tended to distract us – difficulties that members or inquirers [those who had expressed a wish to convert, and who were 'on probation'] have got into, or cases of persecution in which we are asked to interfere, as otherwise the sufferers can get no redress from the authorities. It is most difficult to know just how far to go, so as not to allow these Christians to be unjustly downtrodden, and at the same time not to have recourse to the arm of the law more than one has a right to, in work which aims at exerting a purely spiritual influence.'[16] It would appear however that the necessity to secure converts, especially in the face of stiff opposition from competing Christian churches, ensured that a certain number of individuals entered the church with mixed motives. Crawford became reluctantly embroiled in one such case involving a man named Liu, a shopkeeper whom the missionaries believed joined the church in order to have 'foreign' support in his various transactions. In August 1898 Liu apparently provoked a fight with soldiers as a result of a dispute over money, and marched on the Chinese governor general's office to demand redress.

---

13 A.R. Crawford, *Our Mission in Manchuria* (Belfast, 1900), p. 16. **14** Tan, *Boxer Catastrophe* p. 35. **15** J.W. Esherick, *The Origins of the Boxer Uprising* (Berkeley, 1987), p. 200. **16** Crawford, *Sketches*, p. 108.

Crucially, he did this not in his own name, but in the name of the Presbyterian church. Crawford had therefore to attend a hearing with the governor, adjudicate, hand down a judgement (that Liu and the soldiers should be reprimanded, but not punished), and then spend the following afternoon entertaining the officials at the mission house. The problem did not end there, though. Infuriated by the challenge to his authority implicit in Crawford's judgement, the governor confided that he had lost face through Liu's demands at his gate, and Liu would have to be publicly punished. To this Crawford agreed, apparently in an attempt to demonstrate the missionaries impartiality, although he felt himself manipulated by the governor. On being told to report to the governor for punishment, Liu 'came here to ask me to let him off, as he feared being given over to the hand of the devil, as he put it.'[17] Now certain that Liu was using the church for his own interests, Crawford refused to intervene, and Liu was paraded through the streets, after having received twenty strokes. To crown his conduct, Liu 'preached to the people as he was paraded around', firmly linking the missionaries with his humiliation, and his brawl. The Presbyterian mission of which Crawford was a part was, on this as other occasions, caught up in what has been described as a system of 'informal empire' in China.[18] This was characterised by legal, economic, and administrative rights enjoyed by foreigners, but not by the Chinese. As Europeans, missionaries were inevitably regarded as part of the elite, however much they tried to distance themselves from those whose interests lay in exploiting extraterritoriality or the Open Door policy. In some ways, the privilege granted to foreigners in China was a mixed blessing for the Presbyterian mission, as it drew them into disputes such as those described above. For example, the local officials rarely lost an opportunity to subtly humiliate the missionaries, requesting their intervention in disputes involving Chinese converts. Moreover the gentry had seen the foreigners steadily usurp their power, lending an additional air of tension to these encounters.[19] For their part, the missionaries had to respond to these complaints with every indication of willingness, if they were to avoid accusations of favouritism. Given the fact that some converts blatantly abused the authority conferred by close association with the mission, it was hardly surprising that Crawford and his colleagues spent so much time establishing the grounds for conversion presented to them.

But that is not to minimise the problems facing Chinese Christians. Crawford was acutely aware of the genuine threat of persecution facing converts, and of the necessity to protect them from resentful authorities. He believed that the only way Christianity would gain a foothold in China was through the creation of what he called a 'native church'. Thus those men who had proven their Christian steadfastness were raised to the senior status of elders within the Church, and were active in the field with their European brothers. Chinese workers were crucial to the missionary endeavour, not least in their ability to speak (in many cases) several

17 Ibid., pp. 148–9. **18** Osterhammel, *Britain and China,* pp. 148–9. **19** I would like to thank Rosemary Tyzack for clarification on this and other points.

Chinese dialects. As such, they were invaluable church workers, and Crawford in particular recognised the value of their contribution. Yet there remained a deep-rooted unease that centred on race. When the Boxer rebellion caused the missionaries to flee Kirin, distinctions buried in peace rose again to the surface. Crawford was most concerned about the situation of the native Christians, believing, quite rightly, that they would suffer most in any attacks.[20] He recorded his unease in his journal, which reveals a sense of guilt at the European abandonment of their Chinese fellows:

> During the morning Ch'êntsai (Evangelist at the Street chapel) came over, bringing me $100 which I required. He and the others were of course much disconcerted at the prospect of our leaving Kirin, and it was little one could do or say to comfort them . . . I could only tell Ch'ên that in case of an attack on the Chapel they should make their escape. As to the Xtians [Christians] I advised that they should go as far as possible to a quiet place in the country.[21]

There was however one individual whom Crawford believed should not be left behind. A Mr Sung, an elder in the church, had been the victim of a severe beating in 1895. The missionaries had purchased land to build a hospital in his name, and although permission had been granted by the British ambassador at Peking for the building to go ahead, it had been blocked by the local authorities. They put Sung on trial for 'selling to the foreigners without giving notice to the authorities', a charge denied by the missionaries, who had written proof from the Counsul at Newchang. Sung received one hundred 'stripes' – 'inflicted by means of a wooden lath about an inch wide . . . the strokes were given always in the same place viz. at the top of the right leg' – and the missionaries were warned not to interfere.[22] It was clear that Sung and his family were highly likely to be a target for the Boxers, and they were therefore brought along with the Europeans when they fled northwards to the Russian settlement at Harbin – from there they intended to take a train to Valdivostok. Even in this crisis, though, crucial racial differences were maintained. The barge on which the missionaries and other Europeans travelled towed a smaller boat behind, intended for the accompanying Russian Cossack escort. The Sungs travelled with the soldiers, not with the missionaries. When the travellers arrived at Harbin, they were granted accommodation in an empty Russian schoolhouse. 'Here we had two large rooms, empty except for the school forms, in one of which the ladies and children lived and slept, while we men were in the other – two smaller rooms behind accommodated the Sung family and the servants.'[23]

---

20 'But the brunt is falling, and falling heavily, on the native Church. In all our stations much valuable time is taken up with hearing and discussing and trying to settle such cases of persecution.' Crawford, *Mission in Manchuria*, p. 11. **21** D/2003/B/2/5/1. **22** D/2003/ B/3/2/53. **23** D/2003/B/2/5/1

The ambiguous position of these individuals was a problem not easily resolved. Friendly relations with the local population were crucial for the success of European enterprises,[24] and at a most basic level, Crawford found himself heavily dependent upon converts in his efforts to learn enough Chinese to preach, as his fellow missionaries were too busy to spare the time to teach. Yet he found the notion of too close a relationship with those whom he sought to win to the church disturbing. Throughout his letters there is a clear sense of respect for Chinese culture, and for the Chinese themselves, yet they remain forever too different to be comfortably thought of as true fellows. A letter to his sister Mary, written in 1900, indicates the sense of isolation felt by missionaries, despite the teeming population around them. Mary had apparently neglected to ask specifically after one of the missionary's wives: 'It seems that in writing to Mr Gillespie you made no reference to Mrs Gillespie, but only asked for the children . . . I must also tell you (what perhaps you know but can hardly realise) how life out here tells on ladies who [. . .] for years never have any company but a fellow missionary's wife. The Chinese can never be to us what our own fellow countrymen are – especially Chinese women – and the isolation tends to an exaggerated self inspection and a tendency to brood over anything which seems like a slight to oneself or husband.'[25]

If Crawford and other missionaries were torn over their relationship with converts, there was little ambiguity on the part of many Chinese towards those who had converted. Well before the rebellion, Chinese Christians were a frequent cause of resentment, a resentment that was often given practical expression through beatings and confiscations. Unable or unwilling to attack the missionaries themselves, soldiers and officials vented their displeasure on the Chinese converts. Crawford and others believed that this persecution was directed from the highest levels, although proof was impossible to come by. The clichés of the inscrutable oriental came strongly to the fore at these moments. The missionaries found it frustrating to deal with individuals who welcomed them with great charm and civility to various social functions, but then denied all knowledge of an official sanction of violence against Christians while apparently being both well informed about, and indeed implicated in them. After Elder Sung had been badly beaten over the alleged illegal sale of land to the missionaries, Crawford called on the vice-

24 Crawford worried that that an apparent openness to the Chinese would have dire consequences for both races. Even in the anxiety surrounding European flight from the Boxers in 1900, he noted the following incident with disapproval: 'Mr Daniel, the chief engineer of the Railway in Kirin, came to T'wanshantzu to say farewell to his wife. As he stood on the bank bidding his last adieux he threw his arm (to our considerable astonishment) round the neck of his Chinese interpreter, in a free and easy sort of way, and stood for a good while in this position. I hardly think that this fashion of treating the Chinese as bon comrade raises them in the estimation of the people. It only proves to them how completely the interpreters have sold themselves over to Russian interests. These interpreters are in the habit of shaking hands with and speaking with the Russian ladies quite as unreservedly as a European would.' D/2003/B/2/5/1.   25 D/2003/B/3/7/9

governor in Kirin, seeking reassurance regarding the future of the mission station. Although the official duly gave his word that they were in no danger, Crawford remained uncomfortable:

> Remember that this man is extremely thick with the Governor who is the chief cause of all our troubles, and may be himself for all we know, as bitter against us as any one in spite of all his show of friendliness. To know the heart of such a man is as impossible as to know what there is at the centre of the earth.[26]

In 1898, Crawford met the 'suave' Chinese magistrate of a nearby district at dinner, and enjoyed a cordial conversation. But almost immediately afterwards, Crawford was told of a severe beating given to an inquirer who was left unable to walk: this incident took place as the missionary exchanged pleasantries with the magistrate over their meal. Further investigation revealed that the magistrate 'gave orders in all the places he passed through on his return from the capital to curse and beat all the Christians they met, only not to take their lives.'[27] Much of Crawford's time was in fact taken up in the investigation of these cases, which rarely came to a satisfactory conclusion. Officials denied all knowledge, and pledged their full support to punishing the perpetrators, although soldiers in particular were rarely brought to justice. When the Boxer rebellion broke out, but before actual attacks on missionaries had taken place, placards encouraging the people to act against the 'foreigner' began to appear. Although there was an official denial of any knowledge of them, the district governor made no effort to halt their spread (the placards urged people to copy and distribute them, claiming that 'those who transcribe one such placard [will receive] immunity from his sins, and those who transcribe 10 a similar privilege for his native village, for 100, a whole district').[28] The missionaries were reluctant to remove these placards themselves, as they feared inciting a hostile backlash against their work, so had to suffer the indignity of seeing vividly painted denunciations of themselves as they moved through their missionary districts.

In addition to the uncertainty over Chinese motives in wanting to convert, and in determining official attitudes towards the missionary effort, the Presbyterian workers faced had also to fend off advances from another group with ulterior motives. The Russians, who wished above all else to ensure the success of their railway expansion in China, actively sought the assistance of the missionaries at local level to ensure cordial relations. It was often difficult to maintain a distance between the missionaries and the Russians, especially as in the early years of his work Crawford frequently felt obliged to accept an escort of Russian soldiers, offered to him for his protection. This caused problems in terms of creating links with ordinary people, not least in that inn keepers would often refuse them accommodation in isolated areas, forcing Crawford to camp out in the cold. When rumours of the approach of the Boxers reached Kirin, Russian officials in the town swiftly placed their troops at the disposal of Crawford and his workers. Indeed, a company of 15 Cossacks accompanied the party on their barge when they fled. In return, however, the missionaries were expected to take the Russian side in the conflict, an unwelcome presumption. When Crawford's party finally reached the Russian town of Khabarovsk, en route to Vladivostock, they noted with mixed feelings evidence of a rush towards war:

> [17 steamers laden with troops and equipment passed on the river] In the exuberance of youth we cheered the troopers as they passed. They were allies of our own nation and they seemed to us to be on the side of law and justice rather than of anarchy. If asked, however, what way their presence would affect the Cause for which our hearts were suffering, we should have been at a loss for an answer.[29]

The refugees were treated most cordially in Khabarovsk, but rapidly found themselves drawn more closely into the Russian campaign than they might have wished. One of the Russian officials made the suggestion that 'some of our doctors should offer their services and remain at the base so as to allow their own doctors to go to the front.' Although this strategy implied that the missionaries were part of the Russian war effort, they were only willing to go along with it because 'we of course thought that in the case of our being soon to return to our stations it would be an advantage to be on hand.' The scheme came to nothing: 'It is more than probable that it had been pointed out to him that the presence of English doctors might be open to objection',[30] but it is an indication of the often precarious position of missionaries who claimed to have no material interests in a country, but who in moments of crisis became part of a general European campaign. In the flight from Kirin, Crawford also reflected on the Russian response to the Boxers. Noting that they had placed surprisingly small numbers of troops at important points along the railway, he speculated that this was part of a greater plan: 'That Russia should in this way purposely invite attack in order to give herself a *casus belli*, or the opportunity of annexing the country, I can hardly bring myself to believe.'[31] Even with these doubts, he and his fellow missionaries remained heavily dependent upon Russian assistance, travelling by boat with a guard of Cossacks,

---

29 D/2003/B/2/5/1, July 14. **30** D/2003/B/2/1, July 16. **31** D/2003/B/2/5/1 Crawford's Journal, July 7. Later in his journal, however, he noted that the Russians were most anxious to ensure that no war took place, as they feared the loss of the railway. 'He [the Russian Consular Agent] also expressed the wish that when we should have the occasion we would make known the friendly help we had been given by the Russians, in order to try and counter-balance the false views which are current regarding the Russian Government.'

and staying in Russian accommodation at all of the halting-points on their journey.

There has been a good deal of debate over the precise cause of the Boxer rebellion.[32] However, resentment against foreign missionaries, and the intrusions of foreign political powers, certainly acted as a powerful rallying cry. The rebel group, known as the 'Boxers United in Righteousness', acquired their nickname because they practiced a ritualistic kind of boxing believed to bestow magical powers. Although the group clashed with German Catholic missionaries in 1897, it was to be other factors that gave the Boxers impetus for national action. Between 1887 and 1900 China suffered a series of droughts and floods, and there was widespread harvest failure. These developments were blamed on the foreigners, who became the focus of Boxer attacks. The movement was widespread, but almost entirely leaderless, drawing its support from among the peasantry. However, Empress Cixi, regent from 1875 to 1889, had returned to power in 1898. Although conservative in her politics, she and her court decided in 1900 to support the activities of the Boxers, largely in an attempt to reduce the influence of the foreign powers.[33] This appeared to give official sanction to Boxer activity, and ensured that the movement spread widely. As rebellion flourished, the Europeans moved swiftly, with Britain, Germany, France, Russia, the United States, Japan, Italy, and Austria-Hungary sending a combined force to recapture the city of Tianjin, near Beijing, which had fallen to the Boxers in the summer of 1900. This force put down the rebellion ruthlessly, and China suffered not merely the humiliation of defeat, but the considerable burden of payments for the costs to the allied forces in prosecuting the war.

Foreign concerns over the potential threat represented by the Boxers was well founded. A good deal had been invested in the country, and the struggles over trading and territory that had characterised Chinese affairs for decades had resulted in particular advances, especially with regard to technology. Primarily developed for economic and security needs, the relatively sophisticated network of communications that existed in China ensured that contact was well maintained between missionary workers, at home and abroad. Despite the great distance separating Crawford and his fellow missionaries from Ireland, they kept in constant communication with their families and each other, mainly through letters, but also through telegrams, and occasionally, the telephone.[34] Thus residents in the various mission stations found themselves with access to the most modern of telecommunications, despite the often primitive conditions in which they lived and worked. This factor

---

32 This confusion extends even to its name. It should more accurately be described as the 'Boxer Uprising', as the Boxers were not rebelling against the Chinese (Manchu) government. Their protest was directed against the foreign presence, and to a lesser extent against Chinese Christians, as they were believed to have gone over to the foreigners. **33** Bailey, *China in the Twentieth Century*, pp. 34–43. **34** Kirin was well equipped with telephones, principally due to the Russian presence.

was to assume a particular importance on the outbreak of the Boxer Rebellion, and may in fact have saved a good number of European lives. The Boxers also recognised the importance of the communications network, associating it not merely with the increasing power of foreign forces in China, but with a modernity they despised. In many parts of the country, the cutting of telegraph lines was often the first act of rebellion.[35]

In a certain sense, the Boxers were correct in their association between European encroachments and modern technology. The Kirin mission station was a substantial settlement, with a school, chapel and hospital, and the mission station was located close to a Russian military base on the edge of the town. On 30 June, the rumours that had been circulating about outbreaks of violence were confirmed. The news came in a telegram to Dr Grieg, a mission doctor, and was received by a party of croquet-playing missionaries. The message, from an outlying mission station, warned of the approach of the Boxers, and asked for information regarding the situation in Kirin. Crawford and his companions prepared a reply in Latin *Fama sine tumultu, muscovii auscilium proferimnt* ['Rumours but no trouble, the Russians have offered help'],[36] but did not send it, as the situation rapidly deteriorated. What is extraordinary is the number of communications that passed between the missionaries and others in the few hours before they fled Kirin. In less than a day, they had sent or received nine or ten telegrams, made at least one telephone call, wrote more than four letters (in addition to a 'home mail', sent in the morning before the warnings began to arrive), and sent messengers to alert fellow workers to the danger. What is even more surprising is the fact that Crawford states that almost all of these messages got through, most on the same or the following day. Although these communications fulfilled an important purpose in warning fellow missionaries, they also had the unfortunate effect of confirming hostile Chinese suspicions that the foreigners were in league with each other, a belief that Crawford and his co-workers had difficulty dispelling on their eventual return to Kirin.

The many messages sent and received by the Presbyterian missionaries points up several other issues, in addition to the importance of modern technology. The most striking is the close relationships between the various missionaries, and the concern each felt to warn their fellows of potential danger. It is not surprising to find that representatives of the same church hastened to alert each other to developments, but this concern was extended to European workers of other churches. What is especially noteworthy is the effort made by Crawford to ensure the safety of the Roman Catholic missionaries, a prophetic effort, as Catholic missionaries formed a majority of the European workers murdered during the rebellion. It is estimated that approximately 30,000 Chinese Catholics were murdered, and a further fifty Catholic missionaries were killed. The Protestant churches had a heavier

---

35 Mackerras, *China in Transformation*, p. 17.   36 D/2003/B/2/5/1 Crawford's Journal, describing his journey from Manchuria to Russia as a result of the Boxer Rebellion.

loss of missionary lives – 135 missionaries and fifty-three of their children – but considerably fewer Chinese Christians, at around 2,000, than their Catholic counterparts.[37] On the day he left Kirin Crawford wrote to 'the RC Bishop Lalonyer advising him to go to the Russian colony', and then sent a telegram, fearing that a letter would not arrive as swiftly.[38] Crawford's action reflected his own belief in the necessity for European Christians to present a united front in China. Unlike many other workers, he believed that the importance of mission work was the Christianising of China, rather than a narrow focus upon which particular church achieved the greatest success rate. He viewed all the Christian missions as sharing a common goal, rather than being in competition with each other for souls, as was common in missionary endeavours in Africa and India. It is interesting however to note that it was easier for this liberality to be maintained while in China. Back in Ireland, it was necessary to be rather more circumspect when describing the benefits of association with other churches. Thus in his address to the Presbyterian General Assembly Crawford stressed the necessity for close co-operation with fellow Christians, but tactfully ignored the Catholic dimension:

> A matter of immense importance is that out there the Christian forces present a united front. In Manchuria, not only are we organically united with the Scottish missionaries of the U.F. Church, so that the Chinese don't even know that we come from different churches, but the only other society at work in Manchuria, that of the Danish Lutheran Church is also co-operating with us in a most cordial manner. Still more significant – we are beginning to see quite plainly that the Chinese Christians are not content to perpetuate 'our unhappy divisions'. They are speaking of the "Christian Church of China".[39]

Only in China, it would appear, could Europeans be liberated from religious prejudice, and admit a common goal. In Crawford's letters home he details social meetings with ministers and priests of various religions, to whom he offered hospitality in Kirin. 'Yesterday we had a visit from three Roman Catholic priests, who are here from different stations for their annual conference. I had not met any of these gentlemen before. They had met several of our missionaries, but in many cases they only knew the Chinese name,[40] and inquired of me the English name. They seemed pleased to meet with one who spoke their mother tongue (French).'[41] However, the apparent merging of Christian churches into one undifferentiated mass fuelled Chinese suspicions at the highest levels regarding their impact, and confirmed Christianity as 'a seditious, socially destabilizing heterodoxy'.[42]

---

37 Stanley *Bible and the Flag*, p. 139. **38** D/2003/B/5/1. **39** D/2003/B/2/4/1 'Foreign Mission Speech in General Assembly' by R.A. Crawford, probably 1913. **40** Most of the mission workers took Chinese names, to ease communication. Crawford was known as 'Pastor Tu'. **41** Crawford, *Sketches,* p. 169. **42** S. Bayly, 'The Evolution of Colonial

Despite the Chinese assumptions regarding the close links between Christian missionaries, and Crawford's anxiety on behalf of his Catholic fellows during the Boxer rebellion, the missionaries of different churches were nevertheless wary of potential encroachments on their congregations. Although Crawford maintained a liberal attitude towards association with missionaries of other churches, many of his Presbyterian fellow workers were a good deal more suspicious. New arrivals to the district were scrutinised closely, and their motives questioned. The Chinese converts proved an important source of information with regard to the movements of European missionaries, as they swiftly brought news of potential interlopers to the Presbyterians missionaries:

> Having heard that a foreign priest was in the city, I took the 'boy' with me the following morning, and went to call at a certain inn. On arrival, I found that there were three priests, among them M. Grillon, the Bishop of Moukden. They received me very cordially, and we conversed a good while. I hope the Roman Catholics and we may manage to live at peace with one another. As yet, they have no adherents in this place. The evening of the same day they called on us on our return from a visit to the Arsenal.[43]

Crawford's letters contain tallies of the numbers of converts claimed by the various churches in Manchuria, and it was clearly a point of pride amongst mission workers not merely to save a soul, but to snatch one from a rival mission. One letter records his immediate superior's disappointment that the Presbyterians 'lost' a convert to the Roman Catholics – two brothers had become Christians, one a Presbyterian, and the other a Catholic, and each mission appears to have high hopes of securing the sibling[44] – but when the European missionary movement as a whole was threatened, the churches tended to pull together.

Robert Crawford was a genuinely liberal individual, who recorded his impressions of the Chinese in an even-handed manner. Unlike many other missionaries, he had a great deal of respect for Chinese tradition, and his hope was to encourage the spread of Christianity among a percentage of the population, rather than eliminate native faith altogether. He met with a degree of success in this objective: as early as 1899 the missionaries could point to a total of 7,920 converts, 467 of them in Kirin.[45] Crawford was above all a missionary, devoted to spreading Christianity throughout China. But he was a missionary in the mould of David Livingstone rather more than Mary Slessor, as his obvious delight in the exploration of foreign countries showed. For Crawford, and others like him, missionary work allowed for the expression of deeply held religious beliefs while also satisfying a very secular curiosity about the world.

Cultures: Nineteenth-Century Asia' in Porter (ed.), *Oxford History of the British Empire*, p. 463. **43** Crawford, *Sketches* p. 37. **44** D/200/B/3/3/20. **45** R.H. Boyd, *Waymakers in Manchuria: The Story of the Irish Presbyterian Pioneer Missionaries to Manchuria* (Belfast, 1940), p. 186.

'In general, they do not answer well': Irish priests in the western lowlands of Scotland, 1838–50

MARTIN J. MITCHELL

Historians have been aware for some time of the civil war within the Western District of the Roman Catholic Church in Scotland in the 1860s, between, on the one hand, the Scottish bishops and their senior Scots-born priests, and, on the other, a section of the Irish clergy. The dispute was over the governance of the Church.[1] What is less well known is that this was not the first time that Irish priests in the District had been perceived as being a dangerous and divisive presence. Irish clergymen were recruited from the late 1830s onwards to help to deal with the acute shortage of native priests; however, in the 1840s they were seen by their Scottish colleagues not as a welcome and valuable asset, but instead as a threat to the well-being, and indeed to the identity, of the Catholic Church in the Western District. This chapter, therefore, will look at the attitudes of the Scottish bishops, and their senior clergy, to the Irish priests who served in the District during this period.

I

In the late 1780s there were around 30,000 Roman Catholics in Scotland, of whom only a few lived in the western lowlands (the counties of Lanarkshire, Renfrewshire, Ayrshire, Dunbartonshire and Wigtownshire).[2] The Catholic Church was, not surprisingly, non-existent in this region. Irish immigration from the mid-1790s onwards fundamentally altered this pattern of Catholicism: in the mid-1830s

---

1 See James Handley, *The Irish in Modern Scotland* (Cork, 1947), chapter 3; Vincent Alan McClelland, 'The Irish Clergy and Archbishop Manning's Apostolic Visitation of the Western District of Scotland, 1867', *Catholic Historical Review*, 53 (April and July 1967), pp. 1–27, 229–50; David McRoberts, 'The Restoration of the Scottish Catholic Hierarchy in 1878', *Innes Review*, 29 (1978), pp. 3–29; John F. McCaffrey, 'Roman Catholics in Scotland in the 19th and 20th Centuries', *Records of the Scottish Church History Society*, 21 (1983), pp. 278–88; Bernard Aspinwall, 'Scots and Irish Clergy ministering to immigrants, 1830–1878', *Innes Review*, 47 (1996), pp. 45–68.   2 The population of Scotland at this time was around 1.5 million. In the 1780s, approximately one half of Scotland's Roman Catholics lived in the Highlands and Islands. Most of the other half resided in the north-east of the country (the counties of Aberdeenshire, Banffshire, Kincardineshire, Morayshire and Nairnshire).

there were around 70,000 Catholics in the western lowlands, of whom almost all were of Irish birth or descent.[3] By that time the Catholic Church had managed to establish six missions in the area.[4] The Glasgow Mission had two chapels and four priests, including a bishop; the Greenock Mission supported one chapel, a priest and a bishop; and the Paisley, Dumbarton, Ayr and Wigtownshire Missions each had one chapel and one priest. All ten clergymen were Scottish, of whom nine were natives of the north-east of the country.

Despite the progress that had undoubtedly been made in the western lowlands by the Scottish Catholic Church during the first forty years of significant Irish immigration, it is evident that there remained a severe under-provision of priests and chapels. This is even more apparent when it is recognised that the Catholics of each mission did not all live in the town in which their chapel was located. For example, approximately 43,000 of the 50,000 Catholics attached to the Glasgow Mission lived in the city and its suburbs, while most of the remainder resided in towns and villages throughout Lanarkshire; the Ayr Mission embraced almost all of the Catholics in Ayrshire; only around one-half of the congregation of the Paisley Mission lived in the town, while the rest were scattered throughout several civil parishes in Renfrewshire; and the priest of the Wigtownshire Mission, whose chapel was at Newton Stewart, was in charge of all the Catholics who lived in the county. This was a far from ideal state of affairs, as many Catholics had to travel a considerable distance to attend Mass. The clergymen tried to deal with the problem by occasionally holding services in rented halls in some of the towns and villages which were far from the Mission chapels. Despite this, there was wide-spread recognition that more needed to be done. For example, in 1835 William Thomson, priest of the Ayr Mission, stated that:

> Owing to the great increase of Catholics in Kilmarnock, I have frequently to say mass and preach there & in Ayr on the same day. The fasting, quick driving, & whiles a rainy stormy day is exceedingly trying. The labour here now is too great for one man.[5]

3 For the Irish in Scotland in the first half of the nineteenth century see James Handley, *The Irish in Scotland, 1790–1845* (Cork, 1945); Martin J. Mitchell, *The Irish in the West of Scotland, 1797–1848: Trade Unions, Strikes and Political Movements* (Edinburgh, 1998); *idem*, 'The Catholic Irish in the West of Scotland: "A Separate and Despised Community"?', in T.M. Devine and James F. McMillan (eds), *Celebrating Columba: Irish-Scottish Connections, 597–1997* (Edinburgh, 1999), pp. 50–83.   4 The following discussion of the Roman Catholic Church in the region in this period is based on Martin J. Mitchell, 'The Establishment and Early Years of the Hamilton Mission' in T.M. Devine (ed.), *St Mary's Hamilton, 1846–1996: A Social History* (Edinburgh, 1995), pp. 1–14.   5 Scottish Catholic Archives [hereafter SCA], Blairs Letters, BL6/122/2, William Thomson to Charles Gordon, 30 March 1835.

Almost three years later, the priest in charge of the Paisley Mission complained that his congregation was '. . . too numerous and much too scattered to be properly superintended by one individual'.[6]

To help to deal with the shortage of priests, Bishop Andrew Scott, Vicar Apostolic of the Western District of the Roman Catholic Church in Scotland, decided in 1837 to recruit clergymen from Ireland. Scott's Vicariate consisted of the western lowland counties, as well as the Hebrides, Argyllshire and the southern part of Inverness-shire.[7] In 1838 four recently ordained Irish priests came to work for him.[8] Between 1838 and 1849 a total of thirty-three Irishmen were procured from seminaries in Ireland.[9] The majority were ordained for the Western District, while the remainder were on loan from their bishops in Ireland. In addition to these clergymen, four other Irish priests served in the Vicariate in this period; these men were immigrants who had been educated and trained in seminaries belonging to the Scottish Mission, and who had been ordained for the Western District. The Irish priests were employed almost exclusively in the western lowlands, where, of course, almost all the Catholics were Irish or of Irish descent; at the beginning of 1850, eighteen of the thirty-seven clergymen in this region were Irish born. By contrast, at that time only one of the sixteen priests in the Highlands and Islands portion of the Western District was an Irishman. This was because most of the Catholics here were Gaelic-speaking native Scots, living in rural areas, who needed to be ministered to by clergymen who knew their language and customs. The priests who served in the Gaelic-speaking part of the Vicariate were natives either of that region or of the Highland area of the Northern District.[10]

6 Parliamentary Papers, 1837–8, *Reports of the Commissioners of Religious Instruction, Scotland. Eighth Report,* Appendix I, p. 211.   7 From 1727 until 1827 the Scottish Mission was divided into two Vicariates, the Highland District and the Lowland District. In 1827 it was divided into three: the Western District, the Eastern District and the Northern District. This structure remained until the restoration of the Scottish Hierarchy in 1878.   8 The information in this paragraph, and all subsequent information concerning the numbers and the nationalities of the priests who served in the Western District between 1838 and 1849, is taken from the following sources: *The Catholic Directory for Scotland* for the years 1837 to 1850; Bernard J. Canning, *Irish-Born Secular Priests in Scotland, 1829–1979* (1979); Christine Johnson, 'Secular Clergy of the Lowland District 1732–1829', *Innes Review,* 34 (1983), pp. 67–87; *idem,* 'Scottish Secular Clergy, 1830–1878: The Northern and Eastern Districts' and 'Scottish Secular Clergy, 1830–1878: The Western District', *Innes Review,* 40 (1989), pp. 24–68, 106–52; F. Forbes and W.J. Anderson, 'Clergy Lists of the Highland District, 1732–1828', *Innes Review,* 17 (1966), pp. 129–84.   9 By contrast, during the same period, the Eastern District recruited only four clergymen from Irish seminaries, and the Highland District none.   10 Johnson, 'The Western District', p. 108. The sole Irish priest in the Highlands and Islands portion of the Western District in 1850 was Michael Condon, who was in charge of the Campbeltown Mission in Argyllshire. Condon had been moved there from Glasgow in 1847. Each of his three immediate predecessors at Campbeltown was a young Irish clergyman who, like Condon, had been transferred there from his original posting in Glasgow. The Campbeltown Mission, of all the Missions in the Highlands and

The decision to recruit Irish priests must be examined further, as Andrew Scott had previously expressed his strong opposition to the use of such clergymen in the western lowlands of Scotland. In January 1826, when he was priest in charge of the Glasgow Mission, Scott informed his superior, Bishop Alexander Paterson, that he was 'quite convinced that the Glasgow mission in particular would be most seriously injured by bringing an Irishman to it, even for only a few months. . .' According to Scott, it was

> natural even for Scotchmen in a foreign land to draw together. Irishmen have the same feelings, but less prudence. There has been a cry to get Irishmen to Glasgow, and most certainly an Irish priest would soon associate with his countrymen and naturally fall, into all the habits he was accustomed to see between his own country priests at home and their flocks. He would appear to have all their hearts, which might flatter too much a young mind, and if he had not extraordinary prudence, all Episcopal authority would soon be set aside. This has happened elsewhere. He would also impart to them everything that passed, and many things that he ought not to do . . . I should fear the total ruin of the Glasgow mission in its present circumstances from such a step.

Scott added that many 'respectable protestant Gentlemen' in Glasgow had expressed to him their strong opposition to the use of Irish priests in the city.[11]

Scott soon had first-hand experience of such clergymen. In 1829 James Gibbons, an Irish priest who had been dismissed from his mission in the north-east of Scotland – a region with few Irish Catholics – on account of the scandal that his liking for alcohol had caused, arrived in Glasgow.[12] He quickly inflamed the Irish Catholics in the city against the Scottish bishops (who by this time included Andrew Scott) and the Scottish priests, by telling them that he had been victimised simply because of his nationality. Gibbons argued that '. . .the Irish Catholics, being the most numerous body of Catholics in all the South of Scotland have a right to be served by Irish priests and governed by Irish bishops'.[13] Scott informed Bishop Kyle that 'the paddies' in Glasgow believed Gibbons' claims, and considered him to

---

Islands area of the Western District, was the only one to have a sizeable Irish contingent among its congregation. According to Johnson, 'Here English was widely spoken and the priest did not have to be a Gaelic speaker'. Johnson, 'The Western District', p. 106. See also Handley, *Irish in Scotland*, p.76; Glasgow Archdiocesan Archives (hereafter GAA), Western District Papers, WD5, Michael Condon Memoirs, Miguelide, p. 500.   **11** Andrew Scott to Alexander Paterson, 15 January 1826, quoted in Christine Johnson, *Developments in the Roman Catholic Church in Scotland, 1789–1829* (Edinburgh, 1983), pp. 138–9.   **12** Gibbons had been ordained for the Lowland District in 1827. He was one of only three Irish priests who were employed by the Scottish Mission in the first three decades of the nineteenth century. None was stationed in the western lowlands. See Johnson, *Developments*, pp. 137–9.   **13** SCA, Blairs Letters, BL5/248/14, Andrew Scott to James Kyle, 15 October 1829.

be 'the victim of a Scots persecution . . .'[14] According to Scott, Gibbons spent his time in the city 'venting his rage and calumnies against Scotch Bishops and Scotch priests. Though the generality know him to be a suspended priest, still they give more credit to him than they would do to us'.[15] The crisis was soon over, however, as Gibbons was dismissed from the Scottish Mission and left the country in late December 1829.[16]

Within three years Andrew Scott was faced with a similar problem. In 1832 Revd Byrne, an Irish priest, was stationed at Paisley.[17] He quickly became convinced that he was the victim of an 'injustice' because clergymen who were junior to him were being placed at the Glasgow Mission; Byrne believed that his seniority entitled him to be moved there before them.[18] Byrne was furious about this and in the autumn he inflamed the Irish Catholics in the Glasgow and Paisley Missions against Bishop Scott and the Scottish priests by telling them about the discrimination he had allegedly suffered, and by claiming 'that he was prosecuted merely because he was an Irishman . . .' In November of that year Scott withdrew Byrne's canonical faculties.[19] The rebellious priest, however, was undeterred, and throughout most of 1833 he continued his campaign. According to Andrew Scott, the aim of Byrne and his supporters was '. . . to raise all the Irish Catholics throughout Scotland in rebellion against their superiors and their immediate Scotch pastors'.[20] In September 1833 it was reported that 'a considerable number of the wild paddies' were still attached to Byrne.[21] Before the year was over, however, he gave up the fight. Byrne expressed regret for his conduct and retracted all the allegations he had made over the period. It would appear that he then left Scotland.[22]

The activities of Gibbons and Byrne confirmed Andrew Scott's worst fears about the impact of Irish priests in the western lowlands. Yet in late 1837 Scott had little choice *but* to recruit clergymen from Ireland. By that time not enough Scotsmen had been ordained for the Western District; an insufficient number of boys were training for the priesthood; and he was finding it extremely difficult to persuade others to take up the vocation. Meanwhile, the number of Irish immigrants in the region was increasing daily. Scott made his decision to recruit Irish priests with some reluctance, perhaps even trepidation. He was worried – with

14 SCA, Blairs Letters, BL5/248/17, Andrew Scott to James Kyle, 20 October 1829. Kyle was Vicar Apostolic of the Northern District. **15** SCA, Preshome Letters, PL3/154/25, Andrew Scott to James Kyle, 23 December 1829. **16** Johnson, 'Secular Clergy of the Lowland District', p. 71. **17** Very little is known about Byrne. For example, he is not mentioned in Johnson's clergy lists, nor is he discussed in Canning's biographies of Irish-born secular priests in Scotland. **18** SCA, Preshome Letters, PL3/214/16, Andrew Scott to James Kyle, 22 October 1832. **19** SCA, Preshome Letters, PL3/214/20, Andrew Scott to James Kyle, 21 November 1832. **20** SCA, Preshome Letters, PL3/234/7, Andrew Scott to Donald Carmichael, 22 March 1833. **21** SCA, Blairs Letters, BL6/8/15, Andrew Scott to James Kyle, 3 September 1833. **22** SCA, Blairs Letters, BL6/79/21, John Murdoch to James Kyle, 30 October 1833; Preshome Letters, PL3/234/17, Andrew Scott to James Kyle, 11 December 1833.

good reason given the events of the late 1820s and early 1830s – that the Irish Catholics in the western lowlands would form a strong attachment to the imported clergymen, and that this could have serious repercussions for his Vicariate if he became involved in a major dispute with one, or several, of the Irish priests. It must, therefore, have been of some comfort to Scott to learn that the first priests to be sent to the Western District from St Patrick's Seminary at Maynooth had been given by its president '. . . a most excellent character for piety, talents and docility'.[23]

II

The Irish clergymen who served in the western lowlands between 1838 and 1843 did not attempt to turn their Irish congregations against Andrew Scott and his co-adjutor, Bishop John Murdoch;[24] indeed, it would appear that they did not cause their superiors any great trouble. Nevertheless, Bishop Scott and senior Scottish priests were most unhappy with this Irish presence. For example, the Irishmen who were recruited between 1838 and 1841, nine in total, were not ordained for the Western District, but instead were on short-term loan from their native dioceses. There was a belief among the Scottish Catholic clergy that these priests had no great interest in, or commitment to, the District. For example, in January 1840 Scott stated: 'it is evident that from the hopes of getting some years after this a sit-uation at home, they do not take the same interest in the temporal or spiritual wel-fare of the Mission as Scotch priests do'.[25] The following year John Bremner, priest in charge of the Paisley Mission, complained to Scott about 'Irish clergymen taken by the lump, men, who have no interest in our affairs, & who seem to think they honour us, while they do us only half service . . .'[26] Moreover, it was felt that the young Irishmen whom the Western District had employed, and was seeking to employ, were second-rate clergymen, very inferior in quality to the Scottish priests. In August 1841 John Bremner described them as 'the half educated, & wholly prej-udiced sons of Maynooth . . .'[27] Two months later, the Revd Peter Forbes, who was in Ireland trying to recruit clergymen, informed John Murdoch that the Irish bish-ops kept the best graduates from their seminaries for themselves. Forbes believed, as did John Bremner, that one way of improving the quality of Irish clergymen in the Western District, and of increasing their attachment to the Vicariate, was to find talented Irish boys, and then educate and train them in seminaries belonging to the Scottish Mission.[28]

23 SCA, Blairs Letters, BL6/219/3, Andrew Scott to James Kyle, 22 April 1838.   24 At the end of 1834 Scott had retired to Greenock, leaving Murdoch in charge of affairs in and around Glasgow. Scott reserved 'to himself merely the general superintendence of the District . . .' *Catholic Directory for Scotland for 1867*, p. 140.   25 SCA, Blairs Letters, BL6/281/1, Andrew Scott to James Kyle, 15 January 1840.   26 SCA, Oban Letters, OL2/61/3, John Bremner to Andrew Scott, 9 August 1841.   27 Ibid.   28 SCA, Oban Letters, OL2/62/6, Peter Forbes to John Murdoch, 24 October 1841. Forbes was one of the

Scott's reaction to this suggestion is not known, but it is unlikely that he was favourable to it. For Scott, the main issue was not the intellectual or the pastoral qualities of the Irish priests, but instead their nationality, indeed their very Irishness, and the effect that he believed this had on the Scottish Catholic Church, and on the Scottish people. In December 1841 he stated that although his Irish priests were 'good moral clergymen generally speaking in every respect', they could not 'advance the interests of Religion' in Scotland as much as Scottish priests could do. According to Scott:

> The prejudices of the protestants in this country are so strong against them as to prevent them from listening to any instructions from them, though they might be inclined to listen to those of a Scotch priest. The habits, the ideas, the customs and manners of the Irish priests are in general in such opposition to those of our Scotch population that even those protestants who might be converted by a Scotch priest will not and cannot prevail upon themselves to apply to an Irish priest. Above all the violent political feelings of the Irish clergymen strongly tend to augment the prejudices of the Scotch population against them . . .

Scott added that it was his

> sincere conviction . . . that conversions in any great numbers will not take place, and that Religion cannot be increased in our present circumstances in this country either by Irish or English clergymen but only by native Scotch secular missionaries.[29]

Unfortunately for Scott, there were simply not enough natives coming through the ranks of the Scottish seminaries. For example, in 1842 only two Scotsmen were ordained for the Western District, one of whom was to spend the rest of the decade serving in the Highlands. Yet in that year seven Irishmen were recruited for the Vicariate. Moreover, only one of these men was on loan from Ireland: the others were ordained for the Western District, an acknowledgement by Bishops Scott and Murdoch that Irish priests were now essential for the effective running of the Church in the western lowlands. Despite the serious misgivings which Andrew Scott had about his Irish clergymen during this period, neither he nor John Murdoch encountered any great difficulties managing them. After 1843, however, this situation changed dramatically, largely as a consequence of Daniel O'Connell's campaign for the repeal of the legislative union between Great Britain and Ireland.

Although a Repeal Association was active in Glasgow from at least May 1841 onwards, it was not until 1843 that the campaign for an Irish legislature took off in

priests of the Glasgow Mission.   **29** SCA, Blairs Letters, BL6/330/12, Andrew Scott to James Kyle, 10 December 1841.

Scotland.[30] In July of that year Andrew Scott informed a colleague that, in the western lowlands, 'All our poor people are mad about repeal, and they are convinced that before two months an Irish Parliament will be sitting on College Green in Dublin'.[31] An editorial that month in the *Glasgow Saturday Post* stated:

> such is now the number of natives of Ireland in all our principal towns, and such is their zeal and energy, that were any demonstration against the repeal of the union to be attempted, the repealers would be almost certain to muster, and carry the declaration of public opinion in their favour.[32]

Indeed, from 1843 to 1847 Repeal was arguably *the* major popular movement, in Scotland, for political reform.

Like their colleagues in Ireland, the Irish Catholic clergy in the western lowlands were heavily involved in the agitation for Repeal.[33] For example, in 1843 they chaired and spoke at meetings on the issue, and helped to raise money for the Repeal Fund in Dublin, activities which were both welcomed and applauded by the Catholic Irish in the region. Indeed, the popularity of the Irish clergy among their congregations increased as a result of their involvement in the campaign. This strengthening of the bond between Irish priests and people greatly troubled Bishops Scott and Murdoch, and either in late 1843 or in early 1844 they banned their priests from participating in the movement.[34] Despite this edict, the Irish clergy in the western lowlands continued to promote Repeal. In August 1844 Andrew Scott stated that he had been told that they were spending most of their time going privately among their congregations furthering the cause. Moreover, these priests were, according to the information Scott had received, urging their flocks to donate to the Repeal Fund, yet were not encouraging them, or even asking them, to contribute to the upkeep of their own missions.[35]

The raising of the Repeal Rent in the western lowlands was an issue of great concern to Andrew Scott. The amount of money sent to Dublin was not inconsiderable. For example, in May 1843 the Repealers in and around Glasgow collected almost £130; during the second half of that year they raised over £300.[36] These were funds which Scott could ill-afford to lose, as the Church in the region

---

30 For the Repeal Movement in the western lowlands, see Mitchell, *Irish in the West of Scotland*, chapters 7 and 8. **31** SCA, Preshome Letters, PL3/309/18, Andrew Scott to James Kyle, 12 July 1843. **32** *Glasgow Saturday Post*, 29 July 1843. **33** For the involvement of the Catholic clergy of Ireland in Repeal see Oliver MacDonagh, *O'Connell: The Life of Daniel O'Connell 1775–1847* (London, 1991), pp. 505, 516–17; Gearoid O'Tuathaigh, *Ireland before the Famine* (2nd edition, Dublin, 1990), p. 188; K. Theodore Hoppen, *Ireland since 1800: Conflict and Conformity* (2nd edition, Harlow, 1999), pp. 31–2, 84–5. **34** This in effect was a ban on their Irish clergy, as no Scots-born priest was involved in the agitation. See Mitchell, *Irish in the West of Scotland*, pp. 237–8. Murdoch was in fact opposed to Repeal. See *Glasgow Saturday Post*, 14 December 1844. **35** SCA, Blairs Letters, BL6/442/15, Andrew Scott to James Kyle, 28 August 1844. **36** Mitchell, *Irish in the West of Scotland*, p. 240.

was by no means a wealthy institution. In the years since the beginning of significant Irish immigration it had struggled to raise money for the building of chapels
and the employment of priests. As has been shown, by the mid-1830s progress had
been made although several chapels in the region remained heavily in debt. By that
time, however, the Church had raised enough money to begin a period of expansion, and in the remainder of the 1830s and throughout the 1840s plots of land were
purchased and places of worship erected on them. Debts remained on these buildings, but the practice was, as with the chapels built prior to the late 1830s, that the
money owed would be repaid eventually by the new congregations, through their
seat rents, their weekly contributions and through special collections.[37] The Repeal
Rent, therefore, was depriving the Catholic Church in the western lowlands of
vital funds, and the Irish priests in the region were in part responsible for persuading the Catholic Irish to contribute to it.

By 1845 some of these Irish priests had left the Western District to resume their
vocation in Ireland, while others had been transferred from their original postings
to serve in different missions in the Vicariate. Many within the Catholic community in the western lowlands, and in particular in the Glasgow area, were convinced
that these clergymen had been punished because of their support for Repeal, and
by late 1844 Bishop Murdoch's stewardship was being publicly questioned and
indeed criticised.[38] At least one of the Irish priests was moved because of his role
in the agitation: in November 1844 Revd Hugh Quigley was 'relegated' from St
Mary's Chapel in Glasgow to the Mission at Campbeltown because he had
'earnestly advocated "Repeal".'[39] The following month, Bishop Murdoch, from the
pulpit at St Mary's during Sunday Mass, attacked the Repeal Movement, condemned Quigley 'for his conduct as a Repeal agitator', and denounced those who
had attended a farewell soirée for the Irish priest.[40] Murdoch's outburst infuriated
many of those present, and, according to Quigley's successor at Campbeltown, one
half of the congregation walked out of the chapel during it. It was apparently with
some difficulty that these Irish Catholics were persuaded to again attend the chapel
and contribute to its upkeep.[41]

Murdoch and Scott's fears concerning the close relationship between Irish
priests and people were again confirmed by the subsequent behaviour of Quigley,
and by the activities of another Irish priest, John McDermott, who was in charge

37 For the development of the Roman Catholic Church in the western lowlands during
the first half of the nineteenth century see Mitchell, 'Establishment and Early Years of the
Hamilton Mission', pp. 1–14; John F. McCaffrey, 'The Stewardship of Resources: Financial
Strategies of Roman Catholics in the Glasgow District, 1800–70', in W.J.Shiels and Diana
Wood (eds), *Studies in Church History Vol. 24: The Church and Wealth* (Oxford), 1987), pp.
359–70; Johnson, *Developments in the Roman Catholic Church*, esp. chapters 17, 18, 20, 25.
38 Mitchell, *Irish in the West of Scotland*, pp. 238–9.   39 GAA, Western District Papers,
WD5, Michael Condon Memoirs, Miguelide, p. 460.   40 *Glasgow Saturday Post*, 14
December 1844.   41 GAA, Western District Papers, WD5, Michael Condon Memoirs,
Miguelide, pp. 459–60, 462.

of the Dalry Mission in Ayrshire. The two clergymen, who had been classmates at St Mary's College in Youghal, disobeyed orders and instructions from Bishop Murdoch, who eventually gave them permission to seek employment outwith the Western District.[42] Shortly after this, in April 1846, they attended a Repeal meeting in Glasgow at which, according to Bishop Scott, Quigley 'made a most violent harangue' against Murdoch. Scott added that the two priests had 'raised by their calumnies a very bad feeling among the Catholics of Glasgow against Dr Murdoch . . .'[43] The following month they left the Vicariate for good. A relieved Andrew Scott described them as 'the most self conceited, ungovernable beings that I ever knew among clergymen'.[44]

The activities of the Irish priests in the western lowlands from 1843 onwards reinforced the view of Andrew Scott that only Scottish clergymen should be used in the region. In November 1844 he stated:

> Experience has already proved that Religion will not advance in this part of the Country with so many Irish priests in it. They wish to bring every thing to a level with Irish ideas and Irish practices, and will not encourage the people to contribute for the propagation of Religion. On the contrary, if thwarted in their views they discourage them and even countenance them in resistance to the Bishop.[45]

He therefore redoubled his efforts to obtain as many Scottish boys for the seminaries as was possible, in order to 'do away with the necessity of sending for Irish clergymen'.[46] In letters to colleagues in the Northern District, Scott asked if they knew of, or could find, boys who wanted to be trained for the priesthood and then be ordained for the Western District. For example, in 1845 a Scottish priest recommended an Irishman to Scott for the college at Blairs, but Scott replied that the man did not satisfy the conditions laid down by the benefactors of that institution. He added:

> I will be glad to receive on your recommendation as many Scotch boys from the airds or Strathglass as you can find for me. But you need not recommend any Irishman to me. I have had too much experience of them already.[47]

42 Mitchell, *Irish in the West of Scotland*, p. 242.   **43** SCA, Preshome Letters, PL3/327/5, Andrew Scott to James Kyle, 29 April 1846.   **44** SCA, Blairs Letters, BL6/517/6, Andrew Scott to James Kyle, 28 May 1846.   **45** SCA, Blairs Letters, BL5/442/19, Andrew Scott to James Kyle, 27 November 1844.   **46** SCA, Blairs Letters, BL6/442/20, Andrew Scott to James Kyle, 5 December 1844.   **47** SCA, Blairs Letters, BL6/483/10, Andrew Scott to Angus MacKenzie, 5 June 1845. The Northern District consisted of the Counties of Aberdeenshire, Banffshire, Kincardineshire, Morayshire and Nairnshire – i.e. the north-east – as well as the Highland Counties of Sutherland, Caithness-shire, Ross and Cromarty, and

Moreover, despite there being a major shortage of students for the Western District at Blairs, Scott was extremely reluctant to accept for the seminary boys born in the western lowlands of Irish immigrant parents, as he regarded them, as indeed they regarded themselves, as being just as Irish as those who had been born and raised in the old country. For example, in June 1844 he asked a priest at Auchinhalrig, in the north-east, to recommend to him one or two boys for Blairs, adding that:

> I could get plenty here [i.e. the western lowlands] whose parents were able and willing to pay for them, and the boys in the mean time seem well enough disposed. But we have too few Scotch priests in this part of the country, and I would rather have Scotch boys if I should pay for them the first years board myself.[48]

Scott was unable to rid the Western District of Irish priests and died in December 1846. He was succeeded as Vicar Apostolic by John Murdoch. Murdoch shared Scott's opinion of the Irish who served in the Vicariate, but soon realised that the dream of an all-Scottish priesthood was not going to become a reality. There were simply not enough Scottish boys who wanted to become priests and afterwards serve in the western lowlands; meanwhile, the number of Irish immigrants was increasing rapidly as thousands flooded into the towns of the region to escape the Great Famine. As John Murdoch wearily stated in May 1848: 'I am sadly annoyed by the unsteadiness of the Hibernian portion of my clergy. I wish to heaven I could do without Irish priests; for, in general, they do not answer well: But it is impossible for me to get on without them'.[49]

III

From 1838 until his death in 1846, Bishop Andrew Scott was hostile towards the presence of Irish clergymen in the Western District. The Catholic Church in Scotland was a missionary church, and Scott was convinced that conversions in significant numbers were not occurring largely because the Scottish Protestant population was prejudiced against clergymen from Ireland. Furthermore, the Irish priests had disobeyed episcopal directives, in particular after 1843 when they continued to promote Repeal despite being told not to participate in that campaign. Such defiance was completely unacceptable to Scott; he was a strict disciplinarian

---

the northern part of Inverness-shire, along with the Shetland Islands and the Orkney Islands. Most of the Roman Catholics in this Vicariate were Scottish. **48** SCA, Blairs Letters, BL6/442/10, Andrew Scott to William Caven, 28 June 1844. **49** SCA, Blairs Letters, BL6/587/6, John Murdoch to James Kyle, 31 May 1848. In August 1850 Murdoch claimed that there were at least 100,000 Catholics in the Western District. *Catholic Directory for Scotland for 1851*, p. 68.

who believed that the Catholics in his Vicariate – priests and people – had to submit to his will on all matters, both spiritual and temporal.[50]

The main reason for Andrew Scott's hostility, however, concerned the future governance of the Western District of the Roman Catholic Church in Scotland. Scott was conscious of the fact that the Irish laity and clergy in the western lowlands had a strong sense of national identity. In 1829 he stated that his 'Paddies' were 'poor, ignorant people, enthusiastically attached to every thing that bears the name of Irish'.[51] Fifteen years later, he told the Poor Law Inquiry that the Catholic Irish in the region 'were very national in their ideas and sentiments – rather too much so in some cases'.[52] The Irish priests in the Western District were equally nationalistic, as, for example, their overwhelming and enthusiastic support for Repeal demonstrated. Andrew Scott was fully aware that a strong bond, based on their love of Ireland and all things Irish, had been formed between the Irish clergy and laity, and he believed that this posed a serious threat to his authority and to the position of the Scottish Catholic clergy in the Vicariate. After all, such a close relationship had previously resulted in trouble within the District: during their disputes with the Church, Revd Gibbons and Revd Byrne, in 1829 and 1832–3 respectively, played the Irish card to inflame the people against Andrew Scott and his Scotsborn colleagues.

Scott had been able to weather these storms because he was dealing with only one priest at a time, and was able to use the full weight of Church authority to impose his will on each man. The situation in the 1840s was potentially far more serious for him. Irish priests were now a significant presence in the western lowlands. At the beginning of 1844, 10 of the 22 clergymen in the region were Irishborn; by the time Scott died, in December 1846, the proportion was 16 out of 30. Moreover, the atmosphere within the region was more nationalistic, as O'Connell's Repeal agitation had intensified the sense of national identity of both the Irish clergy and the Irish laity. The campaign had also strengthened the already close relationship between Irish priests and people, while at the same time it had helped to widen the social and cultural gulf between the Scots clergy and the Catholic Irish since the former remained aloof from Repeal activities. Indeed, during the peak years of the agitation two Irish priests (Hugh Quigley and John McDermott) used their influence among the laity to foment hostility towards Bishop Murdoch.

These developments greatly alarmed Andrew Scott, particularly as he was aware that his Irish clergymen, who by the mid-1840s were regarded as a 'party among the Priests',[53] wished 'to bring every thing to a level with Irish ideas and practices . . .' In 1829 Revd Gibbons had argued that because the Roman Catholics in the western lowlands were mostly Irish, they should be served by Irish priests and be

---

50 See, for example, Mitchell, *Irish in the West of Scotland*, chapters 4 and 5.   **51** SCA, Blairs Letters, BL2/248/16, Andrew Scott to Alexander Paterson, 23 October 1829.   **52** Quoted in Handley, *Irish in Scotland*, pp. 284–5.   **53** SCA, Blairs Letters, BL6/492/7, John Bremner to William Caven, 29 December 1846.

governed by Irish bishops. This view found great support among the laity at the time. In the 1840s Scott was undoubtedly worried that the strongly nationalistic – and truculent – alliance of Irish priests and people would lead ultimately (and perhaps very quickly) to demands that Irish clergymen should play the dominant role in the Vicariate, and perhaps even in the Scottish Mission given that the majority of Catholics in the country were Irish or of Irish descent.

Irish ascendancy within the Church was something which Scott, Murdoch and their Scottish colleagues were simply not willing to countenance. The Roman Catholic Church in Scotland had a long history, and a tradition which was distinct from that of the Church both in England and in Ireland. Native Catholics had kept the faith alive in the country since the Reformation of the sixteenth century. The Scottish bishops and clergy did not want to see their Church, the *Scottish* Catholic Church, taken over by Irish priests and bishops, or, even worse, by the Catholic Church of Ireland.[54] Therefore until his death Scott was determined to rid the Western District of Irish clergymen. John Murdoch also wanted an all-Scottish priesthood but circumstances dictated that this was not to happen. Fortunately for him, the threat posed to his Vicariate by the Irish priests receded considerably shortly after he became Vicar Apostolic. The Repeal agitation in the western lowlands was already in decline at the time of his succession, and government repression in 1848 killed off the Movement throughout the United Kingdom.[55] Moreover, from 1847 until the early 1850s the attention of the region's Catholic clergy – Scottish and Irish – was focused mainly on how to deal with the huge influx of poverty-stricken refugees from the Famine in Ireland. Throughout the 1850s, the issue of Irish priests in the western lowlands was not one which appears to have troubled the Scottish bishops and their senior clergy to the same extent as it had done in the previous decade. This was probably because the priests and people were more concerned about preserving a united front against the upsurge of anti-Catholic hostility and Protestant proselytism.[56] In the 1860s, however, the 'Irish issue' within the priesthood in the Western District re-emerged in spectacular fashion, and resulted in a major conflict which ended only when Rome appointed an Englishman, Charles Eyre, to take charge of the Vicariate.

In the 1840s Bishops Scott and Murdoch hoped – and perhaps prayed – that the presence of Irish priests in the western lowlands would be only temporary. In that decade, however, and in subsequent ones, the shortage of Scots-born priests, combined with the continued growth of the Catholic Irish community, ensured that clergymen from Ireland became a permanent, and important, fixture in the region.

54 These views were also held by the Scottish clergy during their conflict with a section of the Irish clergy and laity in the 1860s. See n.1.   55 See Mitchell, *Irish in the West of Scotland*, chapter 8.   56 For this anti-Catholic hostility see Handley, *Irish in Modern Scotland*, pp. 93–113.

Fenian dynamite: dissident Irish republicans in late nineteenth-century Scotland

MÁIRTÍN Ó CATHÁIN

Political dissent takes many forms. It is most commonly applied in the circumstances of non-compliance by groups and individuals with regard to a particular government or state. It also occurs between and within certain organisations as a regular feature of political culture. When however it manifests itself among violent revolutionary movements, the consequences can go beyond the esoteric realm of political theory into the lives of ordinary people, often with explosive force. This paper and this story is about just such incursions, why and how they occur, and what they eventually result in. Such a survey takes us from a mental ward in Perth Prison Hospital to a lonely garret in a backstreet of a small Belgian town, and from exploding hatboxes in Glasgow and London to the blind and naked figure of a Glasgow Irishman in the so-called 'zero cells' located in Portland Convict Prison in England.

In the last two decades of the nineteenth-century Scotland's Irish-born population, probably to the great relief of the majority of Scots, did not increase to any great extent, in fact it actually decreased. In the 1881 census the Irish numbered 218,745 in a total population of 3,735,573, and by 1901 it was 205,064 from 4,472,103, a decline of 1.27 in percentage terms within the intervening twenty years.[1] Glasgow, of course, was the hub around which this Irish wheel spun and its Irish population was not far short of 100,000 strong at this time in a city with almost half a million inhabitants within approximately three square miles of the city centre.[2] Throughout industrial Scotland the socio-economic conditions of Irish immigrants were notoriously poor, as indeed they were for much of the working class in general. However, as an early Scottish socialist was to perceptively note, 'It would be wrong to say that we were one people'.[3] Divisions and inequalities between hosts and immigrants were many and the defensivist badge of a begrudging 'exile', alongside historical animosities towards British and Protestant Scotland, intensified the anti-Irish and anti-Catholic feelings of many Scots. Many Irish therefore found their society shaped by external as well as internal forces

1 J.E. Handley, *The Irish in Modern Scotland* (Cork, 1947), pp. 241, 247. 2 I.G.C. Hutchison, 'Politics and Society in Mid-Victorian Glasgow 1846–1886', Ph.D., University of Edinburgh (1974), pp. 486–7; J.F. McCaffrey, 'Politics and the Catholic community since 1878', in D. McRoberts (ed.), *Modern Scottish Catholicism, 1878–1978* (Glasgow, 1978), p. 154. 3 D. Kirkwood, *My Life of Revolt* (London, 1935), pp. 60–1.

which determined their immigrant identity. This view of the Irish in Scotland has however been critiqued by Martin Mitchell in his study of Irish immigrants and Scottish political and radical movements in the first half of the nineteenth century. That study found substantial evidence for Irish involvement in such bodies but also noted that a great many, and I would contend probably the majority, of immigrants were involved in and/or concerned primarily if not solely with Irish nationalist politics.[4] This in a sense was always likely to exaggerate pre-existing anti-Irish and anti-Catholic antagonisms in Scottish society because Irish nationalism represented not only a challenge to the integrity of the British Empire, but its presence in Scotland threatened violent tumult and civil unrest. Consequently, the Scottish reaction intensified Irish immigrant defensiveness, and the two peoples consequently became locked into a contest of identities, leading to further polarisation. Against this background the rise of Fenianism in Scotland was quite literally a potentially explosive element.

Although it has come to be used in a generic sense to describe militant Irish republicanism in the later nineteenth century, the term 'Fenianism' is most readily employed as a shorthand for the Irish Republican Brotherhood (IRB), founded in a Dublin timberyard in 1858. It appears to have arrived in Scotland within about a year of its establishment though the movement's perceived antecedents in the country are of some antiquity.[5] Pioneering works by Elaine McFarland and Martin Mitchell have clearly delineated an exiled Irish republican movement in Scotland of some size in the years after the 1798 rebellion. This body partially integrated itself into the Scottish radical movement and was partially submerged by the developing Irish immigrant secret society culture of Defenderism/Ribbonism.[6] This latter culture, it must be emphasised, was solely republican. It was a form of indigenous Irish nationalism shaped by ethnic criteria and focused firmly, though never exclusively, on opposing and attacking Orangeism.

From about 1863 the IRB had managed to impose a fairly ordered structure upon its organisation in Scotland and instead of scattered groups and enthusiastic individuals, various so-called 'circles', usually of no more than 100 men were established in all the major towns. In addition, larger urban centres such as Glasgow, Edinburgh and Dundee had district circles for areas such as the Gorbals, Anderston, the Cowgate and Lochee. The commanding officers or 'centres' of these circles also had extra tiers of various rank down to the humble private. Authority appears to have been based on military experience and popular leadership, and the Fenians in

4 M.J. Mitchell, *The Irish in the West of Scotland, 1797–1848* (Edinburgh, 1998).   **5** The idea of an Irish republican continuum stretching back to the 1790s attracted criticism from numerous historians but particularly R.V. Comerford in *The Fenians in Context* (Dublin, 1985), and T. Garvin in *The Evolution of Irish Nationalist Politics* (Dublin, 1981). A recent study, however, by A.M. Breen, *The Cappoquin Rebellion 1849* (Suffolk, 1998), has greatly elaborated on the themes of continuity of personnel and ideology from the Young Irelanders to the Fenians brought out in the early work of M. Bourke, *John O'Leary* (Tralee, 1967).   **6** E.W. McFarland, *Ireland and Scotland in the Age of Revolution* (Edinburgh, 1994); Mitchell, op. cit.

Scotland who held leading positions in the 1860s were or had been involved in either volunteer corps or had served with the US Army.[7] An agenda was never explicitly developed, but the IRB in Scotland were more concerned with fostering insurrection in Ireland than attempting disruption, sabotage or violence in Scotland itself. Nevertheless, as McFarland has illustrated, the very presence, secrecy and perceived threat of Fenianism created a 'moral panic' of some proportions in mid-Victorian Scotland. This reached a crescendo in the wake of incidents in England such as the 'Smashing of the Van' escape in Manchester, and the failed escape attempt and explosion at Clerkenwell in 1867.[8] This high profile was not however maintained. By 1870, with arms siezures in Glasgow, the arrest of Michael Davitt, the execution and emigration of several prominent Fenians, and a general malaise following an attempted re-structuring after 1868, the Fenian movement was apparently in decline.[9] It is important to realise that the Fenian movement was not as monolithic as it is generally represented. From the foundation of the IRB Supreme Council governing body in 1868, the movement, broadly speaking, contained three quite distinct identities: namely traditionalists, reformists and Ribbonmen. An understanding of these tendencies is necessary to trace the origins of the fissures which opened up within Fenianism during the 1880s and 1890s.

The collapse of the 1867 insurrection followed by failed attempts to renew the struggle had left the IRB with a legacy of disappointments and divisions over personalities, strategy and finances.[10] But from the early 1870s a more formalised structure and ideology gave the IRB some stability and authority. This coincided with the rise of a Home Rule movement which won increasing public support, largely at the expense of Fenianism which could offer little as an alternative. It was therefore at this juncture and as a result of past failures alongside future challenges that the Fenian movement in Scotland presented its three faces. The first were the IRB traditionalists – those men wedded to the all or nothing ideal of complete separation from Britain, through armed insurrection. Second were the reformists who challenged the efficacy of the physical-force and conspiratorial tradition, arguing for an 'open' movement and a whole-hearted cooperation with the emergent Home Rulers. The third element were the Ribbonmen who had been part

7 J. Rutherford, *The Secret History of the Fenian Conspiracy* (London, 1877), p. 296; J. Denieffe, *A Personal Narrative of the Irish Revolutionary Brotherhood* (1906; repr. Dublin, 1969), p. 204; S. Ó Lúing, *Fremantle Mission* (Tralee, 1965), pp. 13–14; National Archives of Ireland (NAI), Habeas Corpus Suspension Act (HCSA), 1866, Book ICR, Vol. II, p. 293, entry for Scottish IRB commander Michael MacLaughlin; and Mitchell Library (ML), Glasgow City Archives (GCA), Chief Constable's Letter Books, letter dated 28 February 1866 from Glasgow Chief Constable to District Superintendent A. McCall, Calton, E4/2/14; T. Bell, *Pioneering Days* (London, 1941), p. 94.   **8** E.W. McFarland, 'A reality and yet impalpable: the Fenian panic in mid-Victorian Scotland', in *Scottish Historical Review*, 77, 2: No. 204 (October 1998).   **9** T.W. Moody, *Davitt and the Irish Revolution 1846–82* (Oxford, 1981), p. 74; P. Quinlivan, P. Rose, *The Fenians in England, 1865–1872* (London, 1982), pp. 29–31; *Glasgow Herald*, 4 April & 3 June 1870.   **10** Comerford, op. cit., p. 145 & pp. 156–7.

of Fenianism since the movement began in the 1860s. Although intensely parochial and undistinguished by the national organisation and coherency of the Fenians, the Ribbonmen did represent a quite specific tradition of their own, combining elements of an agrarian egalitarian, Catholic and nationalist ideal overlain with a strong animosity towards Orangeism. The Ribbonmen had deep roots in Scotland's immigrant community and were able to integrate with Fenianism over many years.[11] They were divided over whether to support the traditionalists because of their attachment to the secret society culture, or the reformists whose work with the Home Rulers would allow Ribbonmen to resurrect their parading tradition and face down their Orange opponents on the streets. Ultimately, the Ribbon elements in the Fenian movement passed increasingly from the reformist into the Home Rule camp proper during the 1870s. This left the IRB traditionalists and the reformists to fight it out among themselves. The first round undoubtedly went to the reformists and an unwritten accord with Isaac Butt's Home Rule Confederation, reputedly for a trial period of three years, was agreed to by the Supreme Council.[12] The Council itself was split over whether this accord of toleration and non-interference rather than open support for Home Rulers should be brought into operation. The representative for Scotland, John Torley of Duntocher in Dunbartonshire, appears to have been against the accord while his deputy, Neal Fallon of Edinburgh was very much in favour, and it is therefore likely that the traditionalist-reformist split ran right down through the ranks of the IRB in Scotland.[13] Always tense, consensus collapsed entirely after the three year time limit and was followed by widespread attacks, some of them physical, by the traditionalists on both the reformists and Home Rulers. However, the subsequent rise of Charles Stewart Parnell and a more dynamic and aggressive Home Rule organisation replaced confidence in the movement and neutralised the threat of militant action. In retreat and facing isolation the IRB, also under pressure from influential Fenians in America, decided again to compromise with the forces of constitutional nationalism and the growing land agitation movement under Michael Davitt.[14] Agreement was forced and fragile however, and Davitt himself was expelled from

11 Ibid., p. 204; T. Garvin, 'Defenders, Ribbonmen and others: underground political networks in pre-famine Ireland'; M.R. Beames, 'The Ribbon societies: lower class nationalism in pre-famine Ireland', both in C.H.E. Philpin (ed.), *Nationalism and Popular Protest in Ireland* (Cambridge, 1987); McFarland, 'Fenian panic', op. cit., p. 205; Public Record Office (PRO), Colonial Office Papers, Reports, 1839–41 by P. McGloin on Ribbonism in Scotland, CO/904/8.   **12** T.W. Moody, L. Ó Broin, 'The IRB Supreme Council, 1868–78', in *Irish Historical Studies*, 9 (March 1975), p. 290; D. Thornley, *Isaac Butt and Home Rule* (London, 1964), pp. 90–1; L. Ó Broin, *Revolutionary Underground* (Dublin, 1976), pp. 6–7. **13** Moody, Ó Broin, ibid., pp. 294, 320, & 329, note 22; *Irishman*, 10 & 24 January 1874. **14** *Glasgow Herald*, 21 September 1877; M. MacDonagh, *The Home Rule Movement* (Dublin, 1920), pp. 123–4; *Irishman*, 29 September 1877; *Glasgow Observer* 19 August 1905. The towns of Dumbarton and Hamilton witnessed serious clashes between IRB men and Home Rulers and their Ribbon supporters in 1877; Comerford, op. cit., pp. 226–8.

the Brotherhood in 1880 at a time when the group was losing many members to the Land Leagues. Pinned back once more to a tight conspiratorial network commited to insurrection yet doing little to activate it, and harking back to a mythical republican past, the IRB was becoming somewhat irrelevant. It was at this point that the dynamite men launched their dissident challenge to the sterile Fenian orthodoxy of the Supreme Council and its supporters.

Thus stood the IRB in the period immediately preceding the first dynamite campaign phase of 1881–6. I now want to give a picture of the IRB in Scotland at this time and in the 1890s. Its leader, John Torley (1852–97), was a second-generation Irishman from Duntocher, once a small village heavily populated by Irish immigrants and now forming part of greater Clydebank. His parents were originally from Newry, Co. Down and his father set up a small hawking enterprise selling delfware in the Scottish village in the years after the Great Famine. Torley's father was not himself a Fenian but both parents raised their child in an Irish nationalist atmosphere and Torley certainly never regarded himself as a Scot. He became a clerk and later cashier of a chemical works in Clydebank, and married the manager's daughter, also of Irish extraction.[15] It seems likely that John Torley joined the IRB in Paris in 1869 after seeking out the organisation's exiled leaders. He thus became involved at the time of the Brotherhood's restructuring and by 1873 at the age of twenty-one he represented Scotland on the Supreme Council (which saw itself as the de facto Provisional Government of the Irish Republic in waiting). Torley never had command of more than a few thousand men and this declined as members drifted into the Home Rule camp as well as onto the transatlantic emigrant ships throughout the 1870s. He did, however, appear to establish a close and cordial relationship with the Belfast radical John Ferguson, who led Glasgow's Home Rulers and was for more than a generation the most prominent of all Scotland's Irish nationalists.[16] This alliance undoubtedly eased tensions between the two streams of Irish immigrant politics and allowed a mutual respect to grow up between Torley and Ferguson.

Torley also helped develop the IRB's various 'front' societies during the 1870s. These mainly commemorative groups allowed IRB circles to meet regularly, privately conduct their affairs (when meetings ended), but also formulate a public face which articulated the physical-force separatist alternative to Home Rule. The most notable of these was the Young Ireland Society, branches of which sprung up under IRB patronage in a number of Scottish towns soon after its Dublin foundation in 1881.[17] Such societal nationalism was fairly mild and conservative, and for some disenchanted IRB members it represented a drift into nostalgic retrospection and

15 *Glasgow Observer*, 4 April 1897; and the *United Ireland*, 3 April 1897; private information donated by P.G. Torley, Clydebank, 1994. 16 *Glasgow Observer*, 7 January 1888 & 18 February 1893; J. Devoy, *Recollections of an Irish Rebel* (New York, 1929; repr. Shannon, 1969), p. 317. 17 PRO, Colonial Office Papers, Secret Societies Reports, CO/904/16, p. 301/1 & p. 301/2; Ó Broin, op. cit., pp.36–7.

inactivity. It may just have been however, that this Fenian preoccupation with the past and an allied emphasis upon Gaelic culture which was increasingly popular amongst Irish immigrant communities merely reflected the changing social structure and priorities of the IRB.

Consistently composed of young men from the industrial working class, miners, ironworkers and labourers, for example, the IRB from the mid-1870s appears to have included, at least at leadership level, a more skilled working class and even lower-middle class profile. Apart from Torley himself, the prominent Scottish IRB officers featured a journalist, a whitesmith, a mason builder, a house painter and ship's carpenter, while by the 1890s Torley's staff included a publican, a smith, a master tailor, an insurance agent, a cabinetmaker and a tobacco spinner.[18] Many of these men lectured to the Young Ireland Society on Irish history and literature, and they were an articulate and well-read group. Most had an interest in politics generally and some involved themselves in Scottish municipal affairs in addition to the many bodies, from the Irish National Foresters to the C. Reunion Committees, to which Irish immigrants were drawn.[19] This diversity of interests may be explained by the Fenian strategy of 'entryism', through which IRB men sought to extend their influence and win recruits. The Young Ireland Society itself was very open about wishing to attract nationalistic young immigrants and it meant to select the most promising for the Brotherhood while acting as a sort of revolutionary 'hedge school' for those who had newly joined. It is true to say though, that the IRB at this point in its history was in a sort of 'silent running' mode – merely seeking to politely posit an alternative to Home Rule, maintain a physical-force tradition, and await an opportunity to take to the field once again in another insurrectionary venture. In Scotland, its main illegality only extended as far as purchasing and smuggling small quantities of arms and ammunition to Ireland, and the occasional drill exercise.[20] This was not enough for a number of IRB men and other non-aligned Fenians who were impatient of the organisation's drift into more pedestrian pursuits and radicalised by the tensions and passions released during the Land War.

18 New Register House (NRH), Registrar General's Office (RGO), Register of Births, Deaths and Marriages (Scotland), Death Certificate 1936, Registration District 564/1, Entry No. (140), Death Certificates 1900, 644/8 (702), 1902, 573/1 (1097), 1916, 644/4 (395), 1914, 647 (56), 1948, 574 (73), Marriage Certificate 1876, 685/5 (23), Death Certificate 1922, 558 (114); Census of Scotland 1881, Registration District 644/9, Enumeration Book 89, entry for Thos. Morris & family; and NAI, Crime Branch Special (CBS), S Files, reports dated 7 Nov. 1900 & 13 Dec. 1894, 23367/S & Dec. 1894, Special Precis, Box 1.   19 NAI, CBS, S Files, report dated 7 Feb. 1905, 29995/S. The case of Glasgow IRB man Pat Scullion is not untypical: he was vice-president of Cumann na nGaedheal, a member of the Ballieston IRB circle in Glasgow's suburbs, secretary of the local Ancient Order of Hibernians, a member of the Gaelic League branch, and a local Gaelic Athletic Association stalwart. John Torley was a Dunbartonshire C. Councillor, and at least two senior Glasgow IRB men, Bernard Havelin and Pat Mulheron were involved with the Independent Labour Party in Anderston and the Calton districts of Glasgow respectively.   20 NAI, CBS, S Files, report dated 20 March 1895, 9775/S; and *Scottish Weekly Record*, 30 May 1903.

The origins of the 'dynamite policy' as it was euphemistically termed, are to be found in Irish America. Two men were to feature prominently in its dissemination but their actions were in many ways merely individual responses to an experience shared by many Irish Americans in the mid-1870s. When economic depression became acute in America by 1877, the Irish immigrant community markedly came to take a greater interest in workplace struggles, class conflict and criticism of the debilitating effects of industrial society. This was perhaps most evident in the Molly Maguireism of the Pennsylvania coalfields where an agrarian secret society combining aspects of Irish nationalism, Ribbonism and a proto-trade union role provided a mechanism for resistance. This adaptation was connected to a need among the immigrants to use the familiarity of peculiarly Irish groupings against oppressions, real or perceived, in an unfamiliar environment. Such a 'return to the native' was but one aspect of what a number of Irish American historians have recognised as a wider retrenchment of identities and a more intense attachment to being Irish in response to declining American socio-economic conditions. Ironically, these perceptions of 'exile' and 'banishment' from Ireland turned emigrant resentment not on American society but British.[21] This orientation was partly a result of the efforts of Irish-American journalist Patrick Ford and the Fenian Jeremiah O'Donovan Rossa. Both men edited widely-read newspapers and Ford's backed a so-called 'Skirmishing Fund' launched in 1876 to gather subscriptions for a campaign supported wholeheartedly by Rossa (and his secret 'United Irishmen' group), aimed at various acts of sabotage and general destruction in Britain.[22] Control of the 'Skirmishing Fund' was a major area of contention among the various Irish American associations and individuals as the war chest grew with donations from Irish people throughout the world, including Scotland and England where the attacks were to take place. The money for a number of years though, was put to other uses including the liberation of Fenian prisoners from New South Wales and the development of a submarine for attacking British shipping.[23] But this changed dramatically in the first weeks of 1881 when the first explosion of the dynamite campaign took place at Salford Barracks in England, and the 'United Irishmen', known colloquially as 'the Skrimishers', were activated.

In the first phase (1881–7) of the 'dynamite war' within which different 'teams' of Fenian dynamiters regularly replaced those arrested or killed, two separate Irish American secret societies were active. The first was Rossa's so-called 'Skirmishers'

21 T.W. Moody, 'Irish-American nationalism', in *Irish Historical Studies*, 15: 60 (September 1967), pp. 438–9; J.P. Rodechko, *Patrick Ford and his search for America: A case study of Irish-American journalism 1870–1913* (New York, 1976), pp. 56–7, pp. 214–15 & pp. 272–3; J.F. Donnelly, 'Catholic New Yorkers and New York Socialists, 1870–1920', Ph.D. thesis, New York University (1982), p. 58; W.G. Broehl Jr., *The Molly Maguires* (Cambridge, 1964); and L. Adamic, *Dynamite: A century of class violence in America 1830–1930* (London, 1984), pp. 11–15. **22** S. Ó Lúing, *Ó Donnabháin Rosa*, ii (Baile Átha Cliath, 1979), pp. 61–70 & pp. 87–8. **23** W. O'Brien and D. Ryan (eds), *Devoy's Post Bag*, i (Dublin, 1948), pp. 207–11, pp. 292–3 & pp. 408–11; K.R.M. Short, *The Dynamite War* (Dublin, 1979), p. 45.

and these appear to have been led by an Irish American named James Moorhead about whom virtually nothing is known – even contemporary Fenians regarded him as a 'man of mystery'. The first activists involved with Moorhead's group were James McGrath, a young Glaswegian who worked as a steward on a steamship plying between Dundee and London, and a dock labourer from Warrenpoint in C. Down living in Liverpool called James McKevitt. Their targets were in the north of England and included Salford and Liverpool itself. Both were captured in 1881 after just a few months of their campaign and given heavy prison terms.[24] It is possible that McGrath was recruited in Glasgow by the senior Skirmisher there, an IRB veteran who was also a Ribbonman named John Francis Kearney. Kearney worked as a railway signalman at the Buchanan Street Railway Station in Glasgow and had become disillusioned with the IRB during the late 1870s. In America in 1880 he met O'Donovan Rossa and agreed to return to Glasgow to set up a dynamite squad of like-minded individuals from the IRB and the Ribbonmen disenchanted with Fenian inaction.[25] The result was the formation of a core group of about four men and a greater number of active sympathisers who supplied premises and helped obtain explosive materials. Aided by the expertise of Moorhead and another two Irish Americans, Edmund O'Brien Kennedy and John O'Connor, who all visited Glasgow throughout 1882, lignine dynamite bombs were manufactured and placed at three locations in the city on the night of 20 January 1883. All three – at Tradeston Gasworks on the south side of the city, Buchanan Street Railway Station, and Possil Road Bridge in the north, exploded or partially exploded causing some destruction and injury, but no deaths. The gasworks bomb blacked out a substantial part of the city while a goods shed was destroyed at Buchanan Street. The bomb in a hatbox at Possil Road Canal Bridge only partially exploded after a slightly inebriated off-duty soldier tampered with it. Had it fully detonated and destroyed the bridge, as well as the inquisitive squaddie, the resultant torrent of water from the Forth and Clyde Canal would have caused substantial damage including, perhaps purposefully as has been suggested, the predominantly Orange district of Oakbank Street, a scene of fierce party riots in 1880, which lay directly in its path.[26] A similar hatbox bomb detonated with more success at the London offices of *The Times* newspaper in March 1883 was later found to be the work of Moorhead aided by Terence McDermott, one of the

---

24 *Devoy's Post Bag*, i, p. 194, biog. note & ii, p. 343, biog. note; Short, *Dynamite War*, pp. 63–7 & 46–7. **25** *Irishman*, 24 February 1877; Trinity College Dublin Archives (TCDA), Michael Davitt Papers, Miscellaneous items on the Skirmishers, DP/AE 9381; *Devoy's Post Bag*, i, pp. 208–10; and J.T. McEnnis, *The Clan na Gael and the Murder of Dr. Cronin* (Chicago, 1889), p. 57. **26** Mitchell Library (ML), Glasgow City Archives (GCA), Chief Constable's Letter Book, letters dated 20 February & 3 March 1882 from Chief Constable Alex. McCall to C.H.E. Vincent, Scotland Yard, E4/2/44; Short, op. cit., p. 123 & pp. 104–5; *Glasgow Herald*, 22 January 1883; Handley, op. cit., p.274. I am indebted to Thomas Fyfe, Garngad, Glasgow for his theory on the choice of Possil Road bridge as a target with specific reference to the sectarian riots in the Garscube locality in August 1880.

Glasgow men. By the close of the year, however, ten Glasgow Irishmen had been arrested and convicted of the bombings, largely on the evidence of two informers, one of whom was Kearney himself. Five were given life sentences at Edinburgh High Court in December 1883 and five received terms of seven years each, though unlike James McGrath who died in an English prison in 1891, they all survived with the exception of one – Patrick McCabe who died in the insane ward of Perth Prison hospital exactly one day before he was due for release. The rest of the men did not count themselves overly lucky – two were prevented after their release from earning a living in Glasgow by a trade union and the Chief Constable respectively. All had suffered prison punishments of rations and solitary confinement, often merely for conversing with other prisoners, in the so-called 'zero cells' of Portland Prison (usually located beneath ground level). At least two became insane as a result of their experiences, one became blind and had both diseased eyes removed, while another was 76 years old by the time of his release. A pathetic epitaph to the case came when the wife of one of the men, James Kelly, wrote a barely literate letter to the founder of the Fenian Brotherhood, John O'Mahony, soon after Kelly's conviction, requesting £10 to help herself and her family make ends meet. O'Mahony had neither part in nor knowledge of the dynamite campaign, as he had died six years earlier in New York on 6 February 1877.[27]

In jail the Glasgow men joined a group which included an Irish American medical pratitioner born in Milton of Campsie, near Glasgow, already imprisoned for planning a separate dynamite campaign on behalf of the larger Irish American Fenian grouping, Clan na Gael (or rather a wing of that body which was divided over dynamiting). Clan na Gael also sent Fenian dynamiters to Glasgow but more apparently with the intention of using the city as a base of operations rather than a target, and they did not try to recruit locals, relying instead on Irish American activists to carry out the bombings.[28]

The second phase of the dynamite campaign was in some senses, less spectacular than the first despite a reputed explosion caused by dynamite at Glasgow's Dawsholm Gasworks in 1890.[29] It involved another batch of disaffected IRB men and possibly one or two members of the rejuvenated Irish National Invincibles (responsible for the 1882 Phoenix Park stabbings of the Chief Secretary for Ireland and his assistant). The Invincibles had a small group in Glasgow and working in

27 Short, *Dynamite War*, pp. 105–6 & 159; C.T. Couper, *Report of the Trial of the Dynamitards* (Edinburgh, 1884), pp. 141–93; *Glasgow Herald*, 17, 18, 19, 20, 21 & 22 December 1883; Ó Lúing, *Ó Donnabháin Rosa*, ii, op. cit., p.102; *Glasgow Observer*, 27 December 1890, 22 October 1892, 1 April 1899, 22 August 1896 & 20 April 1895; T.J. Clarke, *Glimpses of an Irish Felon's Prison Life* (Dublin, 1922), pp.13 & 101; ML, GCA, Chief Constable's Letter Book, letter dated 14 September 1886 from Chief Constable Alex. McCall to unnamed source, E4/2/48; S. Pender, 'Fenian papers in the Catholic University of America: a preliminary study', in *Cork Historical and Archaeological Society Journal*, 82: 235 (Jan.-Jun. 1977), p. 129. **28** Short, *Dynamite War*, pp. 125–7, 131 & 134.   **29** A. Goldsmith, 'Glasgow on show and the boys in blue, 1888–1938', in *History Today*, 47: 2 (February 1997), p. 57.

tandem with Clan na Gael's European sister organisation, the Irish National Brotherhood, another dynamite campaign was planned. One of the leaders, Edward Bell (or Ivory) was already under observation when he arrived in Glasgow in 1896 to organise that city and was arrested soon after. At the same time police rounded up the other chief characters in the drama, including none other than John Francis Kearney, who had with an accomplice, set up a small dynamite factory in a rented apartment in the small Belgian town of Berchem, near Antwerp.[30] Kearney's involvement was highly suspicious given his past work with Scotland Yard's Special Irish Branch, and there was already a highly-placed *agent provocateur* involved with the Irish National Brotherhood. This casts serious doubt over the veracity of the Scottish mission which newspaper sources claimed was hatched with Russian Populists or anarchists on the continent to assassinate by dynamite both Queen Victoria and Czar Nicholas II when the latter landed at Leith before a visit to Balmoral. When the *agent provocateur* element was revealed in open court the subsequent cases brought against this group of dynamiters collapsed and the second and final phase of the dynamite policy came to a hasty and ignoble end.[31]

The so-called Glasgow dynamitards of 1883, consistently and somewhat incongruously identified as 'Ribbonmen', differed to quite an extent from the Glasgow IRB. Not only were they committed to a policy that the Brotherhood judged rash and dangerous, especially for the Irish communities in England and Scotland who would bear the brunt of retaliation from the host society, but their social background was crucially different. Most of the dynamiters were labourers with large families in poor circumstances, only one of the ten convicted was fully literate and five were completely illiterate. A number were regular applicants for relief from the Poor Law Board and they would have suffered considerable deprivation as a result of the 1879 recession. The Invincibles and Irish National Brotherhood men of the 1890s were similarly from poor backgrounds and unskilled occupations though their attachment to dynamiting was born out of a much clearer rejection of IRB conservatism and inertia.[32] Like the Irish in America, their collective response would have been an increased support for a form of Irish nationalism dedicated to attacking Britain in a very literal manner. Neither the Ribbonmen or the IRB, showed any likelihood of pursuing such a course and in fact, appeared both in the 1880s and the 1890s to be moving away from any form of direct action.

In Russia the failure of the Narodnik 'to the people' agitation of the early to mid-1870s created an impatience and frustration among many anarchist and nihilist elements within the Populist movement. Developments in the science and technology of warfare (and especially the creation of dynamite), greatly excited

30 *Devoy's Post Bag*, ii, pp. 342–4; M. Gonne McBride, *A Servant of the Queen* (Dublin, 1950), pp. 168–79. **31** *Glasgow Herald*, 15 & 16 September 1896; and NAI, CBS, S Files, report dated 14 September 1896, 12446/S. **32** Couper, op. cit., pp. 116–26; ML, GCA, Poor Law Relief applications 1879, D-HEW 17/206, p. 55208; 1880, D-HEW 17/228, p. 61132; 1881, D-HEW 10/462, p. 227; 1882, D-HEW 17/242, p. 66035 & 1889, D-HEW 10/381, p. 41.

these revolutionary factions, but they also possessed a powerful and sentimental idealised attraction towards the Russian *banditi* tradition and its many European counterparts. This made them view violence itself almost as inherently revolutionary insofar as it kept up a constant 'war of resistance' against the laws and precepts of bourgeois society. Thus anti-state and even some criminal violence appeared heroic and the heroic motif was a mobilising one among Russia's intellectual youth, especially when combined with the failures of the Narodnik experiment.[33] The sort of 'deed propaganda', as it was known, which they and others adopted in the 1880s and 1890s was, significantly, developed firstly by Italian anarchists. They also had a strong romantic attachment to what Hobsbawm famously refers to as 'social brigandage', which was rife throughout rural Italy. Little research has been done into the anarchist borrowings from the tradition of rural banditry, but we know that the mythologisation of the rural bandits was largely the realm of urban intellectuals – which the Italian 'deed propaganda' formulators mostly were. The forms of violent activity created a pattern contemporaneous with and closely resembling the *banditti*, and the anarchist Mikhail Bakunin with his brigand-praising theories of revolt all fed into the construction of 'deed propaganda' activism.[34]

Ireland, of course, had a strong and much more politicised tradition of rural banditry which had expressed itself in the Houghers of the early eighteenth century, the Whiteboys and the Defenders of the mid- to late eighteenth century, and the Ribbonmen of the nineteenth century. Each group was born out of the specific conditions of time and place but also in some respects, were an elaboration of the previous one, and as in much of continental Europe, were highly localised.[35] We already know that Ribbon elements became active in Fenianism at a fairly early stage but they brought their theories of action – their direct action methods – into the heart of the new movement. Most senior IRB men consistently resisted this influence and stuck doggedly to the Blanquist revolutionary methods favoured by most European democratic nationalist groupings. However the influence of the Ribbon tradition was inescapable, and manifested itself in the rural activist, as opposed to urban insurrection, strategy of the March 1867 rising. In addition, some of those activities which did take place in an urban setting were often characteristically Ribbon in character, for example the liquidation of informers, the sabotage

---

33 R. Wortmann, *The Crisis of Russian Populism* (Cambridge, 1967), pp. 81–6; J. Billington, *Mikhailovsky and Russian Populism* (Oxford, 1958), pp. 23 & 99–101; U. Linse, 'Propaganda by deed and direct action: two concepts of anarchist violence', in W.J. Mommsen & G. Hirschfeld (eds), *Social Protest, Violence and Terror in Nineteenth and Twentieth Century Europe* (London, 1982), p. 208. **34** D. Miller, *Anarchism* (London, 1984), pp. 94–108; R. Hingley, *Nihilists* (London, 1967), pp. 52–9 & pp. 81–3; Carl Levy, 'Italian anarchism, 1870–1926', in D. Goodway (ed.), *For Anarchism: History, Theory and Practice* (London, 1989), pp.27–8 pp.36–41; E.J. Hobsbawm, *Bandits* (London, 1972), pp. 13–21. **35** P. Alter, 'Traditions of violence in the Irish national movement', in Mommsen, Hirschfeld, op. cit., pp. 139–41 & 147–9; M. Beames, *Peasants and Power* (Brighton, 1983), pp. 93–7; T. Garvin, *Nationalist Revolutionaries in Ireland, 1858–1928* (Oxford, 1987), p. 34.

of communications in Liverpool and London, the shooting of policemen, and the Clerkenwell escape attempt by using a bomb.[36] It is noticeable though, that most of these incidents took place among the Irish in Britain, indicating a Ribbon influence there which was largely peripheral to Fenianism in Ireland, outside of agrarian outrages.

Obviously, the fact that a number of those Fenians involved in the dynamite campaign in Scotland came out of Ribbon tradition is relevant to their advocacy and practice of direct action methods. But it is more important, I believe, to realise that they were for the most part extremely alienated individuals on two separate levels. Firstly, they had severed ties with an IRB characterised by fairly mundane and cautious activism and thereby demonstrated their frustration with its societal nationalism and entryist political strategy. Secondly, drawn overwhelmingly from an Irish immigrant underclass which could find no 'caution prompt' in the poorer, brutal denizens of Glasgow's Irish quarters amid the filth, sectarianism, unemployment, crime and disease surrounding them, the dissident Fenians turned to dynamite as resistance by proxy to their heightened sense of exile.

This then, is why and how Fenianism fragmented in nineteenth-century Scotland and produced dissident elements who attempted to destroy the city in which they and their families lived. However, maybe that cannot be entirely answered by the historian without the help of people from other disciplines, but perhaps this article goes someway towards initiating that process.

36 H. Senior, 'The place of Fenianism in the Irish republican tradition', in M. Harmon (ed.), *Fenians and Fenianism* (Dublin, 1968), pp. 67–73; T. Garvin, 'Defenders', op. cit., p. 243; C. Townshend, *Political Violence in Ireland* (Oxford, 1983), p. 28 & 239; Comerford, op. cit., pp. 137–9, 148–50 & 158–60; Quinlivan, op. cit., pp. 11–12, 67–8 & 43–93; W.J. Lowe, 'Lancashire Fenianism, 1864–71', in *Transactions of the Historical Society of Lancashire and Cheshire*, 121 (1977), pp. 168–70, 172 & 176.

Landscape, place and memory: towards a geography of Irish identities in colonial Australia

LINDSAY PROUDFOOT

The continuing interest in the history of Irish emigration to Australia forms part of a wider academic engagement with the Irish diaspora, characterised by method-ological diversity and ideological debate. Calls for comparative analyses of the processes and outcomes of Irish emigration to different countries – which them-selves have not gone unchallenged[1] – point to a growing awareness of the need to situate Irish migrant experience, as indeed that of any migrant group, within the wider histories they shared with others. In Jan Ryan's words, the perceived need now is to explore the migrants' 'shared experience of a shared world' and avoid nar-row ethnic histories which 'exclude and contain' their subjects[2]. Even so, the diver-sity of the Irish migrant experience *per se* still exerts its own fascination, and in North America in particular, the burgeoning diaspora literature continues to explore the social, political, economic and – increasingly – gendered construction of Irish migrant experience in a wide range of historic material environments.[3]

In Australia, academic engagement with the nature and consequences of Irish immigration has undergone its own paradigmatic shift. Earlier work by various scholars, notably Fitzpatrick, MacDonagh, McClaughlin, O'Farrell, Reid and Richards[4] has established in broad outline the contribution made by nineteenth-

---

1 D.H. Akenson, *The Irish Diaspora* (Belfast, 1996); M. Campbell, 'Exploring Comparative Histories. The Irish in Australia and the United States' in R. Pelan (ed.), *Irish Australian Studies. Papers delivered at the Seventh Irish-Australian Conference, July 1993* (Sydney, 1994), pp. 342–53. 2 J. Ryan, 'Chinese Australian History' in W. Hudson and G. Bolton (eds), *Creating Australia, Changing Australian History* (St Leonards, 1997), pp. 71–8. 3 For example, B. Elliot, *Irish Migrants to the Canadas* (Belfast, 1988); C. Houston and W. Smyth, *Irish Migration and Canadian Settlement* (Toronto, 1990); Kerby Miller, *Emigrants and Exiles* (New York, 1985). See also volumes one to six in P. O'Sullivan (ed.), *The Irish World Wide. History, Heritage, Identity* (Leicester, 1992–6). 4 See for example, D. Fitzpatrick, 'Emigration 1801–70' in W. Vaughan (ed.), *A New History of Ireland. V. Ireland under the Union I. 1801–1870* (Oxford, 1989), pp. 562–622; *idem* (ed.), *Home or Away? Immigrants in Colonial Australia* (Canberra, 1992); *idem, Oceans of Consolation: Personal Accounts of Irish Migration to Australia* (Cork, 1994); O. MacDonagh, 'The Irish in Australia: A General View' in O. MacDonagh and W. Mandle (eds), *Ireland and Irish-Australia* (London, 1986), pp. 155–74; *idem*, 'The Irish in Victoria in the Nineteenth Century' in P. Jupp (ed.), *The Australian People. An Encyclopedia of the Nation, its People and their Origins* (North Ryde, 1988), pp. 578–82; T. McClaughlin, *Barefoot and Pregnant? Irish Famine Orphans in Australia* (Melbourne, 1991); *idem* (ed.), *Irish Women in*

century Irish settlement to the construction of Australia's demographic profile as a *congerie* of colonial 'settler' states. The Conventional wisdom suggests that the European 'settler' population rose from around 7,000 in 1800, twelve years after the 'First Fleet' under Captain Philip made its precarious landfall at Botany Bay, to approximately one million by 1858 and to around four million by 1905.[5] By contrast, recent estimates suggest that the indigenous population fell during the same period from a conservatively estimated minimum of between 200,000 and 600,000 ca. 1800 to no more than 93,000 by 1901, as a result of dispossession, casual European violence, systematic local warfare and imported diseases.[6]

Research on the Irish component within this particular demographic transition has emphasised the mechanisms, aggregate statistics and population characteristics of both free and penal Irish migration, as well as the experience of the Catholic majority among the migrants. Consequently, the likely numerical scale of the Irish migrant stream (about a third of a million between 1840 and 1914 – the number of 'Irish born' rising from *c*.46,000 in 1846 to *c*.228,000 in 1891), their relative distribution (mainly in New South Wales, Victoria and Queensland), and the assisted migrants' general 'ordinariness', low occupational status, regional origins in Ireland and gender distribution are reasonably well attested. So too, are aspects of the social, cultural and political role of the Roman Catholic Church, the one institution which is pre-eminently associated in the popular historical imagination with Irish Australian identity.[7]

If these broad demographic patterns are reasonably clear, their interpretation remains contested and subject to at least some of the discourses which inflect the production of Australian history in general. Chief among these as far as Irish Australian historiography is concerned are issues of ethnicity, religion and gender. In a complex and diverse literature, two characteristics stand out. First, the growing recognition of the need to augment earlier aggregate analyses and general readings of Irish Australian emigration with accounts that privilege the individuality and diversity of the emigrant experience. And second, the continuing emphasis

Colonial Australia (St Leonards, 1998); P. O'Farrell, *Letters from Irish Australia, 1825–1929* (Belfast, 1984); *idem, The Irish in Australia* (Sydney, 1986); *idem*, 'The Irish in Australia and New Zealand, 1790–1870' in Vaughan (ed.), *New History V*, pp. 661–81; *idem, Vanished Kingdoms* (Sydney, 1990); R.E. Reid, 'Aspects of Irish Assisted Emigration to New South Wales, 1848–1870' (unpub. Ph.D. thesis, National University of Australia, Canberra, 1992); E. Richards, 'Irish Life and Progress in South Australia' in *Irish Historical Studies*, 27 (1991), pp. 216–36. **5** Australian Bureau of Statistics, Canberra. For slightly lower estimates, see S. Macintyre, *A Concise History of Australia* (Cambridge, 1999), pp. 81, 110–11. **6** J.R. Short, *Imagined Country* (London, 1991), p. 127. Macintyre suggests the rather higher figure *c*.1788 of around 750,000. Macintyre, *Concise History*, p.14. **7** C. Kiernan, 'The Irish Character of the Australian Catholic Church' in Jupp (ed.), *Australian People*, pp. 568–73; P. O'Farrell, *The Catholic Church and Community. An Australian History* (Sydney, 1985); *idem, Vanished Kingdoms*.

placed on arguably narrowly-defined and culturally-disabling notions of ethnicity as a major referent for Irish migrant behaviour.

Patrick O'Farrell's *Letters from Irish Australia, 1825–1929*, published in 1984, was the first in a series of anthologies which sought to recover the detailed trajectory of individual migrant histories and explore their meanings through the textual analysis of migrant correspondence. It was followed by Clarke and Spender's *Life Lines* (1992), Fitzpatrick's *Oceans of Consolation* (1994), and Frazer Simons' *Tenants no More* (1996).[8] These studies represent a self-conscious departure from attempts at aggregate analysis, and a significant affirmation of the importance of the mental, social and material worlds inhabited by Irish migrants both in Ireland and Australia in accounting for their experience of emigration. Fitzpatrick in particular envisages migrant letters as a method of ritualised negotiation, which used formulaic greetings and content to deny the growing cultural distance which separated correspondents in Ireland and Australia, but which nevertheless still frequently portrayed imaginative evocations of 'home' which remained firmly grounded in Ireland.[9]

The individualism and sense of origins which characterise the migrant trajectories recovered in these anthologies have been mirrored in other recent readings of Irish migrant experience which have privileged the particular over the general. Reid's analysis of Irish assisted migration to New South Wales between 1848 and 1870 grounds this process firmly in the localities in Ireland where these people originated, while Malcolm Campbell has reiterated his call for a heightened awareness of the regional and cultural diversity of emigrant origins and experience in Ireland and Australia.[10] Similarly, accounts of female orphan migration and of the experience of Irish women migrants in Victoria and Queensland, as well as 'microstudies' of the Irish communities in Geelong, Gippsland (Victoria) and Adelaide have all contributed to the particularist turn in Irish-Australian historiography.[11] They predate but accord with Hudson and Bolton's recent assertion that 'mono-

---

8 P. Clarke and D. Spencer (eds), *Lifelines. Australian Women's Letters and Diaries, 1789–1840* (Sydney, 1992); P. Frazer Simons, *Tenants No More. Voices from an Irish Townland and the great Migration to Australia and America* (Richard, 1996); Fitzpatrick, *Oceans*; O'Farrell, *Letters*. 9 Fitzpatrick, *Letters*, pp. 535–627. 10 M. Campbell, 'The Irish in South West New South Wales: The Validity of a Regional Approach?' in O. MacDonagh and W. Mandle (eds), *Irish Australian Studies. Papers delivered at the Fifth Irish-Australian Conference* (Canberra, 1989), pp. 25–41; *idem, The Kingdom of the Ryans* (Sydney, 1997); Reid, 'Aspects'. 11 C. Macintyre, 'The Adelaide Irish and the Politics of St. Patrick's Day, 1900–1918' in Pelan (ed.), *Seventh Irish-Australian Conference*, pp. 182–96; McClaughlin, *Barefoot and Pregnant?; idem* (ed.), *Irish Women*; P. Morgan, 'The Irish in Gippsland' in P. Bull, C. McConville and N. McLachlan (eds), *Irish-Australian Studies. Papers delivered at the Sixth Irish-Australian Conference, July 1990* (Melbourne, 1991), pp. 120–35; R. Reid and C. Morgan, *'A Decent Set of Girls'. The Irish Famine Orphans of the 'Thomas Arbuthnot', 1849–1850* (Yass, NSW, 1996); P. Rule, 'Irish Immigration to Geelong: A Microstudy of Success and Failure' in Bull, McConville and McLachlan (eds), *Sixth Irish-Australian Conference*, pp. 201–16.

lithic' understandings of 'Australia' are no longer possible, and their call for studies which recognise the multiplicity (and by implication, instability) of historic identities which operated simultaneously at individual, local and national levels.[12]

If the individualism inherent in these studies represents a necessary corrective to the generalising assumptions of previous aggregate analysis, it may also have helped to destabilise the essentialist ethnic assumptions which have underpinned much of the discussion of Irish migrant identity and behaviour in Australia. The central tenets of this essentialist discourse are first, that the primary explanation for migrant behaviour is to be found, not in the material conditions the Irish encountered in Australia, but in their innate ethnicity, a view which Campbell argues also underpins the 'exceptionalism' of Irish-American historiography.[13] And second, that the only *authentic* Irish ethnicity was, by implication, Gaelic and Catholic. The epistemological status of these assertions has rarely been considered, and the assumption of Gaelic/Catholic authenticity frequently accepted unreflexively as a 'given', though some recent studies, notably by Akenson and Payton, have begun to address its meanings.[14] Here we follow Ashcroft and Isajaw, and consider an ethnic group to be a population subset defined or set apart by itself and/or others, primarily on the basis of cultural or national characteristics. These include a common ancestral origin, shared cultural traits, traditions, language and social patterns; and a shared sense of 'people-hood' or group belonging, expressed in terms of experiences, consciousness of kind, memories and loyalties.[15]

When defined in these terms, it seems hard to assert that the Anglo-Irish and Scots-Irish minorities among the Irish migrants were less deserving of separate ethnic status than the Gaelic Irish majority. Although as migrants, these three groups shared a common origin in Ireland, they did not share a common ancestry there. Equally, while they might have been defined on occasion in Australia as a collective 'Other' – and been willing to accept this designation – they remained deeply conscious of their own defining localism and separate identities. And finally, above everything else, they remained divided by possibly the most powerful cultural referent of all: religion and its attendant narratives of empowerment and dispossession. Whether, in the end, this made the Anglo-Irish and Scots-Irish less *authentically* Irish, is entirely a matter for subjective judgement. We merely conclude

12 Hudson and Bolton, *Creating Australia*, pp. 2–18. **13** Campbell, 'Comparative Histories'. **14** D.H. Akenson, *Small Differences. Irish Catholics and Irish Protestants 1815–1922* (Dublin, 1988); *idem*, *Diaspora*, p. 112 ff; C. Cumming, '"In the Language of Ossian": Gaelic Survival in Australia and New Zealand – A Comparison' in *Australian Studies*, 12 [2] (1997), pp. 104–121; P. Payton, 'Re-inventing Celtic Australia: Notions of Celtic Identity from the Colonial Period to the Era of Multi-Culturalism' in *Australian Studies*, 12 [2] (1997), pp. 78–90. For a wider theorisation of representations of identity in Australia, see M. Dixson, *The Imaginary Australian. Anglo-Celts and Identity – 1788 to the present* (Sydney, 1999). **15** B. Ashcroft, G. Griffiths and H. Tiffin (eds), *Key Concepts in Post-Colonial Studies* (London, 1998), pp. 80–4.

that the migration stream from Ireland to Australia contained members of each of these three population groups who, while they were in many ways quite clearly distinguishable in ethnic terms, also shared a highly contested history in Ireland, which at times blurred and shaded their identities both there and, subsequently, in Australia.

It is therefore noteworthy that despite the well-attested evidence for significant Protestant Irish migration to Australia, much of the discussion of Irish Australian history continues to ellide their history with that of the Catholic majority. Protestants are estimated to have accounted for up to 45 per cent of Irish-born migrants in 1844–5 (in New South Wales), and by 1891 still numbered perhaps one-fifth of the total of c.228,000 Irish-born in Australia, yet their presence in the historiographical record remains curiously muted. Obvious exceptions include studies of various Anglican gentry families and of the Anglo-Irish in general, as well as the textual analysis of letters from Protestants in the migrant anthologies referred to above, but in general the non-Catholic Irish have attracted only generalised comment.[16]

The existence of these 'hidden histories' of Irish Protestant migration are an apt reminder of the silences and absences which inflect all attempts at historical under-standing. The remainder of this paper argues that in the case of Irish migration (of all descriptions) to Australia, one of the most significant silences relates to the geo-graphical construction of the clearly diverse identities this created in that country during the colonial period. While rejecting assertions of Gaelic Catholic ethnic authenticity in Ireland, the discussion recognises that this particular community nevertheless stood in a cultural relationship with British authority there which was not shared in its entirety by others. Accordingly, after considering first, how geo-graphical space might be implicated in general in the reproduction of Irish iden-tities in Australia, the paper concludes with an analysis of the implications for these identities of what has been argued to have been the 'colonial' relationship between Britain and Ireland up until the nineteenth century.

I

With the notable exception of Malcolm Campbell's *The Kingdom of the Ryans*, [17] scholars working on the history of Irish settlement in colonial Australia have eschewed detailed engagement with the geographical contexts in which it

16 G. Forth, 'The Anglo-Irish in Australia. Old World Origins and Colonial Experiences' in Bull, McConville and McLachlan (eds), *Sixth Irish-Australian Conference*, pp. 51–62; *idem*, '"No Petty People": The Anglo-Irish identity in colonial Australia' in P. O'Sullian (ed.), *The Irish World Wide. History, Heritage, Identity. Volume Two. The Irish in the New Communities* (Leicester, 1992), pp. 128–42; T. McClaughlin, 'Protestant Irish Settlement' in Jupp (ed.), *Australia People*, pp. 573–76; O'Farrell, *Irish Australia, passim.*   17 Campbell, *Kingdom.*

occurred. Rather, and on the basis of spatial statistical analyses that have gone largely unchallenged, conventional wisdom has it that Irish migrants were widely distributed throughout the settled areas as opposed to the outback, but showed no particular preference for agricultural districts. Moreover, while they might have been slightly under-represented in urban Victoria but over-represented in urban New South Wales between 1861 and 1901, they displayed no tendency to congregate in the sort of urban ghettos that characterised New York or Boston. The overall pattern has been variously explained in terms of social and geographical mobility and urban growth, but has also been held to reflect the Irish settlers' 'caution, prudence and good economic sense'.[18]

There are, however, considerable limitations to this formulation. It is based on the consensus that since by the late nineteenth century, the overwhelming majority of Irish migrants were Catholic, in the absence of census data relating to place of birth, data on religious affiliation can be used as a surrogate measure of the distribution of 'Irish' settlement. Figure 1 exemplifies this, and identifies those census enumeration districts where the number of Catholics exceeded 34 per cent of the recorded population in 1891. Whether it is acceptable as a representation of the distribution of *Irish* Catholics at that time depends, first, on the accuracy of this consensual estimate that around 80 per cent of Irish migrants were by then Catholic, and second, on the status of Macdonagh's assertion that the overwhelming majority of Catholics in Australia were Irish. Even if both these conditions hold true, the depicted distribution quite clearly excludes Protestant Irish settlement, and yet it was originally published as an acceptable surrogate representation of the distribution of the Irish in south-east Australia.[19] In reality, therefore, the map is culturally-disabling, and constitutes a form of erasure which reinforces the essentialist assumption of synonymity between authentic Irish ethnicity and Catholicism.

Moreover, there are sound reasons to suggest that this form of areal statistical representation is itself inherently misleading, and certainly does not support the thesis that Irish settlement was characteristically evenly distributed. This involves what has been termed an 'ecological fallacy',[20] the assumption that the population characteristic which is under consideration (in this case the proportion of Catholics), is uniformly distributed throughout the geographical space represented by each enumeration unit. This is plainly not necessarily the case. Figure 1 tells us nothing about the micro-geographies of Catholic settlement either in the enumeration units which it highlights, or in others where the *overall* proportion of Catholics was lower. We cannot determine from the threshold proportional statistic whether Catholics were concentrated in particular parts of any enumeration district, or whether they were indeed evenly spread across its entire area. Both outcomes are entirely plausible irrespective of the overall proportion of the

18 Summarised by Fitzpatrick, *Oceans*, pp. 16–18.   **19** Kiernan, 'Irish Character', p. 569.
20 D. Martin, *Geographic Information Systems and Their Socio-economic Applications* (London, 1991).

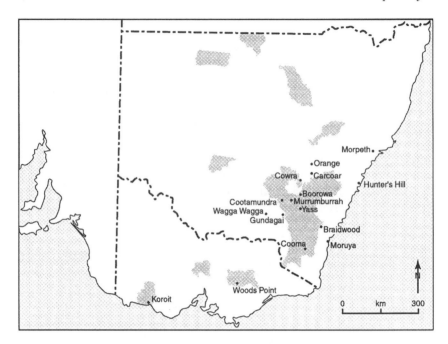

Figure 1. Census enumeration districts in south-east Australia recording over
34 per cent of the population as Catholic in 1891, after Kiernan in Jupp (ed.),
The Australian People (Sydney, 1988), p. 569.

population represented by the Catholic community, and both have significant –
and significantly different – implications for the *communitaire* construction of this
particular form of Irish identity in colonial Australia.

If this form of essentialist approach to the recovery of the geographies of Irish
Australia is problematic, more recent readings by cultural geographers of the ways
in which individuals and communities create, manipulate and 'consume' space, may
offer further elucidation of what geographers would claim to be the defining spatiality of Irish (as indeed of all) identities there (as elsewhere), and thus go some
way to end the geographical 'silence' alluded to above. The emphasis in these readings has been on the unstable, not to say ephemeral nature of these spaces, and on
the complex, multi-faceted meanings they convey to those whose lives are imbricated in them. Central to this analysis is the belief that individuals occupy not only
materialist or physical space, but also – continuously and simultaneously – a complex variety of other, ever-changing, socially-constructed abstract spaces – ethnic
space, religious space, political space, economic space and so on. Crucially, it is the
meanings which individuals invest in these spaces, and which they contest and
reproduce in a continuous process of self-identification, which provides a sense of
'rootedness' or 'rootlessness' to their individual and collective identities.

Fundamental to this rereading of the relationship between space and identity are the related concepts of 'landscape' and 'place', which are argued here to offer a *trope* through which the detailed textures of the everyday spaces inhabited by Irish migrants of all ethnicities might be recovered and their invested meanings read. Following Althusser, landscape has been conceived of by the Duncans, Williams and others as a socially-constructed 'text', which encodes the prevailing system of signifying symbols (or culture) through which the world is experienced and the prevailing social order communicated, reproduced and explored.[21] As cultural practice, therefore, landscape is also thoroughly implicated in the processes of social and economic reproduction, since these both shape and are shaped by it.[22] Accordingly, landscape can be deconstructed to reveal the continuously emerging power relations or ideology which underpins the prevailing social order. In the case of nineteenth-century Australia, this ideology was that of the capitalist-driven colonialism which, in progressively modified form, constituted the immediate and specific expression of British imperial engagement there. When construed in these terms, the socially-constructed landscapes of nineteenth-century Australia might be read for evidence of the economic, social and political power relations which were implicit in the reproduction of British imperial interests, and in the tense and ambiguous core-periphery relationships which characterised the progressive delegation of metropolitan authority to individual colonies after the establishment of responsible government between 1855 and 1890.

But implicit in this decoding is the assumed existence of subordinate as well as hegemonic groups or 'textual communities'. These textual communities 'cohere around shared visions, languages and codes of practice'[23] and thus share a common understanding of landscape's textual content, and order aspects of their lives in compliance with or resistance to the prevailing ideology. The landscapes representing these hegemonic values are therefore never entirely innocent, but always contain the potential for encoded subterfuge geographies of resistance. In the context of colonial Australia, this concept of landscape as a terrain of resistant alterity, encoding the values of subaltern textual communities, resonates strongly with contemporary and modern representations of the Gaelic Catholic Irish as a colonial 'Other', who were viewed from the very beginnings of the colony as potentially subversive. According to O'Farrell, this projection of alterity eventually led to an essentially positive outcome, insofar as the Irish Catholics' peculiar sense of displacement and marginality led them to pursue social and economic objectives

---

21 The key text is J. and N. Duncan, '(Re)reading the landscape' in *Environment and Planning D: Society and Space*, 6 (1988), pp. 117–26. See also J.S. Duncan, 'Landscapes of the self/Landscapes of the other(s):cultural geography 1991–2' in *Progress in Human Geography*, 17 (1993), pp. 367–77; *idem*, 'Landscape geography, 1993–94' in *Progress in Human Geography*, 19 (1995), pp. 414–22; E.R. Hills, 'The Imaginary Life: Landscape and Culture in Australia' in *Journal of Australian Studies*, 29 (1991), pp. 12–27; R Williams, *The Sociology of Culture* (London, 1988). **22** C. Harris, 'Power, Modernity, and Historical Geography' in *Annals of the Association of Amercian Geographers*, 81: 4 (1991), pp. 671–83. **23** K. Anderson and F. Gale (eds), *Inventing Places. Studies in Cultural Geography* (Melbourne, 1992), Introduction, *passim*.

which, though they at first set them at odds with the English colonial elite, later acted as a major catalyst in the formation of what O'Farrell describes as 'an Australian national identity'.[24] In a such a reading, the meanings of resistance and alterity encoded in the landscape for and by Irish Catholics can be construed to have given way to more positive affirmations of power, as the abstract spaces defined by Irish Catholicism were renegotiated in ways which enhanced their centrality in the projection of Australian nationhood.

This conceptualisation of landscape as text is essentially generic, and thus we may talk of 'colonial' or 'imperial landscapes', of 'feudal landscapes' or 'landscapes of oppression' and so on. The constitutive relationship between landscape as text and the specific and the particular – the individual self and its experience of the world – has been envisaged in terms of 'place'.[25] Traditionally, geographers have conceived of 'places' as closed, static and essentialist micro-locations in physical space, as nothing more than a synonym for physical location. However, as sites of individual understanding and of the memory which forms part of this, places may be more usefully conceived of in ways which foreground the slippery relationship between the abstract and the material spaces created and consumed by individuals. Thus as material locales, places possess a topographical identity, but one which is ambiguous and only loosely bounded.[26] Moreover, as these material locales represent shared space, they are imbued with multiple and, as we have seen, continuously changing or emerging individually-constructed social and cultural meanings, geared to the signifying systems of the hegemonic and subaltern ideologies encoded in the textual landscape.[27] Through such places, individuals make sense of their world and create and seat their own sense of identity – their 'rootedness' in the world around them. Places, therefore, are held to be multivocal and possessed of no single authentic essentialist meaning, but are instead the sites of individually-constructed memories which are imbricated into multiple, overlapping, identities.

Figure 2 provides one example of how some of the individual meanings attached to place in the spaces of Irish Australia might have been signified. It depicts the cross raised over the grave of Timothy Twomey at Hamilton, Victoria. As the inscription attests, Twomey was born in C. Cork in 1830, and died, at no great age, at Barewood sixty four years later. The cross is remarkable for the complexity and seeming accuracy of its 'Celtic Irish' ornamentation, but is in fact not particularly unusual in its use of the Ring or Celtic cross design, nor in its attesta-

24 Most cogently stated in the Introduction to *Vanished Kingdoms*, p. xiv ff. **25** Recent geographical literature on the topic is usefully summarised in J. Nicholas Entrikin, 'Place and Region' in *Progress in Human Geography*, 18 (1994), pp. 227–33; *idem*, 'Place and Region 2' in *Progress in Human Geography*, 20 (1996), pp. 215–21' *idem*, 'Place and Region 3' in *Progress in Human Geography*, 21 (1997), pp. 263–8. **26** S. Daniels, 'Place and the Geographical Imagination' in *Geography*, 77 (1992), pp. 310–22; D. Massey, 'Questions of Locality' in *Geography*, 78 (1993), pp. 142–9. **27** A. Pred, 'Place as Historically Contingent Process: Structuration and the Time-Geography of Becoming Places' in *Annals of the Association of American Geographers*, 74 (1984), pp. 279–97.

Figure 2. Commemorative cross, Hamilton, Western Victoria.

tion of Twomey's place of origin. Jordan and Greiner have identified over eleven hundred Irish epitaphs from a sample of seventy-nine graveyards in Queensland, Victoria and New South Wales.[28] The particular significance of this cross, and of others like it, lies in the various meanings which may be ascribed to it.

The first and most evident of these meanings is the cross' testimony to one particular form of Irish identity. The cross was presumably erected shortly after Twomey's death in 1894, at a time when the 'Gaelic Revival' in Australia was creating a resurgence of interest in the Celtic language and in Early Irish material cultural forms in general among the Irish community. The Revival was not, however, simply a cultural celebration of the presumed antiquity of Gaelic Irish roots in pre-Norman Ireland; rather, it was also an expression of support for the thoroughly modern – and largely (though not entirely) sectarian – political project of Home Rule for Ireland. In these circumstances, the Twomey family's choice of a carefully-proportioned Irish High Cross of perhaps tenth or eleventh century design, lavishly decorated with intricate (and expensive) Hiberno-Norse strap-work, is unlikely to have been accidental. Rather, we may speculate (admittedly in the absence of direct proof), that it was intended as a commemorative assertion of Timothy Twomey's continuing sense of Gaelic and presumably Catholic Irishness. If this was indeed the case, it points to a Jansenist ambivalence in his own location of the self, something which has been argued by O'Farrell to have been widespread among Irish Catholic migrants. O'Farrell links this to what he describes as their deeply-rooted and intensely localist identities, and to the importance within this of a place-centred, 'Irish' funerary culture.[29] In Twomey's case, this statement of identity may be read as an assertion of the Gaelic Irish 'Other', all the more subversive and potentially destabilising because it was embedded in the spaces of Hamilton, the regional 'capital' and political hearth of the wealthy, anglophile, conservative 'squattocracy' of western Victoria.

II

Closer inspection of Twomey's High Cross reveals, however, that it is not altogether what it at first appears to be. While the proportions are those of a tenth- or eleventh-century cross such as the High Cross at Monasterboice, Co. Louth, the strap-work, but more particularly the absence of any figural Biblical decoration is much more typical of earlier crosses, such as the eighth-century example at Ahenny, Co. Tipperary.[30] However powerful its symbolism, Twomey's cross is in fact

---

28 T.G. Jordan and A. Greiner, 'Irish Migration to Rural Eastern Australia: a Preliminary Investigation' in *Irish Geography*, 27 (1994), pp. 135–42.   **29** P. O'Farrell, 'Landscapes of the Immigrant Mind' in J. Hardy (ed.), *Stories of Irish Migration* (Sydney, 1988), pp. 33–46; *idem*, 'Defining Place and Home. Are the Irish Prisoners of Place?' in D. Fitzpatrick (ed.), *Home or Away? Immigrants in Colonial Australia* (Canberra, 1992), pp. 1–18.   **30** P. Harbison, *Guide*

a work of fiction: an inauthentic rendition of an imagined past. As such, it raises the issue of the *efficiency* of memory in the construction and reproduction of Irish identities of all traditions in Australia; and the character of the 'Ireland' or – more probably – 'Ireland*s*', which these memories invoked.

Recent analyses have suggested that although evocations of 'home' require an increasing act of the imagination among diasporic communities as time passes and generational shifts occur, they are nevertheless capable of retaining a very power-ful, if increasingly illusory, symbolic message. Mcleod argues that migrant con-structions of the 'old country' become increasingly imaginary and discontinuous with the real location. The *idea* of the 'home country' becomes divorced and split from the *experience* of returning 'home', and thus 'home' becomes a mythic place of desire in the diasporic imagination, ever further removed in space and time from the migrant's real 'here and now'.[31]

This is certainly implicit in the imaginings rendered in Timothy Twomey's Cross. Its ellision of a complex archaeological reality indicates concern with the *idea* of an anciently-rooted Gaelic Irish past, rather than an engagement with the *reality* of its surviving material legacy. Yet as Maureen Strugnell suggests, the increasingly mythic quality of such evocations of home or identity does not nec-essarily diminish their importance as cultural references for subsequent generations of the diasporic community. Strugnell develops her argument in the context of twentieth-century Catholic Irish identities in Australia. She suggests that the mythic quality of evocations of 'home' in Ireland only served to heighten their potency for subsequent generations of this particular Irish diasporic community. Shorn of all ambiguity by the simplifying passage of time, they served to reaffirm the experiences of kind and collective consciousness that underpinned Gaelic Irish ethnicity. Strugnell concludes that these effects rapidly led to the re-invention of locally-born generations of Catholic Irish Australians as a notably essentialist Gaelic Catholic group, characterised by both Anglophobia and sectarian mistrust.[32]

Central to Strugnell's argument is the idea that the Catholic Irish in Australia defined themselves as a community in relation to the 'Otherness' of English and Protestants, and this invites consideration of the possible sources of this 'Otherness' in the migrants' origins in Ireland. Put simply, the question is what sort of 'remem-bered Irish past' drove the construction of Irish identities of all descriptions in place and landscape in Australia? And what was there about the allegedly 'colonial' past in Ireland, with all its connotations of alien domination and indigenous subordi-nation, which might explain the sense of Self and Other encountered by Strugnell?

Although there are strong historical arguments against representing the rela-tionship between England and Ireland in formal colonial terms, it nevertheless

to the National Monuments of Ireland (Dublin, 1975), pp. 16–17. **31** J. Mcleod, *Beginning Postcolonialism* (Manchester, 2000), pp. 208–11. **32** M. Strugnell, 'It's a Long Way from Home: Irish Exiles in Australian Drama' in Pelan (ed.), *Seventh Irish-Australian Conference*, pp. 111–19.

effected seemingly 'colonial' cultural outcomes in the creation of an unevenly divided pluralist society in Ireland. Although historians have stressed, first, that English policy towards Ireland during the sixteenth and seventeenth centuries was marked more by opportunism, inconsistency and incoherence then by any colonial master-plan; second, that significant feelings of colonial difference were notably absent in Ireland during the eighteenth century; and third, that the Act of Union of 1801 spelt the end of any conceivably colonial relationship between the two countries, Ireland nevertheless still experienced unilateral colonisation by significant numbers of English and Scots.[33] This created a society which was divided along the multiple, but by no means conformable axes of language, religion, wealth and ethnicity, and in which the Catholic majority and their representatives were formally or informally excluded from political power from the early eighteenth to the early nineteenth centuries. Unsurprisingly, this led to a highly contested constitutional, political, social and economic relationship between the State and its citizens, both during the brief period of constitutional autonomy under the Crown in the late eighteenth century, and after the Act of Union with Britain in 1801. Despite, or perhaps because of, Ireland's accelerating but regionally-uneven pattern of modernisation and demographic change, this underlying dialectic continued to find overt cultural and political expression – either through complicity or resistance – throughout the nineteenth century.[34]

Whether formally colonised or otherwise, Ireland's ambiguous relationship within the Empire as Britain's constitutional yet culturally subordinate partner after 1801 seems to be appropriately captured by Mitchell's description of Imperialism at large. This, he notes:

> 'is not a one-way phenomenon but a complicated process of exchange, mutual transformation and ambivalence. It is a process conducted simultaneously at concrete levels of violence, expropriation, collaboration and coercion, and at a variety of symbolic or representational levels whose relationship to the concrete is rarely mimetic'.[35]

Central to these 'complicated processes of exchange, mutual transformation and ambivalence' in more unambiguously colonial situations was the interpellation or 'naturalisation' of the colonial ideology in the beliefs and mind sets of the colonised, for only in this way could the material practices of colonialism work.

---

33 These arguments are most recently summarised in S. Howe, *Ireland and Empire: Colonial Legacies in Irish History and Culture* (Oxford, 2000).   **34** In an extensive specialised and general literature, useful summaries may be found in K. Theodore Hoppen, *Ireland Since 1800: Conflict and Conformity* (London, 1989); D. George Boyce, *Nineteenth-Century Ireland. The Search for Stability* (Dublin, 1990); and C. Ó Gráda, *Ireland. A New Economic History 1780–1939* (Oxford, 1993).   **35** W.J.T. Mitchell, *Landscape and Power* (Chicago, 1994), pp. 9–10.

This 'colonisation of the mind' among the Empire's subjects involved both alterity, the 'Othering' of groups who would not be complicit in the business of colonisation, and flattering invitations to (near-) 'selfhood', as other groups among the colonised were invited to participate in this.[36] In Ireland, the bitterly-contested issue of land rights and agrarian reform, the gathering pace of democratisation and the growth of sectarian politics, and the changing and unstable geographies of identity bound up with the regionally-uneven processes of industrialisation, modernisation and urbanisation, all point to the existence of analogous patterns of individual and collective collaboration and resistance, assimilation and alterity, and provided the context for emigration.[37] Quite how far these conditions were echoed in the spaces of meaning created by Irish migrants in Australia has yet to be fully assessed. But they bear witness to the individualism and diversity of the Irish identities which were bound up in the emigration process, and to the uneven spaces of meaning in Ireland from which these were derived.

This paper has argued for a new spatial awareness in the exploration of the symbolic identities that attached to Irish settlement in colonial Australia. Its central thesis has been that any understanding of the human condition demands recognition of its inherent value-laden abstract spatiality. It has demonstrated the limitations to essentialist ethnic representations of Irish migrant identities, and proposed that concepts of 'place' and 'landscape' which privilege the multiple and unstable meanings with which we invest the everyday spaces of our lives, provide an appropriate *trope* through which the complex abstract and material geographies created by Irish migrants to Australia might be recovered. In this way, we might hope to contribute to what Stuart Macintyre has called the reworking of an 'inescapably present' Australian history, which 'provides a capacity to determine what still might be'.[38]

The author wishes to acknowledge the generous funding provided by the British Academy for the research in Australia on which this paper is based.

---

36 Mcleod, *Beginning*, pp. 37–40.   **37** Hoppen, *Ireland, passim;* Boyce, *Nineteenth-Century Ireland, passim.* See also G. Hooper and L. Litvack (eds), *Ireland in the Nineteenth Century. Regional Identity* (Dublin, 2000).   **38** Macintyre, *Concise History*, p. 280.

Worlds apart: the Anglo-Irish gentry migrant experience in Australia

IAN McCLELLAND

> Throughout all Australia, there is a sympathy for the ideal of a gentleman. This gives a moral aristocracy. Sustain it by showing a store set on integrity, honour and civilised manners; not by preferences of birth, which belong to old countries.[1]

The continuing interest in the role of Irish migration in the historical construction of an Australian identity (or, as scholars would more recently have it, identities), has produced a wide-ranging and extensive literature. However, until recently, this has been dominated by discussion of the Catholic majority within the Irish migrant stream thus marginalizing other religious groups such as presbyterians, methodists and anglicans.[2] As this implies, religion continues to be accepted as an adequate surrogate for ethnicity in Irish-Australian studies while considerations of class as another factor determining the nature of Irish experience in colonial Australia have only rarely been considered.[3] On both counts, one group which has largely been ignored in chronicles of Irish migration and settlement is the Anglo-Irish gentry. In terms of the English gentry, Bolton has argued that despite the fact that they wielded a dominant share of social and political power in Great Britain, at least until the early years of the twentieth century, their younger sons did not migrate in sufficient numbers to have a direct influence on the structure and development of any colonial society within the Empire.[4] Moreover, he argues that even where significant numbers of gentry did migrate, the distinctions between them and other classes tended to become blurred and shaded following their arrival overseas. In Australia this view is disputed. Forth and Kiddle, for example, both suggest that there was a *marked* distinction between 'ordinary' assisted migrants and the minority of gentry migrants to colonial Australia in terms of their instrumental role within society.[5] Although these divisions were not always immediately obvious at

1 Letter from Edward Lytton, Secretary of State for the Colonies, to Sir George Bowen, the governor-elect for Queensland, 29 April 1859 in S. Lane-Poole *Thirty Years of Colonial Government: a selection from the dispatches and letters of the Rt. Hon. Sir George Ferguson Bowen, G.Co.M.G., &c'* (London, 1889), p. 62. 2 D.H. Akenson, *The Irish Diaspora* (Belfast, 1996), pp. 91–122. 3 P. de Serville, *Port Phillip Gentlemen* (Oxford, 1980), pp. 13–34. 4 G. Co. Bolton, 'The Idea of a Colonial Gentry', in *Historical Studies*, University of Melbourne 13: 51 (Melbourne, 1968), p. 307. 5 G. Forth, 'No Petty People: the Anglo-Irish Identity in

first glance, they may be argued to have had a profound effect on the whole nature of colonial Australian society throughout its development.

Many gentry migrants exhibited both social and political leadership in the colony and were prominent through their work as government officials, business-men, industrialists, politicians and pastoralists. Similarily, although the Anglo-Irish gentry constituted a very small minority when viewed within the context of the entire Irish migrant stream, they also enjoyed a prominence within Australian colo-nial society beyond that which their minority status would have suggested. This distinction was partly attributable to the wealth and economic power wielded by these migrants as well as to their superior educational background. Through this power base they obtained prominent roles in Australian society and, as a result, the legacies of many are still visible throughout the Australian landscape. To assist in the examination of the Anglo-Irish gentry migrant's role in colonial Australia we must first determine who the Anglo-Irish gentry were, the number who came to Australia, their contribution to the development of Australia's nationhood and the extent of the relationship between their cultural identities and the surrounding cultural landscape.

In terms of definition, the phrase 'Anglo-Irish gentry' is highly subjective. The majority of Anglo-Irish gentry migrants were defined by their social class, wealth or landholding. However, although many statistics are available for assisted migrants to Australia between 1840 and 1900, there are virtually none which relate specifi-cally to gentry migrants. The main reason for this is that most of the gentry migrants paid for their own passage to Australia while assisted migrants relied on some sort of financial aid either from the imperial or colonial government or from their landlord. Consequently, fairly meticulous, though not unproblematic, gov-ernment records are available to ascertain the developing nature and context of the assisted schemes. The gentry, on the other hand, had barely more than their name recorded on a ship's passenger list and, upon arrival in Australia, their name listed as an arrival in the colony – itself a standard procedure for all arrivals of every class. Although the gentry were unassisted migrants, they were not synonymous with these, as there were other 'ordinary' migrants who also arrived in Australia unas-sisted. Moreover, due to the subjectivity of the definition of the Anglo-Irish gen-try it should be remembered that any emigration statistics that do exist for gentry migrants tend to be fairly speculative and are often predominantly based on land ownership records, as a large number of these migrants established pastoral runs across the Australian countryside.

Colonial Australia', in P. O'Sullivan (ed.), *The Irish in the New Communities* (London, 1992), pp. 128–42; M. Kiddle, *Men of Yesterday* (London, 1961).

I

Upon arrival in Australia, Anglo-Irish gentry migrants gravitated towards various social and cultural milieux and occupational 'worlds'. At one extreme there were squatters, men like Mervyn Archdale, originally from Castle Archdale in Co. Fermanagh and James Moore from Dublin, who took up land with Charles James Griffith from Co. Kildare. Others included Hugh Glass from Portaferry in Co. Down and Charles Augustus Von Stieglitz from Co. Tyrone. These men took up leases of many thousands of acres of land and ran extensive pastoral enterprises. At the other extreme, some gentry entered the colonial bureaucracy and established themselves in public life as lawyers, barristers, or politicians. For example, migrants like Thomas Strettel Clibborn from Co. Westmeath was secretary of the Australian Jockey Club (*c*.1873), while Sir William Foster Stawell from Co. Cork, was chief justice of Victoria from 1857 and Sir Robert Molesworth from Dublin was a prominent judge. Others dwelt in both domains combining life as pastoralists with work in the public sphere as bureaucrats. In some cases, such as that of Thomas Budds Payne from Co. Carlow, the transition from pastoralist to lawyer was part of on-going career progression, while some gentry members such as Acheson French from Co. Galway maintained their pastoral interests, also undertaking employment in the colonial bureaucracy, becoming, in his case, a local police magistrate.

According to De Serville, property was the economic prop of gentility and thus pastoralism – 'squatting' – attracted men from all ranks of society in both Britain and the other colonies. These well-to-do economic migrants included younger sons of the aristocracy and gentry, army and navy officers, clergymen, lawyers and doctors as well as young men with capital but no occupation.[6] Indeed the whole concept of squatters ran deep in the Australian psyche as many regarded them as the essence of colonial Australia and the embodiment of the colonial experience. Along with other iconic figures such as bushmen and diggers, squatters were seen as the quintessential colonial Australian. Even in the words of Australia's de facto national song, 'Waltzing Matilda', the squatter denoted property, style and prosperity:

> Up rode a squatter, mounted on his throughbred;
> Down came the troopers, one, two, three . . .

Thus, not only did squatters span the history of 'White' Australia from the arrival of the first sheep to the emergence of the modern developed country in the twentieth century, but they have also figured in public constructions of Australia's past as heroic and romantic figures who 'discovered' the land, settled it through some danger to their own lives and regularly experienced hardships such as drought and bushfires, all to produce enduring and renewable wealth. However, in the 1860s public sentiment turned against them when anti-squatting feeling found expres-

6 De Serville, *Port Phillip Gentlemen*, p. 82.

sion in the Land Selection Acts passed by Victoria, New South Wales, Queensland and South Australia between 1861 and 1869. These represented an ultimately unsuccessful attempt to create a class of agricultural smallholders, as much in response to the perceived inequalities of the developing monopoly of landowner-ship as any realistic appraisal of the agricultural potential of the land itself.

Amongst the squatters themselves, however, there were deep and still frequently unrecognised social divisions. These were highlighted by Captain Foster Fyans, a military officer originally from Dublin who was appointed Crown Lands Commissioner in 1840.[7] His classification of the squatters is revealing. First, there were the gentlemen squatters, then the 'shopboys' who were rich and successful men but who lived in primitive squalor with little or no regard for comfort and status; and finally shepherds and other servants who had grown rich over time, and were eventually able to buy out their masters. However, Fyans himself was a mem-ber of the Irish landed gentry and his opinion on the matter was undoubtedly biased. Of all these groups only the gentlemen squatters earned his respect. In his view, 'many of the squatters are gentlemen, worthy and excellent men, of undoubted character and well connected at home.'[8]

For other Anglo-Irish gentry migrants, the colonial bureaucracy offered an alternative form of employment. For some such as Sir Robert Molesworth (1806–90) and George Higinbotham (1826–92), their careers in Australia as judge and chief justice were a natural progression from their previous employment in Ireland. Molesworth had been called to the Irish Bar in 1828 and Higinbotham to the English Bar in 1853. Whether such men migrated to Australia purely in order to increase their prospects in life is uncertain, but it is reported that Higinbotham migrated because he felt that as a barrister at home he saw 'little reason to hope for advancement in his profession, or even for any work at all in it.'[9] Like many of his contempories in the 1850s, Higinbotham's original intention had been to make his way to the gold fields to seek his fortune but once he landed in Melbourne, work at the Bar offered itself in abundance and his previous aim was forgotten.[10]

II

Lowenthal and Bender[11] have argued that in many settler societies, ideological notions of landscape and identity inherited from the 'mother country' were quickly discarded as migrants sought to establish a new ideological basis for the cultural landscapes being created in the 'new' country. For example, Lowenthal argues that newly independent Americans (of European descent) gloried in their felt lack of

7 Foster Fyans Papers 1844–1870, MS.10594, MSB.616, State Library of Victoria, Melbourne. **8** De Serville, *Port Phillip Gentlemen*, p. 84. **9** E.E. Morris, '*A Memoir of George Higinbotham*', (London, 1895), p. 29. **10** Ibid., p. 30. **11** B. Bender (ed.), *Landscape: Politics and Perspectives* (Oxford, 1993).

history and, seeing Europeans burdened by the past, rejoiced in their own supposed freedom from its shackles.[12] In Australia, similar conceptions have been addressed by O'Farrell, who argues that many early migrants also aspired to independence from Britain and shared the view that the new 'pristine' country they had arrived in was suitable for the construction of a new identity and landscape.[13] Arguably, the fact that many migrants may have aspired to create an identity and landscape separate to that of the Old World which they had left was a result of the circumstances surrounding their departure. Many had been transported and it is understandable that they may have felt a degree of resentment towards the motherland. Others who were voluntary migrants may also have felt that the very action of migration involved a new beginning and a new landscape. McCalman argues that for many 'ordinary' nineteenth-century migrants, emigration involved a deliberate and self-conscious act of 'erasure' as they sought to escape their 'embattled, impoverished or otherwise negative' experiences in the 'homeland'.[14]

It is thus debatable whether the intentions and expectations of ordinary migrants had very much in common with those of the gentry. Many of the latter, perhaps more familiar with the heritage of the Old World, seemed quite unprepared for the apparent lack of 'human' history in the Australian landscape. Some at least appear to have actively searched for significance in the landscape to connect them with the world they had left. As Morphy argues, they brought with them an 'old' past in the form of the distant landscapes they had experienced elsewhere and which influenced their conceptualisation of and attitude towards the 'new' land. That this was so is demonstrated by gentry migrants such as Charles James Griffiths (1840–63) who felt mixed emotions about the new country. On 23 November 1840 he wrote in his diary:

> The aspect of this country gave me I don't know why something the idea of the Co. of Meath everything about this country is done so much in the English style that I sometimes find it difficult to believe that I am in a foreign country. This I merely mention incidentally the hand of man being nowhere visible on these plains . . .[15]

This theme continues in his book *The Present State and Prospects of the Port Phillip District of New South Wales*, published in 1845. In the chapter dedicated to practical tips and hints for prospective migrants to Australia he wrote:

12 D. Lowenthal and M. Bowden, *Geographies of the Mind* (Oxford, 1976), p. 89.   **13** P. O'Farrell, *Vanished Kingdoms: The Irish in Australia and New Zealand* (New South Wales, 1990), pp. 1–21.   **14** J. McCalman, 'The Originality of Ordinary Lives', in W. Hudson and G. Bolton (eds), *Creating Australia* (St Leonards, 1997), p. 87.   **15** Diary of Charles James Griffith 1840–1841, MS 9393, State Library of Victoria, Melbourne.

> It was the custom amongst the ancient Greeks and Romans to carry with them, when they migrated, their household gods, their Lares and Penates, not more as the objects of religious observance, than as memorials of their former homes, and symbols of their national identity; and thus, in the spirit of this beautiful emblem, the old world customs and the polished usages of English civilization should be cherished round the hearth of the Australian settler, as momentos of the home of his fathers, and to identify his children with the race from which they are sprung.[16]

Thus, as with America, so too, Australia appeared to be a new land, unburdened by history and unhampered by forebears. To the European settlers the landscape was a blank canvas on which they could begin to build their nation. However, their 'white' landscape ideology was consciously ignorant of the fact that the land they were populating was already imprinted with the cultural landscapes of the indigenous population. The aboriginal population was neither white nor settled and as the landscape bore no marks of an agrarian society or an industrial order, consequently many of the early European settlers took it upon themselves to rid the land of the indigenous peoples in order to make the land profitable. Even though it has been estimated by Short that the total pre-contact Aboriginal population of Australia was between 200,000 and 600,000, the arrival of the European marked the end of their way of life as the white European invasion led to the loss of their land, the destruction of their culture and the superimposition of white economic and cultural power.[17] In the early decades of European settlement in Australia the aboriginal community was often used as a measuring stick against which the settler community could compliment their own achievements and their civility compared to the native 'savages'. However, it has only been in more recent decades that the aboriginal population has been given full recognition as a legitimate culture. With this gradual acceptance has come a substantial range of books and articles focusing on the history and culture of the indigenous community. Perhaps it is somewhat ironic that scholars are now suggesting that the discourse of the aboriginal community should no longer be narrated by others and instead should only be narrated by the aboriginal community themselves.

Yet for all this, compared with Europe, the new colonists found Australia a country untamed, a land which was scarcely lived in and a landscape which conveyed little sense of historical depth. Initially, mediated through its experience of Empire, Australia deployed British notions of culture, politics, nature and society as it began the process of nation-building but gradually these became blurred and hybridized as the relationship between the Australian state and the Imperial power took on a new and increasingly independent tenor.

---

16 Co. Griffiths, *The Present State and Prospects of the Port Phillip district of New South Wales* (Dublin, 1845), p. 132. **17** J.R. Short, *Imagined Country* (London, 1991), p. 127.

III

If, as suggested by Lewis, we accept that vernacular landscapes provide strong evidence of the kind of people we are, were, and are in the process of becoming, what can be said about the landscape surrounding the early colonial gentry settlers to Australia? Using Samuels biography of landscape as a basis, it is possible to argue that there is a strong bond between landscape and its authors. This 'biography of landscape' has as its central concern the role of individuals – authors – in the making of landscape. Its central geographical task is to follow through on Hartshorne's complaint that geographers, including those engaged in the study of 'decision making processes', have underestimated the importance of key individuals and thousands of lesser figures who have left the mark of their leadership on the geography of every country, even if their names are no longer known. This is probably the case for many of the early gentry settlers in Australia as either most of their records and traces have gone or else we are as yet unaware of the role they played in colonial society. However, the records of a substantial number *are* available and in many cases it is easy to see their roles at local and national level. One such man was William Rutledge (1829–76), originally of Co. Cavan who, although his influence was largely on a local scale, became something of a legend in the Western District of Victoria.

Little is known about Rutledge's activites in Australia between his arrival in 1829 and his visit in 1843 to the coastal town of Port Fairy, two hundred miles west of Melbourne. During this visit Rutledge bought a local merchant firm and acquired a Special Survey in the area. Special Surveys were introduced by the Colonial Office in London in 1840 as a means of opening up Australian land. Any person who paid the sum of £5120 into the Treasury could thereupon obtain an order to be given as many acres, or eight square miles in the colony. The main enterprise of Rutledge's new firm was shipping wool, tallow and, later, gold direct to London and importing all the necessities and luxuries required by the settlers. According to Irish gentry migrant and leading Australian politician Charles Gavan Duffy, Rutledge was a leading member of a 'Syndicate of Irish Gentry' and at one stage owned approximately 6,367 acres around Port Fairy. Regarded as a considerate landlord due to his provision of rations, seeds and implements for his tenants, it is likely that Rutledge either brought out families from Ireland to work as tenants on his farms or at least encouraged Irish men to rent them, as local maps show many of his tenant families had Irish names.[18] Most of these farms ranged in size from 150–200 acres. Rutledge's influence around Port Fairy was considerable and it was through his constant petitioning of the government that the land within a ten-mile radius of Port Fairy was declared a settled zone and a new county. Such petitions were frequent with Rutledge who bombarded government departments with letters complaining about the state of the roads, delays in the mail and peo-

---

18 M. Rutledge, 'An Australian Pioneer', in *Victorian Historical Magazine*, 36: 3., p. 110.

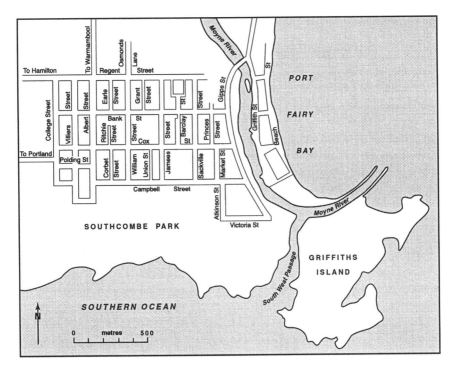

Figure 1. Map of Port Fairy

ple unlawfully occupying his land. His constant petitioning demonstrates the difficulties experienced by early governors in trying to rule from a distance men who, during their struggle against a harsh environment during the 1830s and 40s, were a law unto themselves.

With James Atkinson from Co. Armagh as a business partner, Rutledge decided to attempt to increase the size, wealth and importance of Port Fairy by improving its harbour, thus allowing the easy export of agricultural goods from the surrounding area. As Port Fairy was the only worthwhile port between Melbourne and Portland, and as the area around Portland was already dominated by the Henty family, Rutledge and Atkinson invested heavily. The local volcanic soils were very fertile and, in addition to this, the existing natural harbour was already suitable for trade with the whole of the western district of Victoria. The proposed township was laid out on a rectangular plan typical of colonial town planning in Australia, with streets running due east, west, north and south to form blocks of equal size. Rutledge and Atkinson renamed the settlement 'Belfast' after the city in their native Ireland. Visualising the town as a place of importance, with all the trappings of civilization, Rutledge and Atkinson granted land for churches and other buildings including a hospital, a cemetary, a town hall and several banks.[19] Town

19 J.W. Powling, '*Port Fairy: The First Fifty Years*', (Melbourne, 1980), p. 49.

promotion would not have been altogether unfamiliar to men of Rutledge and
Atkinson's background as similar activities had been undertaken by members of the
gentry in Ireland throughout the eighteenth and early nineteenth centuries.
Rutledge and Atkinson had hoped to encourage widespread emigration to the area
but this never materialised on the scale they had proposed, and although the town
experienced some success as a port it remained relatively small. The two local
newspapers, the *Banner of Belfast* and the *Belfast Gazette*, were opposed to Rutledge
and Atkinson's plans from the start and represented both men as members of the
Irish Ascendancy who were primarily interested in looking after their own interests rather than those of the town's inhabitants. Both papers complained that
Rutledge and Atkinson's ownership of the town inhibited both government
investment – and its growth.

Rutledge and Atkinson's actions at Port Fairy would have reflected similar
activites undertaken by other Anglo-Irish gentry members back in Ireland where
the landowning minority frequently planned the creation of new settlements and
the replacment of buildings or streets – for example, John D'Arcy's foundation of
Clifden, Co. Galway, between 1815 and 1835. Although directly controlled by the
landlords, the development costs of such estate towns were spread, as long-term
building leases with low ground rent were often offered to many of the tenants on
condition they bore the cost of constructing the property. The primary motivation
behind such ventures was the reproduction of the prevailing economic system. As
long as landlords continued to delegate property rights to their tenants they
ensured the tenants' continuing interest in reproducing the existing economic formation as it validated the tenants' possession of their property. Moreover, the ten-
urial structures inherent within it validated the tenants' retention of any additional
benefits which might accrue from an increase in their property's value.[20] Thus, the
planning of Port Fairy would not have been an entirely new enterprise for men of
Rutledge and Atkinson's calibre.

If Rutledge and Atkinson's activities at Port Fairy mirrored the urban improvements carried out by Anglo-Irish gentry in Ireland, those of another Anglo-Irish
family, the Ffrenches, mirrored the Irish gentry's equally widespread interest in
landscaping in Ireland. The Ffrenchs were seated at Monivea in Co. Galway, and
were one of the 'Galway Tribes' in that their ancestry traced back to the twelfth-
century Anglo-Norman colonisation of Galway city. These mainly Catholic merchant families invested heavily in land, buying out the impoverished Gaelic
proprietors in its hinterland and over time established a social and economic dom-
inance over Galway and into Mayo. The Ffrench family had a large network of
estates with over twenty houses in Co. Galway alone and others in Roscommon

20 L.J. Proudfoot and B.J. Graham, 'The Nature and Extent of Urban and Village
Foundation and Improvement in Eighteenth and Early Nineteenth Century Ireland',
Planning Perspectives, 8 (1993), pp. 259–81.

Figure 2. Belfast Bakery

and Mayo. Their three major estates were Tyrone, (50,000 acres), Monivea, (10,000 acres), and Castleffrench of (5,000 acres), all located in Co. Galway.

Patrick Ffrench, father of Robert Ffrench, had spent time in London training to enter the legal profession. Upon his return to Dublin in 1707, an act was passed requiring all barristers to attend communion with the established Church of Ireland. Having invested considerable time and effort in his training, Patrick vaulted the barrier which would have excluded him from a lucrative career by conforming to Protestantism. It was this decision which facilitated the Ffrench family's social and professional ascent and started a process of assimilation which was completed within the family well before the century had ended.

The conversion to Protestant ideals, values and traditions was clearly shown in Patrick's son, Robert who inherited the family's landholdings. He can be looked upon as an example of a 'broker' figure who mediated between his locality and the wider world. Robert travelled widely throughout Europe and also spent some time, almost every month, in England where he often marvelled at the widespread use of steam engines. The ease and regularity with which the Irish aristocracy, gentry and professionals, such as the Ffrenches, travelled to and fitted into England spoke more of a provincial rather than a colonial relationship. Britain simply lengthened and strengthened the networks which had already spread throughout Ireland and along which commodities, as diverse as roots and saplings for the garden, geological curiosities and political patronage, were distributed. Although familiar with the country, Ffrench neither lived nor owned property in England and was rarely away from his native Galway for any considerable period of time. Happy with his inheritance in Ireland, he did not need to build a career elsewhere.

It was Robert Ffrench's son, Acheson Jeremy Sydney Ffrench, who eventually migrated to Australia in 1840. In his letter book Acheson French tells how, while still living in Ireland, he had a difference of opinion with the archbishop of Tuam concerning his own belief that the bible should be abolished as a text book in schools. French believed that by its abolishment and the amalgamation of youth of different persuasions the wounds of his unhappy country would be healed and the prejudices smoothed. He continued:

> As I could not coincide with his Grace's view of this subject I suddenly found all my prearranged plans of life frustrated; I was obliged tho' with many a heart's pang to tear myself from a people and tenantry who were endeared to me, and amongst whom I had hoped to use what influence or talent I might have possessed for their amelioration. Accordingly a few weeks after . . . saw me on the seas for Australia.
>
> In French's own words he became an *Exile from Erin*.[21]

Upon arrival in the colony he modified the spelling of his surname so that it only had one 'F' and after approximately a year, took out a licence for land at a

---

21 Acheson French Letterbook, MS 10053 1298/1, State Library of Victoria, Melbourne.

place named 'The Grange' which he proceeded to re-register as Monivae. He was also appointed Stipendary Magistrate for the New South Wales Government in order to maintain the peace between the aborigines and the white settlers of the district.

At this time the area around Monivae was newly settled and disturbances between the indigenous aboriginal population and the settlers were frequent. In his capacity as police magistrate French regularly reported such incidents to the state's Governor Charles La Trobe. Although he was regarded as an extremely honest and fair man, there are several occasions when French is shown to have taken the side of the settlers during various disputes with the aboriginals. This may have been due both to his wish to keep on moderate terms with his closest neighbours in the area and to the circumstances surrounding many of the incidents where, in his view, the settlers were having a difficult time as they were under regular attack from the abo-riginals. On one occasion a neighbouring settler and acquaintance, Mr McKenzie, was murdered by the aboriginals and his 700 sheep taken. According to French, Mr McKenzie had 'behaved with kindness to the natives frequently feeding them with flour and meat.'[22]

The realm in which Acheson French lived and moved in was, in many ways, similar to that which he had left back in Ireland years before. Most obvious were the similarities between physical objects such as his homestead and the layout of the surrounding land. Not only did he name his residence Monivae after the fam-ily home in Galway (although he changed the spelling from v-e-a to v-a-e) but the layout of home was reported to have closely resembled the original house with a long sweeping drive up to the front of it and two lines of non-native English oak trees running either side to the bottom of the property. In Ireland, the construc-tion of similar houses by the wealthy landowning elite and the subsequent land-scape ornamentation of the surrounding lands would have been relatively common throughout the nineteenth century. Such spatial organisation was to be found across the country and not only did this landscape transformation reflect social and economic axes of difference between the gentry and the 'ordinary' Irish, but they also acquired additional ethnic and colonial meanings.[23]

While many newly settled areas in Australia were named after places back in Ireland, for example the towns of Killarney and Coleraine, the fact that French altered the spelling of Monivea slightly suggests that perhaps he too had a desire to weaken ties with the Old World he had left yet at the same time he didn't wish to let go of them completely. At this time people with money living in Australia imported many goods and Acheson Ffrench was no different, importing many pre-fabricated pieces of ornate iron from England with which to build his house. The

22 Ibid.   **23** L.J. Proudfoot, 'Hybrid Space? Self and Other in Narratives of Landownership in Nineteenth-Century Ireland', *Journal of Historical Geography*, 26: 2 (2000), pp. 203–21.

new Monivae consisted of sixteen rooms with detached servants quarters as well as stables, harness room and coach house.

Socially, French was extremely well respected within the local community and was the driving force behind many of the changes initiated within it. These included the construction of a new school for which he was the main benefactor, as well as the main contributor to the Benevolent Institute at Hamilton. In 1845 he also set up a local book club which he ran from his house and which had about ten regular subscribers who all lived in the local area. In his diary he lists the members names and their purchases throughout the year. Many of the subscribers were also gentry members and their purchases were wide-ranging from Mr Cameron's purchase of a volume entitled 'Highland Sports' to Mr Thomson's order for a volume of the 'London News' as well as two volumes named 'Memoirs of a Physician'.[24] The purchases alone illustrate the type of people French associated with: they were well educated and from a similar background to French himself. The books gentry migrants purchased also show how their new worlds in Victoria still revolved to a certain degree around the homeland: they frequently bought literature that would keep them informed about life back in Ireland and England.

Many of French's friends and close companions in Australia were gentry migrants like himself who originated from Ireland. When he married Anna Watton in 1842 he held a joint wedding with a close acquaintance, James Moore, whose father George was a political representative of the city of Dublin.[25] Other associates included Cuthbert Featherstonhaugh from Westmeath and Charles James Griffith from Kildare. In his autobiography Featherstonhaugh writes that he became great friends with the Ffrench family and describes Acheson as the 'well bred Irish gentleman, a most delightful man, none more hospitable, and full of Irish humour.' 'At Monivae' he wrote, 'you got a real Irish welcome.'[26]

Although relatively little work has been undertaken into the role of the gentry class as a whole in Australia, much of the research that *has* been carried out often makes the assumption that the gentry were a homogenous class. This is debatable. As French himself makes clear, in his opinion a widespread prejudice existed in Australia against the Irish as a nation and in particular against those who had migrated, and this extended to the gentry and included many of his friends and colleagues. He cites as one reason for this the tone taken by the Australian press which he considered to be quite anti-Irish. His belief stemmed from a series of articles and editorial comments printed in the *Argus* newspaper which had launched scathing attacks on the Colonial Secretary and some of his government officials purely because they were of Irish origin. In one incident French responds to the Scottish editor of the newspaper by reminding him that at the end of the day *all* government officials had been appointed by one of his own fellow coun-

24 Acheson French Diary, MS 10053 1298/2, State Library of Victoria, Melbourne.
25 *Port Phillip Patriot*, 10 February 1842, Marriage Notice, State Library of Victoria, Melbourne.   26 Co. Fetherstonhaugh, *After Many Days* (Melbourne, 1917), p. 62.

trymen who was at the head of the English government.[27] He concludes that 'If the officials are not to this Editor's taste because *they are Irishmen* he should vent his bile on his own Countrymen and not presume to sow the seed of division amongst a mixed people.' This feeling of prejudice against gentry from an Irish background is mentioned by other migrants such as George Higinbotham and George Belcher who also make reference to the same underlying sentiment. As each of these gentry members varied in their religious views it is unlikely that the prejudice was a result of religious differences but rather as a result of perceived ethnicity or political opinion.

The French family archives provide an overwhelming sense that one of the reasons why Acheson French came to Australia was to make a fresh start following ideological disagreement with Church and state in Ireland. He felt that the new nation of Australia could learn from the past histories of the Old World and not make the same mistakes again. However, as the nature of his letters and diaries show, it is obvious that he was restrained to some degree by the baggage of his past. That his past was in many ways replicated in Australia is easy to see but it must be remembered that this replication was a result of French's own actions.

IV

Irish overseas migration, has, and is likely to continue to be, an important facet of the global topic of migration studies. Although considerable work has been undertaken on Irish migrants to a range of destination countries, there is still considerable scope for work to be undertaken. Arguably, it has only been over the last decade that academics have begun to recognise the true complexity of the Irish migrant stream and to comprehend the variety of discourses and narratives this involved. Members of the Anglo-Irish gentry who migrated to Australia represent only one strand in this intricate stream, and even then, were internally diverse as the migrants themselves represented a broad spectrum of occupations and family backgrounds. In addition, each was driven by his or her own reasons and motivations for leaving Ireland and migrating to Australia. Upon arrival, many were assimilated into colonial life with relative ease and undertook leadership and professional roles, some of which they had previously experienced in Ireland. Others followed entirely new pursuits. Many migrants, consciously or unconsciously, recreated similar lives to those they had left in Ireland as it was often the case that their social networks and landscapes in Australia closely mirrored those in which they had once interacted whilst living in Ireland. As well as illustrating how a substantial number of gentry migrants became important members of both local community and wider community, the examples of Rutledge and French also show how their

27 Acheson French Letterbook, *c.* June 1854, Letter to Editor of *Argus*, MS 10053 1298/3, State Library of Victoria, Melbourne.

Figure 3. Current dwelling at the site of Monivae

Figure 4. One of the lines of non-native English Oak trees
running along the boundary of French's land

own landscapes in Australia closely replicated those back in Co. Cavan and Co. Galway respectively. It is the enduring legacy of Anglo-Irish gentry migrants in the cultural landscapes of Australia which this chapter has attempted to address in an endeavour to uncover some aspects of the detail of the Anglo-Irish gentry migrant experience in Australia.

Ireland abroad/broadening Ireland: from famine migrants to asylum-applicants and refugees

JASON KING

'There is no Irish blood in my veins, but there is pity in [my heart] for Irish suffering,' declares Father Caseau, a character in Jim Minogue's unpublished play *Flight to Grosse Ile* which was performed by the Mountjoy Theatre Project before a sold-out audience on 12 April 1999.[1] What made the declaration particularly 'electrifying', according to *Irish Times* columnist Mary Holland, was that the actor/prisoner (Tola Mohmoh) playing Father Caseau was black, and that seated directly in front of him in the audience that night was Irish Minister for Justice, Equality, and Law Reform (whose portfolio includes immigration), John O'Donoghue.[2] It must have been a compelling spectacle, a member of a visible minority preaching to the Minister not in his capacity as a prisoner of the state or as a presumed asylum-seeker incarnate, but in the guise of a French-Canadian priest, invoking the spectre of the Minister's own ancestors and their reception at Grosse Isle, and beseeching him to show compassion for those who arrive unwanted 'on a hostile shore'. 'Have we not got room[?] Just a little space[?]', Father Caseau implores, and the meaning of his question and the ironic role reversals enacted on stage could not have been lost upon anyone in the audience that night: that there is an implicit analogy to be drawn between the historical plight of Irish Famine migrants and asylum-seekers and refugees coming to Ireland today.

No less theatrical, however, have been the declamations of Irish parliamentarians employing this analogy whenever the subject of legislation for immigrants, asylum-seekers, and refugees has arisen in the Dáil. During an *Oireachtas* debate about the drafting of the Irish Refugee Act (1996), for example, the then opposition shadow Minister for Justice, John O'Donoghue, publicly compared the situation of Ireland's Famine migrants with that of asylum-seekers and refugees. Much more explicitly than Father Caseau, he declared to the House that: 'the status of refugees is an issue which should strike a chord with every man, woman and child here who has any grasp of Irish history, our history books being littered with the names and deeds of those driven from our country out of fear of persecution.'[3] Subsequently,

1 I am grateful to Lulu Reynolds, who directed the production, for sharing with me a copy of her working script of Jim Minogue's unpublished play, *Flight to Grosse Ile*. All references are to p. 26. 2 *Irish Times*, 15 April 1999. 3 Private Members Business. Asylum Seekers (Regularisation of Status) (No. 2) Bill, 1998: Second Stage. *Dáil Debates* Official Report –

as Ireland's so-called 'refugee crisis' began to escalate after the Act was passed into law, the election of 1997, and Deputy O'Donoghue's appointment as Minister, that statement would come back to haunt him on a number of occasions. In fact, less than a year after his appointment as Minister, O'Donoghue's statement was invoked several times during a Dáil debate in February 1998 about a proposed amnesty for asylum-seekers in Ireland through their 'Regularisation of Status'. According to opposition Deputy Liz McManus, who tabled the Bill, the very history of emigration from Ireland required the amnesty and implementation of a 'generous and just' asylum policy, as moral recompense for the successive 'generations of Irish asylum-seekers who were driven out to seek refuge among strangers'.[4] 'There are more Irish emigrants buried in that little plot of land [at Grosse Isle] in Eastern Canada,' she added, 'than there are asylum-seekers in the whole of Ireland today'. 'All through [the preceding] debate' about the Irish Refugee Act', stated opposition Deputy Michael Higgins,'there were continual references to the 150th anniversary of the Famine,' 'the ethics of memory' forbid Ireland now to 'visit the same difficulties and disabilities on people which faced our citizens when they went in floods to north America' in 1847.[5] More recently, during a *Seanad* hearing for Ireland's Immigration Bill, 1999, Senator Connor insisted that Ireland 'has a moral duty to take [its] fair share of the thousands of people who are forced to flee economic privation and political persecution . . . because of [Ireland's] historical experience'.[6]

Indeed, throughout the many heated *Oireachtas* debates and much of the press coverage surrounding Ireland's so-called 'refugee crisis', influx of illegal immigrants, and then the speedy passage of the Immigration Act, 1999, Illegal Immigrants (Trafficking) Act, 2000, as well as policy directives that have emanated from the Department of Justice, the discussion of current immigration into Ireland has tended to be framed against the backdrop of the Famine exodus of 1847, and the calamities of Ireland's colonial history. Thus, what each of these statements above have in common is their moral injunction that we exercise our historical imaginations to metaphorically equate the plight of the Famine emigrants of the mid-nineteenth-century with that of asylum-seekers and refugees coming into Ireland now, that we attempt to counter-intuitively envision what would happen if the 'Coffin Ships' of 1847 somehow entered into a historical time-warp and were redirected to land on Ireland's shores in the late twentieth century.

However, such appeals to Irish historical experience, the 'ethics of memory', and analogies of displacement between the Famine migrants and asylum-seekers and refugees can appear merely polemical and superficial when one considers the profound discrepancies between the specific social, economic, political, and cultural circumstances underlying their respective dislocations. It is sobering to realize, for

10–3–98. PRIVATE MEMBERS' BUSINESS. Asylum Seekers (Regularisation of Status) (No. 2) Bill, 1998: Second Stage. (http://www.irlgov.ie/oireachtas/frame.htm). **4** Ibid. **5** Ibid. **6** (http://www.irlgov.ie/oireachtas/default.html seanad.htm. . .).

example, that the vast majority of the Famine migrants of 1847 were economically or ecologically displaced individuals who would have no substantive claim to political asylum or entitlement to refugee status under Irish or even the most liberal interpretations of international refugee law – that very few of them were, in fact, 'driven from the country out of fear of persecution' or could claim refugee protection on that basis. This is not to deny the existence of a durable, humane, and remarkably liberal tradition of granting political asylum in mid-Victorian Britain, one that reached its apogee in the aftermath of the failed rebellions of 1848, when a host of exiles from across the European continent found protection on English soil.[7] Rather, it is to suggest that in the eyes of both contemporaries and current international and Irish refugee law, the desperate outrush of famine migrants and the movements of asylum-seekers and refugees in need of protection from repressive regimes by no means fall within the same category, but represent polarised types of involuntary displacement. Indeed, the very term 'ecological' or 'Famine refugee' is at best oxymoronic in its juridical connotations, to the extent that it collapses the humanitarian function of the alleviation and prevention of hunger with the grant of political asylum under the auspices of a singular protection regime.[8] In other words, if the Great Famine were to happen again in Ireland tomorrow, the international response to such a catastrophe would be coordinated within an institutional framework and discourse of 'development' and the provision of emergency relief, to alleviate the consequences rather than the underlying socio-economic and political causes of hunger.

This is not to deny the utility of historical analogy or of attempting 'to look to the colonial past ... to establish [forms of] cross-cultural solidarity through a shared history of discrimination or oppression', as Luke Gibbons has recently intimated to be the object of a 'post-colonial ethics'.[9] On the contrary, it is to assert that any such 'post-colonial ethics' must be premised *not* upon facile historical analogies but upon careful investigation of the specific areas of resemblance as well as dissimilarity between the types of displacement and modes of personal and cultural transformation as well as reception into different host societies experienced by the Famine migrants and contemporary asylum-seekers, before any such gesture of cross-cultural solidarity can be either effective or meaningful. In other words, the question is not whether 'the status of refugees is an issue which should arouse compassion and strike a chord with every man, woman and child who has any grasp of Irish history', but rather, what are the similarities and discrepancies between the specific administrative, humanitarian, juridical, and political norms of

---

7 See B. Porter, *The Refugee Question in mid-Victorian Politics* (Cambridge, 1979). 8 See G. S. Goodwin-Gill. *The Refugee in International Law*, 2nd Ed. (Oxford, 1996), pp. 3–4. Also see V. Lassailly-Jacob & M. Zmolek (eds), 'Special Issue: Environmental Refugees', *Refuge: Canada's Periodical on Refugees*. 12: 1. June 1992, esp. pp. 1–4. 9 L. Gibbons, 'Guests of the Nation: Ireland, Immigration, and Post-Colonial Solidarity'. Presented at the Red Stripe Seminar, Newman House, Dublin, University of Notre Dame, 4 November 1999, pp. 9, 13.

the institutional framework of the protection regime through which that compassion becomes exercised in relation to either group; and, secondly, in what ways can looking to the past and identifying the asymmetries, specific gaps, and historical instances of failure within the institutional framework designed to protect the Famine migrants lead towards better, more comprehensive, enhanced standards of protection for asylum-seekers and refugees coming into Ireland today.

Accordingly, I want to examine the often perfunctory, rarely elaborated or sustained comparisons made between the Famine migrants and asylum-seekers and refugees, both in the context of the historiography of mid-nineteenth-century Ireland, and also against the more exacting strictures of current Irish and international refugee law. The meaning and legacy of the Famine migration is frequently invoked, for example, either to posit a continuity or make a categorical distinction between the historical plight of Ireland's persecuted emigrants, on the one hand, and those asylum applicants/illegal immigrants who would strategically (mis)represent themselves as political exiles to gain entry into Ireland today. It is this seeming contradiction between the public commemoration of the Famine migrants and modern Ireland as the benefactor of their legacy, and the current widespread and countervailing expressions of hostility both in the *Oireachtas* and many British and Irish media outlets towards economic aliens and asylum-applicants who become conflated under the singular categorization of 'bogus refugees' that I want to focus upon first and that I take as the starting point for my analysis. More specifically, I want to focus throughout my discussion upon the literary and political significance of *typologies of displacement* in Ireland, and the impact of lingering perceptions that Ireland is still an 'emigrant nursery' rather than an immigrant host society in engendering public opposition towards immigrants, asylum-seekers, and refugees settling in the country.

I

To begin with, I want to suggest that one can in fact posit a continuity of displacement between the Famine migrants and asylum-seekers to the extent that each group envisions itself to be politically constituted under the sign of exile. Indeed, I would suggest that there is a remarkable structural affinity between the *self-perception* of the members of each of these groups in that they either naturally envision or strategically (mis)represent the causes of their displacement in narrowly political rather than broadly social and economic terms, interpreting themselves to be the victims of state persecution in place of national or global socio-economic disparities or ecological catastrophe. In the case of Irish emigrants, including many of the Famine migrants, according to Kerby Miller, such a strategic (mis)representation of their cause of displacement had an overtly political correlative: the 'exile motif' provided the cornerstone for Irish-American nationalism, engendered mass-support for Fenianism, and effectively financed Land League agitations through the remittance of vast sums of money from America, while at the same time alleviating the inherent familial pressures that stemmed from a system of impartible inheritance and the creation of numerous 'surplus', landless sons and daughters.[10] Yet 'the paradox remains of a tremendous gap between the exile image and the objective realities of Irish emigration'. For the many 'Famine emigrants [who] had left home voluntarily, without attributable compulsion, cultural characteristics not easily shed predisposed them to view their departures in conformity with communal traditions and nationalist motifs' that collapsed any distinction between economic dislocation and political exile.[11]

In the case of asylum-seekers and refugees in Ireland now, on the other hand, their rationale for leaving home has less a political than a legal correlative: for the difference between political persecution and economic dislocation is absolutely vital when it comes to making a claim for refugee status, and for genuine asylum-applicants, at least, that categorical distinction can mean the difference between life and death. It is only political rather than economic migrants, in other words, who are legally entitled to claim asylum and to the international protection afforded by refugee status, to remain within rather than become removable from the Irish state, not to be subject to deportation. It is in this sense, then, that I want to suggest that the self-image of a large proportion of Irish Famine emigrants and economic aliens coming into Ireland now involves a categorical sleight of hand, to elide the distinction between political and socio-economic causes of displacement, albeit for very different reasons. There are significant qualitative distinctions to be made between the types of displacement experienced by Famine emigrants and contemporary asylum-seekers, in other words, but the movements of both groups take place under the sign of political exile and under a veneer of suspicion.

II

However, I also want to extend the argument a little further to suggest an affinity not just between the self-image of Irish emigrants and asylum-applicants, but also between the mechanisms of exclusion and instruments of deportation employed first by Victorian municipal and English Poor Law authorities and now by the Irish government to control their respective movements. More specifically, I want to argue that the 'removal' provision of the Laws of Settlement inaugurated in the seventeenth century and enshrined within the amended English Poor Law (1834) to a large extent prefigures the rationale behind the European Union's burden sharing agreement on asylum-applicants instituted in the Dublin and Schengen Conventions (1990).[12] What each of these bodies of legislation have in common, I

---

10 K. Miller, *Emigrants and Exiles: Ireland and the Irish Exodus to North America* (Oxford, 1985). 11 Ibid, pp. 6, 341. 12 For comprehensive analysis of the English 'Laws of Settlement' and their 'Removal' provisions, see C. Kinealy, *This Great Calamity: The Irish*

would suggest, is that they provide for the institutional abdication of moral responsibility for the welfare of either the transient poor or the persecuted from other states: not through any disavowal of the validity of their claims, but rather through the erection of procedural barriers that call for their removal to other jurisdictions – whether it be the parish of settlement in the case of the English and Irish Poor Laws, or 'Safe Third Countries' that asylum-applicants have transited through en route to Western Europe and to which they can be repatriated under the Dublin Convention – for the provision of relief or determination of refugee status. Entitlement and status determination, in either case, becomes a function of the control of vagrancy or irregular migration, and is vested in the immobility of the claimant.

Moreover, the institutional logic of both bodies of legislation in the English Poor Laws and Dublin and Schengen Conventions appears more inclined towards the deterrence, exclusion, and stigmatisation of those who would fraudulently avail themselves of and abuse these respective protection regimes, collapsed in the figures of the fraudulent poor or spurious asylum applicant, than enshrining a comprehensive standard of protection. For whether it be in the form of the 'undeserving poor' or the fraudulent asylum-applicant, it is the spectre of the seemingly trans-historical figure of the *abusive claimant* that haunts the historical imagination of Irish refugee policy makers, delimits the institutional parameters, and sets the parsimonious scope of Ireland's regime of refugee protection and resettlement practice, the ultimate prerogative of which becomes the exclusion of what Justice Minister O'Donoghue terms 'manifestly unfounded' and 'frivolous, vexatious or unmeritorious' claims.[13] Indeed, Minister O'Donoghue could effectively be speaking as the chief architect of Ireland's nineteenth century Famine relief rather than contemporary refugee policy in his recent statement that his 'key objective . . . is to minimize the scope for abuse of the procedures to the greatest extent possible'.[14] There are substantive grounds for comparison, in other words, not between the Famine migration and Ireland's so-called 'refugee crisis' in their entirety as discrete historical phenomena, but rather in the common stigmatization of the masses of Famine emigrants and asylum applicants who appear interlinked as seemingly trans-historical agents of clandestine migration and meretricious claimants of assistance: that is, potentially abusive beneficiaries of material relief or refugee status with its corresponding social and economic entitlements, that in turn limits the scope of either form of protection.

The alleviation of the public anxiety engendered by the threatening figures of the undeserving poor or bogus refugees thus becomes the over-riding objective of policy formation: to root out and limit the movements of those who might fraudulently avail themselves of these respective regimes of protection, rather than to

Famine, 1845–1852 (Dublin, 1995), pp. 327–42; as well as F. Neal, *Black '47: Britain and the Famine Irish* (Dublin, 1998), pp. 89–90, 217–37. **13** *Irish Times*, 26 February 2000, p. 10. **14** *Irish Times*, 29 March 2000.

extend it in scope to all those who might genuinely be in need. And yet, it cannot be stressed emphatically enough that there is *no such thing* as a 'bogus' asylum applicant any more than one can have a 'guilty accused' in a criminal justice proceeding: for it is a contradiction in terms that involves the *presumption* rather than adjudication of fraudulent intent on the part of the claimant, and inverts the norms of due process and procedural fairness underlying any respectable regime of refugee status determination.

There are also substantive grounds for comparison, I would further suggest, between the Famine migration to Britain and Ireland's current 'refugee crisis' in terms of the means of exclusion and instruments of deportation employed by each respective host society to deter unwanted migration. In *Black '47: Britain and the Famine Irish*, Frank Neal notes that

> to establish the right to poor relief in a parish, a person had to have the legal status of 'settlement', achieved by being born in the parish or by one of a number of arcane criteria. Alternatively, after 1846, a person who had lived for five years *continuously in a particular parish*, acquired the status of 'irremovable poor'. Outside of these categories, persons claiming poor relief of more than a temporary nature, could be physically removed to the parish in which they had settlement . . . However, the poor law unions . . . had a legal obligation to ensure that nobody died of starvation, malnutrition or 'the want of the necessaries of daily life.[15]

Christine Kinealy further observes in *This Great Calamity* that 'the growth in volume of Irish persons travelling to Britain [in 1847] resulted in a more extensive use of the powers of removal by the British authorities', because 'many parish officials . . . particularly those located in ports, were determined to [prevent] any Irish paupers [from acquiring] the status of irremoveability'. Thus, 'the English, Welsh, and Scottish Poor Law authorities responded to the unprecedented influx of Irish poor with large-scale removal, some of which was not only indiscriminate but also illegal'.[16] The point then is that British Poor Law authorities employed sweeping measures of preventative deportation to alleviate migratory pressures upon their infrastructure of relief by simply transferring Irish paupers out of their jurisdiction rather than taking action to redress either the causes or consequences of mass-hunger.

In a similar spirit, Ireland's accession to and utilisation of the powers of deportation instituted within the Dublin Convention (1990) to alleviate its 'refugee crisis' augurs a potentially historically specific and analogous example of the employment of sweeping removals to deflect migratory pressures upon Irish asylum procedures by simply restricting access to them in the first place. As John Walsh notes in 'Home Is Where the Policy Is', the underlying institutional logic of the

---

15 Neal, *Black '47*, p. 90.   **16** Kinealy, *This Great Calamity*, pp. 334, 335, 336.

Dublin Convention 'is to ensure that all asylum seekers arriving in Europe will be removed to the first country of entry (effectively the 'safe third country') where their application will be processed . . . Therefore, although the Preamble [to the Dublin Convention] speaks of the need to remain loyal to the spirit of [the] 1951' United Nations Convention on the Status of Refugees, which includes an absolute prohibition against *refoulement* or the forcible repatriation of anyone outside of his or her country of origin with a well-founded fear of persecution, 'the Dublin Convention has swiftly become an instrument by which the European Union can move asylum-seekers further away from its core.'[17] Thus, 'the combined effects of the Dublin, External Frontiers and Schengen Conventions,' according to Walsh, 'is a draconian asylum and immigration policy' both in Ireland and in Europe at large that appears 'far removed from the provisions of international human rights and refugee law'.[18] For by framing the question of entitlement to protection as an administrative and procedural rather than ethical and political issue, Ireland's refugee legislation and particularly the Immigration Act, 1999, with its provisions for expedited application of the Dublin Convention, would appear to resemble the *spirit* of the English Laws of Settlement, at least to the extent that both bodies of legislation abdicate responsibility for the vast majority of claimants who would avail of them, not by refusing to recognise their entitlement to the provision of relief or political asylum, but simply by restricting the scope of their jurisdiction and refusing to process the vast majority of claimants.

Moreover, under both bodies of legislation it is precisely the *asymmetry* between the absolute moral prohibition against *refoulement* or for the prevention of starvation that provides the cornerstone of their protection regimes, and the procedural limitations set upon their application, that leads to the employment of preventative deportation and sweeping removals to deflect migratory pressures to prior jurisdictions that the respective applicants have previously transited through: yet, in practice, the abdication of responsibility to adjudicate entitlement to material relief or refugee status functions to inaugurate a chain of deportations or the 'refugee in orbit' phenomenon that ultimately returns migrants seeking protection or relief back to their original situation of persecution or of utter destitution from whence they fled in the first place. To illustrate how the institutional frameworks of the 'English Laws of Settlement and Removal' and Ireland's Immigration Act resemble one another to elide their original protective function and initiate 'chain deportations', I will cite just two case studies that illustrate the 'refugee in orbit' phenomenon. Kinealy notes, for example:

> one such case [which] involved an Irish weaver who had been resident in Scotland for eight years. Following an application for relief in 1851, he was returned to Ireland accompanied by a Poor Law official. The official took

17 J. Walsh, '"Home is Where the Policy Is . . ." European Asylum and Immigration Policy and Procedure: The Irish and Dutch Examples'. University of Dublin (Trinity College): MA in International Relations, 1998–9, p. 32.   18 Ibid., p. 35.

the pauper to his native Strabane, but the local guardians refused to accept custody of him on the grounds that he was legally relievable in Scotland. They returned him to the care of the officer with instructions to take him back to Scotland. The officer, however, deserted the pauper at Derry, on the pretence of buying some tea. The pauper returned to Strabane and again applied to the guardians for relief. Defeated yet undaunted, the Strabane guardians appealed to the Poor Law Commissioners to end the injustice of removal.[19]

Consider now the points of resemblance between this case study of chain deportations under the aegis of the English and Irish Poor Laws and a much more recent 'case documented by ECRE [European Council on Refugees and Exiles]', in which:

a Somali refugee traveling with five dependent children was pushed out of four different European countries, each less safe than the previous one, until UNHCR and ECRE finally lost track of them. The family arrived at Brussels airport on May 29, 1994 and applied for asylum. They were immediately detained and subjected to an expedited procedure in which the application was turned down.

The Belgian authorities returned them to Prague on 8 July. The Czech Republic sent them in turn to Bratislava airport in Slovakia because they had in their passport a genuine, but expired, visa allowing them transit in Slovakia. The Slovak authorities. . . denied them [entry]. UNHCR discovered and interviewed them, and found them to have a well-founded fear of persecution.

Despite UNHCR's intervention, the Slovak authorities refused to register the applicant's claims for asylum . . . and insisted that they be deported to Ukraine, the country of first arrival. UNHCR countered that returning them to Ukraine would be tantamount to *refoulement*. On the night of 25 July, the Slovak authorities put the family on a train to Kiev. At that point, UNHCR lost track of them.[20]

What each of these case studies illustrate in common is a process of chain deportations that leads to the 'refugee in orbit' phenomenon,[20a] a phenomenon that would appear to be an integral aspect rather than unforeseen consequence of the implementation of two distinct regimes of protection that nevertheless resemble one another precisely because they are highly restrictive in the scope of their jurisdiction, largely for reasons of cost reduction. In both cases, the applicants were not just morally but legally entitled to relief or refugee protection in each of the jurisdictions transited through, yet the fact that no single jurisdiction was in its own

---

19 Kinealy, *This Great Calamity*, p. 339.   **20** Cited in *Interpreter Releases: Report and analysis of immigration and nationality law*, 73, n. 8. (February 26, 1996), pp. 222–3.   **20a** In the Irish context, see D. Nozinic, 'One Refugee Experience in Ireland', R. Lentin and R. McVeigh (eds), *Racism and Anti-Racism in Ireland* (Belfast, 2002), pp. 77–80.

right accountable or bears exclusive responsibility for the infringement of their rights does not exonerate any of them from their ultimate violation. The point then that must be made is that in each case the failure to provide relief or political asylum became compounded and diffused through this process of chain deportations until the ultimate prohibition against *refoulement* or to prevent starvation, that is the cornerstone of each of these respective protection regimes under the English Poor Law and the UN Refugee Convention, which the claimants above had sought to avail themselves of, was violated to the core. Or, to illustrate the point of the historical analogy between the Famine migration and Ireland's 'refugee crisis' more succinctly, when refugees are expelled into orbit, they rarely land safely.

III

To illustrate this point more clearly in a nineteenth-century context, I would like to anchor my discussion with a close reading of a well-known incident of a failure to provide relief portrayed in Herman Melville's *Redburn* (1849),[21] a fictional account of the author's own visit to Liverpool during the onset of the Famine, in which the eponymous hero, a sailor boy, discovers a famine stricken family of Irish emigrants sheltering in a cellar on a 'narrow [Liverpool] street called "Launcelott's-Hey"'[22]. He recoils from the spectacle of an emaciated Irish Madonna-figure cradling a dead infant on her breast, 'her blue arms folded to her livid bosom [with] two shrunken things like children, that leaned towards her, one on each side'. 'At that moment I never thought of relieving them,' Redburn declares; 'for death was so stamped in their glazed and unimploring eyes, that I almost regarded them as already no more. I stood looking down on them, while my whole soul swelled within me; and I asked myself, What right had any body in the wide world to smile and be glad, when sights like this were to be seen'.[23] However, Redburn quickly regains his composure and leaves to seek assistance for them, only to be rebuffed with utter indifference from the inhabitants of the area, and from a policeman who refuses his 'help' to '*remove* [the] woman' [italics mine], exclaiming: 'it's none of my business . . . I don't belong to that street . . . go back on board your ship . . . and leave these matters to the town'. Instead, Redburn continues to seek assistance and to 'do something to get the woman and girls *removed*' [italics mine] from the cellar, but even after he procures food for them he is met only with their 'unalterable, idiotic expression[s], that almost made [him] faint'. Ultimately, 'without hope of [procuring] permanent relief', Redburn can only leave them to their fate, although

21 H. Melville, *Redburn: His First Voyage, being the Sailor Boy Confessions and Reminiscences of the Son-of-a-Gentleman in the Merchant Service* (New York [1849] 1957), pp. 173–8. For a more general discussion of Redburn and its representation of Famine emigrants in Liverpool, see R. Scally, *The End of Hidden Ireland: Rebellion, Famine, & Emigration* (New York, 1995), pp. 194–9, 217–18.　**22** Melville, *Redburn*, p. 173.　**23** Ibid., p. 174.

he suffers an 'irresistible impulse' 'to relieve them from their miserable existence', from which he is 'deterred' only 'by thoughts of [that same] law which would let them perish without giving them one cup of water'. Finally, after they have perished, Redburn returns to the same policeman he initially encountered to say that at last 'he had better have them *removed*', only to be informed again by the officer 'that it was not his street' [italics mine] and hence not his responsibility; nor is it that of 'the Dock Police', Redburn is told, when he solicits their assistance, but soon thereafter he discovers 'in place of the woman and children, a heap of quick-lime was glistening'. 'The first time I passed through this long lane of pauperism, it seemed hard to believe that such an array of misery could be furnished by any town in the world,' Redburn concludes; 'but to tell of them, would only be to tell over again the story just told'.[24]

That story in embryo represents a scathing critique of the deficiency of England's Poor Law in accommodating Ireland's indigent and transient populace. Indeed, the institutional abdication of moral responsibility for the welfare of famine stricken emigrants occurs in the novel at the level of individual streets rather than in the wider jurisdiction of Poor Law Unions as a whole, but the widespread indifference revealed towards the fate of the family of Irish emigrants whom Redburn tries to assist exemplifies in microcosm the failure of England's relief programme that was designed for their protection. The eschewal of responsibility by the figures of the individual policeman or the Dock Police thus becomes a synecdoche for the institutional framework of the English Poor Law and the restricted scope of its jurisdiction and operation that they come to represent to the ultimate absurd extreme: refusing to investigate or alleviate suffering that is no further away than a couple of streets, for which 'the town' as a whole if not its various agencies or individual representatives bears a collective responsibility for the prevention of hunger. The procedural intricacies inherent within the implementation of the protection regime of the Poor Law, in other words, lead to oversights and neglect, even when help is very close at hand, for those whose protection and provision of relief it is the very function of that regime to deliver in the first place. Ultimately, then, Redburn is forced to abandon the stricken family he would deign to assist rather than 'drag them out of the vault', because there, if from nothing else, 'at least they were *protected* from the rain; and more than that, might die in seclusion' [italics mine].

Moreover, his failure to provide any form of material assistance leads Redburn to espouse a Judeao-Christian metaphysic of compassion in place of decisive remedial action, albeit one that is tempered by feelings of despair when he reflects upon the magnitude and pervasiveness of suffering amongst 'the remarkable army of paupers' in his midst.[25] 'Poverty, poverty, poverty, in almost endless vistas,' he

24 Ibid., pp. 174–8. **25** p. 179. For an example of Redburn's metaphysic of compassion tempered by despair, consider his remarks immediately after the removal of the bodies of the stricken family has finally taken place: 'But again I looked down into the vault, and in fancy beheld the pale, shrunken forms still crouching there. Ah! What are our creeds, and

laments.[26] As Joyce Rowe remarks, 'Redburn seems able to sublimate his personal pain into a growing sympathy for those around him, but it is precisely the limits of sympathy as an adequate response to social suffering that the narrator himself indicts'.[27]

I would like to push this reading a little further, however, to question, once again in a counter-intuitive fashion, what would have happened if Redburn had actually found the policeman who belonged to the 'narrow street called "Launcelott's-Hey"' and whose responsibilities included the famine stricken Irish family that he was compelled to abandon? The answer to this rhetorical question, I would suggest, contains a much more powerful indictment not just of the limits of sympathy as a response to social suffering, but of the entire paradoxical infrastructure of relief enshrined within the English Poor Law, whereby 'poor law unions . . . had a legal obligation to ensure that nobody died of starvation, malnutrition or "the want of the necessaries of daily life"', yet no further 'legal obligation to provide *long term* assistance to newly arrived Irish,' including 'many Famine refugees [who] stopped claiming relief because of the threat of being removed back to Ireland'.[28] In other words, Melville's very sensibility of compassion and outrage at the seemingly comprehensive neglect of Ireland's indigent migrants is laden with a profound, unintended *ambiguity*, one that overdetermines Redburn's capacity for humanitarian intervention and the remedies he proposes, and especially his terminology of 'removal' and 'relief'. For what neither Melville himself nor the character Redburn ever consider is that he would actually be doing the famine-stricken Irish family a disservice if he had called their plight to the attention of the proper authorities, because their enforced passivity and immobility in the face of starvation – in that 'out of the way . . . silent, secluded spot' – is perhaps the only means of resistance still available to them before a faulty protection regime that would seek to alleviate their hunger not only by 'removing' them from the cellar but from the jurisdiction altogether, and then back to Ireland, where their hunger, suffering, starvation, and death would only be more protracted. In other words, their failure to claim relief is the only way of ensuring their 'irremoveability' from the English jurisdiction in which they have initially sought protection, and their refusal to receive emergency assistance happens not in spite of but as a direct result of the design of the protection regime they choose not to avail of because of the narrow scope of its application.

how do we hope to be saved? Tell me, oh Bible, the story of Lazarus again, that I may find comfort in my heart for the poor and forlorn. Surrounded as we are by the wants and woes of our fellowmen, and yet given to follow our own pleasures, regardless of their pains, are we not like people sitting up with a corpse, and making merry in the house of the dead?' p. 178.   **26** Ibid., p. 194.   **27** J.A. Rowe, 'Social History and the Politics of Manhood in Melville's *Redburn*,' (*Mosaic*, 26/1, 53–68), p. 61.   **28** Neal, *Black '47*, pp. 90, 217.

IV

Finally, charges can be leveled in a similar spirit, I would suggest, against the narrow scope of Ireland's Immigration Act, 1999, and its more recent amending legislation – misnomers in that they legislate for little more than renewed powers of deportation after the provisions of the Aliens Act (1935) were struck down as unconstitutional by the High Court. In a broader historical context, the deportation of failed asylum-applicants from Ireland under the Dublin Convention might seem a complementary type of involuntary return movement to the 'removal' of Famine migrants from England's Poor Law Unions. Both appear to be interlinked processes of preventative or 'constructive deportation'[29] that deflect migratory pressures from asylum or relief procedures through a displacement of jurisdictions in which claims are to be processed that ultimately has the potential to launch migrants into orbit until they land right back where they started from, often a situation of persecution or utter destitution from which they had to flee in the first place.

As a remedy for the 'refugee in orbit' phenomenon, Melville's all-encompassing metaphysic of concern for all who might be in need would appear tempting to embrace: 'that if they can get here, then they have God's right to come . . . For the whole world is the patrimony of the whole world'.[30] In practice, though, such sentiments might prove extraordinarily cumbersome to any conceivable protection regime, and detrimental to the interests of asylum-seekers in the long term. The recommendation of Zolberg *et al.*, on the other hand, that 'optimally . . . a liberal asylum [procedure] must rest on a combination of an open door policy and a discriminating hearing process' should suffice to enshrine a comprehensive standard of refugee protection in Ireland, one that makes no use of preventative deportation to put those genuinely in need of protection at risk of involuntary return without having their claims processed first.[31] In any case, whatever the substance behind historical analogies between the Famine migration and Ireland's current refugee crisis, they are at the very least indicative that Ireland is no longer just a country of origin for its own widely scattered diaspora, but has also come into collision with the diasporas of many other nations.

29 For a definition and comprehensive discussion of the history and uses of 'constructive deportation' in a European context, see N. Mole, 'Constructive Deportation and the European Convention' (5 *EHRLR*), pp. 63–71. **30** Melville, *Redburn*, p. 282. **31** A. Zolberg, A. Suhrke, and S. Aguao. *Escape from Violence: Conflict and the Refugee Crisis in the Developing World* (Oxford, 1989), p. 281.

Notes on contributors

PETER DENMAN lectures in the Department of English at NUI, Maynooth. He has written a number of articles on nineteenth- and twentieth-century literature, including *Samuel Ferguson: The Literary Achievement*.

KATHLEEN COSTELLO-SULLIVAN is a Ph.D. candidate in English at Boston College, where she specialises in nineteenth-century Irish and English literature. She is currently completing a dissertation on Irish and English realism and modernity.

LIAM HARTE is a Lecturer in the Academy for Irish Cultural Heritages at the University of Ulster. His most recent book is *Contemporary Irish Fiction: Themes, Tropes, Theories* (2000). *Writing Home: The Autobiography of the Irish in Britain* (2003) is forthcoming from Four Courts Press.

DIANE M. HOTTEN-SOMERS is a doctoral candidate in American Studies at Boston University, and Lecturer in the Department of English at Boston College. She has published articles on America's response to the Irish famine, Irish women's immigration to America, and the future of Irish Studies.

DECLAN KIBERD is Professor of Anglo-Irish Literature at University College, Dublin. He has published extensively on Irish literature and culture, and is author of the prize-winning *Inventing Ireland* (1995) and *Irish Classics* (2000).

JASON KING was employed as a Lecturer in the Department of English at the NUI, Maynooth, where he recently completed a Ph.D. on nineteenth-century Irish migration writing. He is currently an IRCHSS postdoctoral fellow at the Irish Centre for Migrartion Studies, NUI, Cork, where his research focuses on refugee perceptions of Irish historical memories of migration.

IAN McCLELLAND graduated with a Ph.D. in Geography from Queen's University, Belfast where his research focused upon the symbolic landscapes constructed by Irish gentry migrants in colonial Australia.

ELIZABETH MALCOLM is the Gerry Higgins Professor of Irish Studies at the University of Melbourne, Australia. She previously worked in Dublin, Belfast and Liverpool and has published extensively on Irish social and medical history.

LOUISE MISKELL is based in the Department of History at the University of Wales, Swansea. Her research interests include aspects of industrialisation and urbanisation in nineteenth-century Britain and the experience of the Irish in British towns.

MARTIN J. MITCHELL is Research Fellow at the Research Institute of Irish and Scottish Studies at the University of Aberdeen. He is author of *The Irish in the West of Scotland, 1797–1848: Trade Unions, Strikes and Political Movements* (1998).

MÁIRTÍN Ó CATHÁIN recently completed his Ph.D. at the University of Ulster, and is currently teaching at UU Coleraine. His research interests include the Irish in Scotland, and Irish revolutionary culture.

CLÍONA Ó GALLCHOIR is lecturer in English at University College, Cork. She has published a number of articles on Maria Edgeworth, and her main research interests lie in eighteenth and nineteenth-century writing, in particular works by Irish women writers.

LINDSAY J. PROUDFOOT is Reader in Historical Geography in the School of Geography, Queen's University Belfast. His research interests include representation and cultural identity in colonial societies.

NINI RODGERS is Lecturer in the School of History, Queen's University Belfast. She has publised a number of articles on the rise of anti-slavery in eighteenth-century Ireland, and is currently working on a book entitled *Ireland, Slavery and Anti-Slavery 1645–1860* to be published by Palgrave Press.

OONAGH WALSH is Lecturer in the Department of History at the University of Aberdeen. She is author of *Ireland's Independence, 1880–1923* (2002), and the forthcoming *To Forge or to Follow: Women of the Church of Ireland in Dublin, 1910–1925* (2003).

Index